Saint Francis: Nature Mystic

※

SAINT FRANCIS:
NATURE MYSTIC

The derivation and significance
of the nature stories in the
Franciscan Legend

※

Edward A. Armstrong

University of California Press

Berkeley   Los Angeles   London

University of California Press
Berkeley and Los Angeles, California
University of California Press, Ltd.
London, England
Copyright © 1973 by The Regents of the University of California
First Paperback Edition, 1976
ISBN 0-520-03040-0
Library of Congress Catalog Card Number: 74-149949
Designed by Theo Jung
Printed in the United States of America

For my grandchildren

Acknowledgements

I am very grateful to Professor Séamus Delargy of the Irish Folk-lore Commission for his advice and encouragement and to Dr. T. R. Henn of St. Catharine's College, Cambridge, and Dr. Herbert Friedmann of Los Angeles Natural History Museum for reading and commenting on this essay in manuscript. I am glad to pay tribute to the memory of the Rev. T. B. Allworthy and Professor Thomas Okey who first aroused my interest in Italian studies. The University of Cambridge greatly facilitated my work by including me on its roll of honorary graduates, thus enabling me to take full advantage of its library. Without the easing of my task in countless ways by my wife, Eunice, it could not have been completed.

EDWARD A. ARMSTRONG
Cambridge

Contents

Introduction

Although Saint Francis is regarded throughout Christendom, and especially among the English-speaking peoples, as the saint most closely identified with the love of nature, no serious writer has dealt more than incidentally with this aspect of the Franciscan Legend—understood here in the traditional sense as the stories about him and recorded details of his life and teaching. This is remarkable as few, if any, medieval saints appeal to our age as he does. Among the increasing number who spend most of their time in towns and have less opportunity than they would choose to become closely acquainted with unspoiled nature, many feel an attraction for a man who lived a simple, dedicated life in the Umbrian countryside extending his sympathy alike to human sufferers, animals, and flowers, greeting even the winds and fire as his brethren.

The explanation of the neglect of Franciscan natural history may lie in the complexity of the theme. To concentrate on a scientific treatment with annotations concerning the biology of the species mentioned without discussing the milieu that produced these stories and allusions would be a barren exercise, but the effort necessary to transport ourselves imaginatively into the thirteenth century is far greater than is required to understand the outlook on life of people who lived two or three centuries ago. A naturalist reading the works of John Ray (1628–1705) or Gilbert White's *Natural History of Selborne* (1789) does not encounter points of view much outside his usual experience, although he may smile at White's belief that swallows hibernated in holes, whereas he tends to be puzzled or baffled on turning to the best-known biography of Saint Francis, the *Fioretti* ("Little Flowers of Saint Francis"), and finding himself among strange pieties and animals so docile as to seem unreal. He may thus fail to perceive the interesting problems raised by this abrupt but ephemeral efflorescence of regard for nature in medieval Italy. Indeed, even historians and hagiographers have paid scant attention to the antecedents and explanation of this prominent element in Franciscanism.

It is hoped that this discussion may shed some light on these matters, on the character of the saint who brought Galilee to Umbria, and on the treatment of his life by the biographers, or, at least, may show that the approach to the saint as nature mystic reveals aspects of the Franciscan story and facets of his personality which have been given less prominence than they deserve. He appeared at a time when men were groping after new outlets for their energy, and his single-minded devotion to Christ inspired or influenced, sometimes indirectly and unintentionally, great enterprises in evangelism, exploration, philanthropy, learning, art, and, in the persons of Dante, Jacopone da Todi, and Roger Bacon, poetry and science. He has been called "the real founder of the Italian Renaissance."[1] By tracing some of the rivulets that flowed into what became the broad stream of Franciscan thought and endeavour, the character of the sources and the nature of the momentum they contributed to it may be more clearly discerned.

Although modern biographies give us vivid, colourful portraits of the saint, it is not so easy as some of them suggest to see him clearly. The early biographers on which their successors rely were under strong pressures to depict him acceptably. From the time of his death he was the subject of propaganda campaigns. This is apparent to all who compare the early biographies or consult the critical studies of the sources.[2] In the course of time the exaggerations and distortions increased. Celano, in his *Vita Secunda*, omits any mention of Francis's dissolute youth, which he had described in the *Vita Prima*, but reports his mother as saying: "He will become a son of God by his merits" (2 *Cel.* 3). It has been said of Celano's biographies: "In the *First Life* Francis appears as an extraordinary

---

[1] J. Cartwright, *The Painters of Florence* (London, 1914), p. 3.
[2] J. R. H. Moorman, *Sources for the Life of S. Francis of Assisi* (Manchester, 1940); republished with corrigenda (Farnborough, 1966); R. B. Brooke, *Scripta Leonis, Rufini et Angeli sociorum S. Francisci* (Oxford, 1970).

man, in the *Second* as a saint." [3] Bonaventura, whose *Life* was endorsed as official in 1266 when orders were given for all other biographical material to be destroyed, incorporated almost nine-tenths of Celano's material and framed his narrative to assuage dissension rather than reveal new facts.[4] He eliminated references to some of Francis's personal idiosyncrasies and approximated him to an angel mentioned in the Apocalypse (*Bon.* Prol. 2). It is unnecessary to stress further that the demands of thirteenth-century hagiography, primarily edificatory, were not those of exact history or biography.

If, at times, our inquiry seems to stray beyond the theme of Franciscan natural history, this is because what is related of birds and other creatures must be seen in its medieval setting. The study of the nature stories, and more particularly how they came to be included in the Legend, is of interest for itself; but apart from this, it is a means to the end of understanding the saint and the prejudices of his biographers, as well as the outlook of his age and the character of the movement he created. Moreover, we cannot interpret the relationship of St. Francis to animals, for which he cared so much, unless we interest ourselves in his dealings with people for whom he cared more.

Thus a survey of Franciscan natural history leads us into wide fields and sometimes poses queries concerning such diverse matters as the transmission of medieval legends and the psychology of thirteenth-century biographers. The complexity of the subject is a measure of its interest. We are called on at times to use the methods of the folklorist, as well as those of the historian, theologian, psychologist, and naturalist. But there is a special fascination in detecting clues enabling us in some measure to enter into the mentality of men who lived long ago and even to perceive their unacknowledged motivations. We may thus enlarge our vision and sympathies and at the same time come closer to Saint Francis.

---

[3] W. Goetz, *Die Quellen zur Geschichte des h. Franz von Assisi* (Gotha, 1904), pp. 232, 243.

[4] Fortunately the official decree was not entirely effective. Celano's *Vita Secunda* was recovered in 1798 (but not published until 1806), the *Speculum Perfectionis* in 1898, and the *Legenda Antiqua* in 1922.

Nevertheless no attempt has been made to assess the saint's devotional life and religious achievements or to paint a full-length portrait, though it is hoped that removing some of the gilding and overpainting on the picture left us by the early biographers may reveal the lineaments of the saint more distinctly, enabling us to envisage him and his companions more clearly as they lived, laughed, prayed, and preached in the woods, hills, and towns of central Italy.

Although we are here concerned primarily with Saint Francis and his Legend, this discussion will not have succeeded in its purpose unless it helps the reader to view the saint, not as an isolated figure, but as an outstanding representative of that long line of Christians who, throughout the centuries, delighted in and cared deeply for nature in all its exquisite manifestations. It would be gratifying if it were to encourage others to value their heritage and to love and conserve the natural beauty that still survives but is increasingly threatened to an extent that prompts many to speculate how long the world can sustain man's depredations and still provide an environment in which he can find fulfilment. But those who would like to count themselves as in the tradition of St. Francis do not treat nature compassionately primarily for utilitarian reasons. Moved by the wonder, beauty, interest, and mystery of life's setting on this good earth, they feel impelled to save what they can from spoliation and to increase their own and others' appreciation of the loveliness with which this lonely pearl spinning in the midst of space is clothed. In spiritual fellowship with the Little Poor Man of Assisi, they reflect how great must be God's glory when, despite the limitations imposed by our faculties, His Creation is seen to be so fair.

❈ I ❈

Saint Francis: Nature Mystic

A rich store of Christian nature legends appeared throughout the centuries before the time of Saint Francis, and he was by no means the first saint to show compassion for animals; but the blossoming of Christian compassion for nature in the thirteenth century and the concentration of stories of this kind around the person of Francis, taken for granted by most writers, require explanation. Prior to his appearance, Italy had not been fertile in stories, true or apocryphal, telling of men and animals on friendly terms with one another, nor were Italians then any more renowned than they are now for their kindly treatment of birds and beasts. Why, then, should there have accumulated in connexion with a humble Umbrian friar a galaxy of stories of this kind? Should we accept the tacit and often unchallenged assumption which has prevailed widely hitherto that Francis inaugurated a new outlook on nature in the West? Should we suspect that what is recorded of his relationship to nature was the culmination of a long tradition? Or may the truth lie between the two? It has commonly been assumed that the nature stories in the Legend are, in the main, factual, though it is difficult to believe that this explanation could satisfy any critical, informed reader. Yet such is the aura of piety enveloping Saint Francis and the subtle influence of wishful thinking that their substantial veracity is scarcely questioned by admirers of the saint or even by historical scholars. It is as if the science of animal behaviour, ethology, in which great advances have been made in the last twenty-five years, could be disregarded and even commonsense criteria abrogated. In part the explanation is that minds trained in one discipline are often unsympathetic to the methods of another so that hagiographer and ethologist, the student of legends and the naturalist, have little in common. One views a nature legend historically, the other biologically, and it is easy for each to assume that the other's inquiries have little relevance to his own. Here we shall try to take account of both points of view.

It is evident that many critics feel a certain amount of embarrassment in dealing with the Franciscan nature stories and frequently allow sentimentality to gain the upper hand. Thus, while these legends are given prominence in the popular accounts of the saint, more serious writers and critics tend either to pass lightly over them, apparently regarding them as trivial, or to discuss them in a naïve way. The Wolf of Gubbio still prowls with gory jaws through their pages. Some, perhaps, dismiss these stories as food for babes; yet they are given such importance in the early biographies that any estimate of the achievement of Saint Francis which fails to take full account of them and their antecedents must be inadequate.

This much is clear and needs emphasis: when a man appeared dedicated to living the Christ-life as faithfully as possible, the compassion for nature which constitutes a golden thread in the Gospels and historic Christianity was one of his outstanding characteristics. Furthermore, it must be stressed that to separate compassion for man from compassion for nature in considering the outlook of St. Francis is to make an accurate evaluation of his personality impossible, for his compassion extended to all Creation. If it appears that in what follows a distinction is made between the saint's compassion for man and for nature, this is merely a matter of convenience and should not be allowed to mislead the reader. It has been well said: "All Nature (and there are few more pernicious errors than that which separates man from Nature) is the language in which God expresses His thought." [1]

Our age tends to regard Saint Francis romantically as a person who was kind to animals and friendly toward birds. Thus he is represented in statues at the Carceri in Assisi and the new Guildford cathedral holding doves in his hands. But when emphasis on this aspect of his character involves failure to stress his complete devotion to his Lord and Master, the outcome is a very distorted picture of

[1] W. R. Inge, *Christian Mysticism* (London, 1899), p. 250. Although in what follows "nature" is usually spelled without a capital letter, it is to be understood that it is used in this sense as equivalent to "Creation."

the man and his message. His tenderness toward animals was an expression of his dedication to Christ and of his practical compassion for all Creation. Neither men nor worms were excluded. In thinking of him as one who loved nature, we must not lose sight of the man who served Lady Poverty, tended the diseased, and risked or even sought martyrdom among the Saracens. He endured agony of soul as he came to realize that his exalted ideals were not being maintained by some of his followers and that the fellowship he had founded was being diverted from what he considered the true path. If, in these pages, we concentrate on the animal legends associated with the Poverello and the Franciscan contribution to the Earthly Paradise ideal, harmony between man and beast, this is not to imply that the main influence of Saint Francis and the Order named after him was in encouraging the love of nature. Indeed, his example in this respect was shamefully neglected as controversies developed within the Order and attention was devoted to other matters. Thus, from the time of the General Chapter of Narbonne (1260), it was a rule "that no animal be kept, for any brother or any convent, whether by the Order or by any person in the Order's name, except cats and certain birds for the removal of unclean things." [2]

The Franciscan movement appears as a springtime of piety, compassion, and missionary endeavour spreading over the world. No metaphor can suggest its combination of dynamism with beneficent suasion. Before the death of the saint in 1226, Franciscan missions had reached England, France, Germany, Hungary, Spain, Morocco, Turkey, and the Holy Land; and less than twenty years after his death, two Franciscans arrived at the Mongol court (p. 241). But the accounts of this astonishing peaceful crusade may be found in the pages of the historians.

There are many who, bearing in mind the achievements of St. Francis as the founder of a mendicant Order, devotee of Lady

[2] C. G. Coulton, *From St. Francis to Dante* (London, 1906), p. 86. In a modern convent of Poor Clares there are no inhibitions concerning pets. Sister Mary Francis in *A Right to be Merry* (London, 1907), p. 197, describes how the Festival of St. Francis (4 October) was celebrated by singing the Canticle of the Sun in the vineyard at sunset, the nuns surrounded by cats, a gander, a cow and a rabbit.

Poverty, and evangelist, fail to think of him as an eminent mystic.[3] But his conversion experiences alone are sufficient to place him in this category. How powerful the visitation must have been which forced the enthusiastic young recruit to Count Gentile's troop of horse to return to Assisi! Of his second conversion experience, which involved a state of trance, it was said that "had he then been pricked as with knives all over at once, he could not have moved from the spot" (3 Soc. 7). Celano (2 Cel. 7, 10) says: "Forasmuch as he felt that the change he had undergone was ineffable, it behoves us to be silent concerning that which he himself could not express." Once he rode through Borgo San Sepulcro while the people acclaimed him, cutting off pieces of his habit as souvenirs, so rapt in ecstasy that later he inquired how soon they would be arriving at the village (2 Cel. 98). When a vision came to him of his movement spreading throughout the world, "he was caught up above himself and wholly absorbed in a certain light; the capacity of his mind was enlarged, and he beheld clearly what was to come to pass" (1 Cel. 26). Praying before a crucifix he was "raised up and snatched into Heaven, whether in the body or out of the body God knoweth" (Spec. Perf. 60). The stigmatization in which Christ's wounds appeared in his hands, feet, and side was a mystical experience of the most intense kind.[4]

In the *Fioretti* (14) we hear of corporate ecstatic experiences in which Francis participated. He and his companions "were rapt out of themselves, and lay as though dead and insensible to the world."

---

[3] The virtues of Martha and Mary do not exclude one another. Among outstanding mystics who were doers as well as seers may be mentioned Saint Bernard, a contemplative active in good works, Saint Teresa, and Saint John of the Cross, of whom Inge wrote "his character was one of fiery energy and unresting industry" (op. cit., p. 224).

[4] The reader interested in stigmatization may refer to the data cited by Paul Sabatier in *The Life of St. Francis of Assisi* (London, 1920), pp. 433–443, and the bibliography provided by P. Gratien in his *Histoire de la Fondation et de l'Évolution de l'Ordre des Frères Mineurs au XIIIe Siècle* (Paris, 1928), p. 18. For a more recent discussion, see J. Danemarie, *The Mystery of the Stigmata* (London, 1934). Padre Pio, who died recently in Italy, bore the stigmata, but the Church has been reticent concerning him. Cf. O. de Liso, *Padre Pio* (London, 1961).

We are also told of Friar John's visionary experience and of Friar Juniper's remaining rapt for a long period. It could be argued that the accounts of some of these ecstatic states in conventional terms weaken confidence in them, but experiences of rapture take conventional forms and tend to be described in set terms among communities which regard them as normal, though occasional, ways in which God manifests Himself.

Saint Francis was not only a mystic but a nature mystic. Like Clement of Alexandria before him, he saw nature as sanctified by the Incarnation; and like William Blake later, he could see heaven in a wild flower. The evidence does not depend on the stories of his tender dealings with animals, though these may be cited in support. Celano (1 *Cel.* 80, 81) tells us:

> When he considered the glory of the flowers, how happy he was to gaze at the beauty of their forms and to enjoy their marvellous fragrance! How easily his spirit would take wing and rise to meditating on the beauty of that unique flower that blossomed fair as the approaching spring, from "the root of Jesse" and by its fragrance brought new life to countless men who were dead in their souls!
>
> When he found many flowers growing together, it might happen that he would speak to them and encourage them, as though they could understand, to praise the Lord. It was the same with the fields of corn and the vineyards, the stones in the earth and in the woods, all the beauteous meadows, the tinkling brooks, the sprouting gardens, earth, fire, air and wind—all these he exhorted in his pure, childlike spirit to love God and to serve Him joyfully.
>
> He was wont to call all created things his brothers and sisters, and in a wonderful manner inaccessible to others he would enter into the secret of things as one to whom "the glorious liberty of the children of God" had been given [Rom. viii. 21].

The Christian nature mystic has seldom been described more felicitously than in the last few lines.

Saint Bonaventura (viii. 8) describes Francis as absorbed in an ecstasy of prayer while holding a small waterfowl in his hands. He wrote (ix. 1), "He beheld in fair things Him who is the most fair," and (x. 2), "Ofttimes he was rapt in such ecstasies of contemplation as that he was carried out of himself, and, while perceiving things beyond mortal sense, knew naught of what was happening in the outer world around him." The *Mirror of Perfection* (115) also mentions his being caught up in ecstatic contemplation of inanimate as well as animate things of God's creation: "Nor is it strange," we read, "if the fire and the other creatures were obedient to him and venerated him, for, as we who were with him have very often seen, he was so much drawn to them, and rejoiced in them so much, and his spirit was moved with so much pity and compassion for them, that he would not see them badly treated, and he used to speak with them with inward gladness, as if they had reason, whence by their occasion, he was ofttimes wrapt up to God." Thus he treated even inanimate things as, to all intents and purposes, children of God.

At times his reverence for nature went to extremes reminiscent of Indian ascetics. Because water was used in baptism, he took care not to tread where his wash basin had been emptied; he stepped with awe on stones "for the love of Him Who is called 'The Rock.'" Because Christ suffered on the Tree, he would not allow the whole of a tree to be cut down; and he called for a plot in the garden to be reserved for flowers "for the love of Him who is called the 'flower of the field' and 'the lily of the valley'—an allusion to the allegorical interpretation of the Song of Songs (ii. 1). Wild flowers delighted him: "He bade the gardener not dig up the outlying parts round the garden, in order that in their seasons the greenness of grass and beauty of flowers might proclaim the beauteous Father of all things" (2 *Cel.* 165).[5] Centuries later Robert Browning in "Saul" showed

---

[5] At Farneto, in Northern Italy, there is a legend that a certain tree grew from the staff Saint Francis thrust into the ground. A similar story is told of Irish and other saints. Although the staff was an important item in the equipment of Irish saints, it was not carried by St. Francis and his companions as they kept to the letter of Luke ix.3 (*Bon.* iii. 13) rather than Mark vi.8. The story is in line with the saint's love for trees and also illustrates the pleasure taken by Italian country folk in finding (or inventing) an association between him and their village. Cf. H. E. Goad, "The Dilemma of St. Francis and the Two Traditions," in *St. Francis: 1226–1926: Essays in Commemoration*, ed. W. Seton (London, 1926), pp. 129–162. The origin of the Hospitalers of Saint Anthony is ascribed to a vision of a multitude of diseased people being healed beneath the shade of a tree grown from the saint's tau-headed crutch. St. Francis

that he understood something of the kind of ecstasy experienced by the saint:

God is seen God
In the star, in the stone, in the flesh,
in the soul and the clod.

Brother Giles also participated in this sacramental regard for nature. He would pick blades of grass or lift up stones and kiss them.[6] The writer of the passages from the *Speculum Perfectionis* (118) quotes Francis as believing "every creature cries aloud 'God made me for thee, O man!'" and gives his personal testimony: "Whence we who were with him used to see him rejoice, within and without, as it were, in all things created; so that touching or seeing them his spirit seemed to be not on earth but in heaven."

Possibly the prominence of the nature stories in the early Legend may be due in part to the biographers' aim to forestall accusations of eccentricity and suspicions of heresy by describing his love of nature in pictorial terms which could not be misconstrued. In his attitude to animals he was continuing what the *Lives* of earlier saints showed to be an orthodox tradition. But suspicions that he was inclined to pantheism such as have been voiced from time to time rest on the error of not distinguishing it from sacramentalism. The saint was a devoted sacramentalist (*Bon.* ix. 2). "He had a singular and intimate love of creatures, especially anything pertaining to God or the Order" (*Spec. Perf.* 113). For him nature spoke of God. All created things pointed beyond themselves to their Creator. Even the interlacing twigs in a hedge reminded him of the Cross (1 *Cel.* 45). It was because nature revealed in sight, sound, and fragrance the handiwork and glory of God that he admired and rejoiced in things

---

is said to have stayed at one of their convents in 1209 when he obtained the pope's approval of his movement. Cf. E. Gilliat-Smith, *St. Clare of Assisi* (London, 1914), pp. 18–19. Celano (I *Cel.* 33) and Bonaventura (iii. 10) mention Francis's vision of the bending tree in this context.

6 Like Saint Francis, Brother Giles was enraptured with the love of God, nature, and music. He, too, is said to have played a make-believe viol, quoting Scripture—Isaiah lxiv. 4 and 1 Cor. ii. 9. Cf. *Vita fratris Aegidii*, in *Analecta Franc.* III, 105.

of beauty. He envisaged all Creation, man supremely, as worshipping the Creator. In his sacramental regard for nature, Francis differed alike from the heretics of his time and the philosophers and poets of the nineteenth century whose romanticism was tinged with pantheism. So far was Goethe from admiring or even being interested in the saint that when he visited Assisi he inspected the temple of Minerva but considered the church of San Francesco beneath his attention. Bonaventura (iv. 3) tells us that Francis taught the brethren "to praise God in all things and through all His creatures." The witness of the two scholars, Celano, the elegant writer, author of the *Dies Irae*,[7] and Bonaventura, mystically minded as he was but more at home in the lecture halls of Paris than the Umbrian countryside, is all the more valuable as there is little or no likelihood that they personally enjoyed mystical experiences of nature to such an extent as to attribute them gratuitously to Francis. In this matter they were not conforming to convention. Moreover, what they relate of the saint coheres with the evidence of other informants and rings true to the testimonies of many Christian nature mystics.

Suso, after viewing the countryside, listening to the birds' songs, and reflecting on the pairing of animals and the springtime joy of young and old, cried out: "O tender God, if Thou art so loving in Thy creatures, how fair and lovely must Thou be in Thyself!"[8] Traherne wrote:

> Had I been alone in Adams steed, how should I have Admird the Glory of the World! What a Confluence of Thoughts and Wonders and Joys and Tydings would have replenished me in the sight of so Magnificent a Theatre, so Bright a Dwelling Place, so great a Temple, so stately a Hous replenished with all Kind of Treasure, raised out of Nothing Created for me and for me alone . . . And how Glorious must the King be, that could out of Nothing Erect such a Curious, so Great, and so Beautifull a Fabrick! It was Glorious while new; and is as new as it was Glorious.[9]

7 F. Casolini, *Enciclopedia Cattolica* XII (1954), 277–282.
8 Cited in J. R. Illingworth, *Divine Immanence* (London, 1898), p. 41.
9 *Centuries of Meditation*, First Century, 65. Cf. *Poems, Centuries and Three Thanksgivings*, ed. A. Ridler (Oxford, 1966), p. 194.

Such mingled delight in God and Nature, Creation and Creator, has been experienced by many Christians, scholarly and simple, throughout the centuries. Evelyn Underhill, referring to a passage in the *Phaedrus*, remarked:

> Most men in the course of their lives have known such Platonic hours of initiation, when the sense of beauty has risen from a pleasant feeling to a passion, and an element of strangeness has been mingled with their joy . . . in such moods of heightened consciousness each blade of grass seems fierce with meaning, and becomes a well of wondrous light, a "little emerald set in the City of God." [10]

Although detailed discussion of the characteristics of Christian nature mysticism would be out of place here, some comments on what is implied are necessary because writers today query or deny the validity of the concept and so define religious mysticism that Christian nature mysticism might seem a contradiction in terms. It has been claimed that the *sine qua non* of all strictly religious mysticism is concentration on ultimate reality to the exclusion of all that we normally call nature—total detachment from it. According to Professor Zaehner, "The nature mystic identifies himself with the whole of Nature and in his exalted moments sees himself as being one with Nature and as having passed beyond good and evil." [11] The name of Saint Francis appears only once in this writer's work—mentioned together with other saints and not as a mystic. Another authority, Dom David Knowles, although devoting a chapter to nature mysticism, makes no mention of the saint of Assisi in his *What is Mysticism?* [12] Are we, then, to be content to call Francis merely a "nature lover"?

These writers are able to think in the terms they do because, owing to the fear of Catharism, the imposition of certain disciplines on the Orders, and other influences mentioned later, the roots of what might have become a flourishing tradition of Christian nature

---

[10] Evelyn Underhill, *Mysticism* (London, 1960), p. 364 (1st ed., 1911). For a remarkable description of "the presence of a Great and Holy Spirit" experienced in nature, cf. J. Ruskin, *Modern Painters* (Popular edn., London), III, 309.

[11] R. C. Zaehner, *Mysticism: Sacred and Profane* (Oxford and London, 1961), pp. 33, 109 (1st ed., 1957).

[12] London, 1967.

mysticism were allowed to remain unwatered. It could be argued that the Church failed those who might have become its nature mystics by giving insufficient encouragement to worshipful delight in the natural world. In Christendom even the thanksgiving service for the fruits of the earth, the Harvest Festival, is a comparatively recent institution. Nevertheless, from the Desert Fathers to the present time there has been a succession, albeit intermittent, of Christian nature mystics; but because their biographers—when they had any —did not recognize the authenticity of the tradition to which they belonged, some without realizing their lineage, little has been recorded of them. Their witness has received such meagre acknowledgement that it has been possible for modern writers to discount their influence and even, quoting God's injunction to Adam to subdue the earth (Gen. i. 28) without mentioning that He put him in the Garden "to care for it" (Gen. ii. 15), to taunt the Church with encouraging the ruthless exploitation of nature.[13]

Even today, as Zaehner's comment shows, the compatibility of Christianity and nature mysticism can be called in question or denied by Christian writers. Richard Jefferies, who regarded all organized religion as superstition, is commonly considered the nature mystic par excellence. Nevertheless, despite his views on the irreconcilability of Christianity and nature mysticism, Professor Zaehner states that he "appears in fact as an unwilling witness on Christianity's behalf." [14] This authority does not consider Wordsworth to have been a mystic because he finds no evidence of his having sustained what he defines as a unitive experience—a view with which not all readers of his poetry would agree. Knowles refers tentatively to an external resemblance between his mystical experiences and those of acknowledged Christian mystics but gives insufficient weight to the lines he quotes:

> Communing in this sort through earth and heaven
> With every sort of creature, as it looked

[13] In a later work, *Christian Delight in Nature*, I hope to discuss the treatment of nature in Christian hagiography and the tradition of Christian nature mysticism.

[14] Zaehner, *op. cit.*, p. 48.

> Towards the Uncreated with a countenance
> Of adoration, with an eye of love.

and other more mystical passages.[15] As these two authors find it difficult to accommodate nature mysticism within theistic categories, they have not seriously considered the evidence for Christian nature mysticism.

Because we have no introspective accounts of the raptures experienced by Saint Francis to compare with those so profusely provided by Saint Teresa of Avila and other such eminent religious mystics in their efforts to communicate the incommunicable, it would be idle to discuss the extent to which the Seraphic Father's ultimate ecstasies involved what Zaehner defines as true mysticism, "total and absolute detachment from Nature"; but his contemplation was often conducted in the open air amid chosen wild and beautiful surroundings. The summit of La Verna, the scene of the stigmatization, is thus described:

> Beneath the trees was an undergrowth of beech-scrub and fields of dog's mercury, speckled everywhere with cyclamen. The winding path was stepped by tree-roots and carpeted with pine needles and beech leaves. . . . Outcrops of stratified and moss-cushioned rock made seats by the path on which an exhausted climber, long ago, might have rested. And all the wood was stippled with sunlight and aflicker with butterflies." [16]

It was there that Friar Leo, betrayed by the rustling of his feet in the beech leaves as he approached in the moonlight, came upon St. Francis and was told that he had been given two lights within the soul, the knowledge and understanding of himself and the knowledge and understanding of the Creator: "Then was I illumined by the light of contemplation, whereby I beheld the depths of the infinite goodness and wisdom and power of God" (*Fioretti, 3rd consid. of stigmata*). To seek a distinction between this and "unitive experience" is a barren exercise. Even supposing that the raptures of Saint

---

15 "The Prelude," II, 411–414, XIII, 275–277. Cf. M. Moorman, *William Wordsworth* (Oxford, 1965), I, 35–40; Inge, *op. cit.* pp. 305–316.

16 E. Raymond, *In the Steps of St. Francis* (London, 1938), p. 306.

Francis and certain other Christian visionaries did not involve complete detachment from nature, this would not preclude their being rightly regarded as nature mystics. In defining a mystic it is much easier to identify the lower rungs of the ladder on which he sets foot to begin the heavenly ascent than to describe the transcendent characteristics of the region to which he climbs. The points of importance are the degree to which a religious mystic's experiences of enlightenment or exaltation is inspired by or dependent upon his attitude toward nature and the extent to which he regards nature as a manifestation of the divine. For nature viewed in this way, we may conveniently use the traditional term Creation. A Christian nature mystic is therefore one whose mystical experience, whatever form it may take, is based on Christian beliefs and involves an appreciation of Creation as God's handiwork.

Such a mystic's *point d'appui* for the ascent to the spiritual empyrean normally includes certain symbols, outward forms, ritual acts, or postures found effective in inducing ecstasy. Saint Catherine of Siena passed into prolonged states of rapture on receiving Holy Communion, Denis the Carthusian entered into ecstasy on hearing the Veni Creator, Julian of Norwich and Saint Francis became entranced while gazing on a crucifix.[17] But Francis also became rapt during his contemplation of the "creatures of God" and while clasping a bird; Saint Douceline, who continued the nature mysticism of the Poverello, went into ecstasy while looking at a flower or listening to a bird's song;[18] and Saint Teresa remarked that to look on trees, water, and flowers enabled her to recollect the Presence of God.[19] In our own time Teilhard de Chardin was led by his geological and palaeontological investigations to an intellectual mysticism in which all Creation was seen to be sacramental.[20] Thus, while some Christians have found symbols contrived or administered by man means to lead them to the heights, others have enjoyed ecstasies and received grace

[17] Underhill, *op. cit.*, p. 364.
[18] Abbé Albanes, *La Vie de Sainte Douceline* (Paris, 1879).
[19] *Vida*, ix. 6.
[20] Cf. *La Messe sur le Monde, Le Milieu Divin*, and other works listed by Claude Cuénot in *Pierre Teilhard de Chardin, les grandes étapes de son évolution* (Paris, 1958).

and inspiration through the intensity of their enjoyment of the works of God.

The theologian or psychologist might define the Christian nature mystic as a person of Christian faith who, through the apprehension of the beauty, goodness, and glory of God revealed in Creation, is uplifted to an ineffable experience; but there are many gradations between the pangs of delight and thankfulness in the presence of earth's loveliness felt by ordinary Christian folk and the raptures of such as Saint Francis. Those who would not claim more than—to use John Wesley's phrase—to have felt their hearts "strangely warmed" on perceiving some beautiful scene, sound, or scent can claim to be of the company of Saint Francis.

He is the patron saint, not of those who view the enjoyment of nature as an end in itself nor in pantheist appreciation, but of those who, taking pleasure—sometimes rising to ecstatic delight—in the exuberance and diversity of Creation, thankfully regard them as expressions of divine splendour, sacramental intimations of glories beyond human apprehension:

> The meanes therefore which vnto vs is lent,
> Him to behold, is on his workes to looke,
> Which he hath made in beauty excellent,
> And in the same, as in a brasen booke,
> To read enregistred in euery nooke
> His goodnesse, which his beautie doth declare.
> For all thats good, is beautifull and faire.[21]

[21] E. Spenser, "An Hymne of Heavenly Beautie," in *The Poetical Works of Edmund Spenser*, ed. J. C. Smith and E. de Selincourt (Oxford, 1924), p. 597.

❈ II ❈

Traditions that
Influenced Saint Francis

Before discussing the natural history in the Franciscan Legend, we may survey briefly some of the influences that affected the saint and his brotherhood because much of what follows is designed to show in some detail that the Legend owes a great deal to earlier traditions. Having stressed what was personal to himself in Francis's nature mysticism, we must note, so far as is relevant to our theme and space allows, the extent to which he was the child of his age, in debt to the past and the ambience into which he was born.

The epoch was in some obvious respects one of confusion, and to many the outlook appeared grey. It seemed to reflective folk that they were living *in vespere mundi tendentis ad occasum*. But from our vantage point we can see that there was a stirring among the bones of medievalism. It was a time of lively thought and initiative. The verdict of the Oxford Regius Professor of Modern History that the period around 1250 marks the highest point of the European Middle Ages does not differ greatly from that of Taine who regarded Saint Francis as the summit of medieval civilization.[1] This opinion is acceptable to those who endorse, "No Saint Francis, no Dante." But the liveliness of the age declined, and spiritual enthusiasm yielded to administrative discipline. One has only to mention the persecution of the Franciscan Spirituals and the recurrent famines culminating in the Black Death (1348) to realize the extent to which spiritual aspirations were checked during the century after the first rapid expansion of the Franciscan Order.

In seeking to understand how Francis came to be what he was and

[1] H. Taine, *Voyage en Italie* (Paris, 1914), pp. 25–28; H. Trevor-Roper, *The Rise of Christian Europe* (London, 1965), pp. 161 ff.

why his biographers depicted him as they did, it is not implied that he, or for that matter anyone else, can be regarded in simple terms as the product of his age. We must not fail to take account of that which he would have said was supremely important—the hand of God upon him. God's lightning strikes, illuminates, and kindles unpredictably. Moreover, in all cultures the nature mystic is apt to appear unexpectedly although we may identify aspects of the particular society which favour his appearance. Other visionaries besides Francis who showed tenderness for nature, notably William Blake, came on the scene when nature mysticism was at a low ebb.

Together with his love of God, Saint Francis manifested three outstanding characteristics: delight in nature, joyfulness, and devotion to poverty. We have already considered the first of these insofar as it was a spiritual endowment and an inward impulsion. Later in this chapter and throughout most of this book, we shall review the traditions and influences that contributed to this aspect of the saint's character and the accounts given of him by his biographers. But his response to nature cannot be understood without taking into consideration how closely it was linked with his gaiety and devotion to Lady Poverty.

Gaiety

A number of environmental influences fostered the joyous element in the saint's character, among which his feelings of affinity with France were of major importance. The *Legend of the Three Companions* (2) mentions that, although he was christened Giovanni after Saint John the Baptist, his name was changed to Francesco when his father returned from a business visit to France; but this source cannot always be relied on. Probably he received this soubriquet later because of the flamboyant way he aired his smattering of the language. Latin was still spoken in Italy by people other than scholars in his time, and it was taught at the school run by the canons of San Giorgio near his home which, according to Celano, he attended.[2] There is no reason to suppose that French was included in the curriculum. Francis may have picked up most of his French

[2] Cel. 23; *Legenda ad usum chori*, 13. *Analecta Franciscana* X, 124.

from his father, who, we may assume, had sufficient command of
the language for business transactions. If so, we might, perhaps, infer
that father and son were not always on such ill terms as the episode
in which he returned his clothes to his father might suggest (1 *Cel.*
14–15; 3 *Soc.* 20). However, "he was a merrier man than his father,
given unto jests and songs" (3 *Soc.* 2). French was the language of
commerce, and cloth merchants were probably the greatest travellers
of the time. The story (1 *Cel.* 8–9; 3 *Soc.* 16) of Francis's sale of
some of his father's merchandise at Foligno—a questionable transac-
tion—suggests that he may have had some knowledge of the trade.
If we were to suppose that Pietro allowed his high-spirited son to
accompany him on some of his trips, perhaps as far as Provençe, it
would explain Francis's love of that land and its troubadour songs.
He would thus have acquired his thirst for travel and have rubbed
shoulders with an assortment of people no less varied than those
depicted in *The Canterbury Tales*. Frenchmen, Germans, and Irishmen were among the folk frequenting the roads and inns. Contacts of
this kind explain the traffic in ideas from one region of Europe to
another which, despite the primitive means of communication, was
at this period remarkably rapid.

Francis went through the woods singing in French (3 *Soc.* 33;
Bon. ii. 5), and "whenever he was filled with the ardour of the Holy
Spirit he would utter ardent words in French" (2 *Cel.* 13). Celano
remarks: "He loved France as the friend of the Lord's Body, and
longed to die there by reason of her reverence for hallowed things"
(2 *Cel.* 201). He broke into French on all sorts of occasions although
"he spake it not aright" (3 *Soc.* 10). Whenever he was filled with
the ardour of the Holy Spirit, "he would burst out into a French
song of joy" (2 *Cel.* 127). "The love and compassion of Christ would
fill Blessed Francis like strong wine, and the rapturous melodies that
rose in his heart found expression in Gallic song, the stream of
divine whispers which he alone could hear rushing out in a flood of
jubilation in the French tongue" (*Spec. Perf.* 93; 3 *Soc.* 24).[3]

[3] The authenticity of the story that he used French when asking folk to help
him repair St. Damian's (3 *Soc.* 24) has been questioned. Cf. *Testamentum S.
Clarae*, 4; Fr. P. Robinson, *The Writings of S. Clare of Assisi, Archivum Franciscanum Historicum* XIII (1920), 442–449.

Chivalry and the knightly ideal, so prominent in French culture at this time, inspired him. Celano (2 *Cel.* 10) refers to the vision of the Crucified as deflecting him from his ambition to win knighthood. He calls him "Christ's strenuous knight" (2 *Cel.* 21). The ideal remained with him, and he acted as one who regarded courtesy as one of the attributes of God.[4] In the thirteenth century the connexion established between religious devotion and chivalry was based on the cult of Our Lady which involved a romantic and mystical idealization of womanhood, as is apparent in Dante's *Divina Commedia.* It contrasts with the misogyny of Francis's biographers (pp. 231–235). "He was as though by nature courteous" noted the author of *The Three Companions* (3), and it was said that he even greeted sheep courteously (*Bon.* viii. 7). When about to submit to the cauterization of his face with the object of remedying his defective eyesight—such was the crude medicine of the time—he besought Brother Fire to be courteous (2 *Cel.* 166; *Spec. Perf.* 115; *Leg. Ant.* 24, 46, 49).

According to a remark recorded in the *Mirror of Perfection,* Francis as a youth had been inspired by the romances of King Arthur. He said of his friars: "These are my companions of the Round Table" (*Spec. Perf.* 72; *Leg. Ant.* 71–2). He thought of himself and the other friars as *joculatores domini:* "We are the minstrels of the Lord," he used to say; and he asked, "What are the servants of the Lord but His minstrels, who should raise the hearts of men and move them to spiritual joy?" (*Spec. Perf.* 100). We might almost call him the mountebank of God, acting as he did with gay abandon, giving his clothes away, preaching half-naked if only he could save souls, singing like a troubadour in French while stroking one stick on another as if he were bowing a fiddle, and then, much moved and "raised to Heaven," dissolving in tears (*Spec. Perf.* 93; 2 *Cel.* 127). Thus he threw open his soul to beauty, goodness, truth, and joy, and in so doing pioneered the way for men to cast off the bonds that prevented their seeing the world, God's world, as it is. Celano's testimony is all the more valuable because it is so evident that he found it difficult to reconcile his hero's gaiety with his austerity and the

---

4 "La cortesia è una delle proprietà di Dio" (*Fioretti* 37). "Cortesia" includes the concept of generosity.

severe disciplines which, according to Celano's own statements (2 *Cel.* 206), he imposed on the friars. The biographers depict him as embodying the contrasting qualities, exuberance and austerity, which make the culture of the age so fascinating. Francis "strove ever to be gladsome of heart" (2 *Cel.* 125). His counsel to his followers was: "Let them show themselves rejoicing in the Lord, merry and joyful, and gracious as is meet" (2 *Cel.* 128). Through renunciation perfect joy could be attained (*Fioretti* 8). The *Regula Prima* prescribed that: "Wherever they found themselves the Brethren should abstain from murmuring; that they should avoid appearing sad and sombre like the hypocrites; that they show themselves, on the contrary, joyous in the Lord, amiable and gay as it became them to be." More than five centuries earlier, Saint Aldhelm († 709), abbot of Malmesbury and patron saint of Dorset, had practised similar evangelistic methods, singing and dancing on a bridge like a professional travelling minstrel and then proclaiming the Gospel and the wonders of Creation. Less than twenty years before Francis was born, a troubadour singing by the wayside was responsible for bringing about Peter Waldo's change of heart. Francis was following the same tradition when, arriving at Montefeltro during a *festa* on the occasion of the knighting of a young page, he jumped on to a low wall in full view of the concourse of gorgeously attired men and ladies and took as his text lines from a vernacular ditty in which the lover pledges all to his lady, drawing from them the lesson that men should abandon all for Christ:

> *Tanto il bene ch'io aspetto,*
> *Ch'ogni pena m' è diletto.*

> So great the good I hope to gain
> I find delight in every pain.
> (*Fioretti, 1st consid. of stigmata*)

Francis held that the surest remedy against the wiles of the devil was spiritual joy (2 *Cel.* 125). If this Christian jubilation was unusual in the thirteenth century, ample precedent could be found in the Gospels (John xvi. 20–24), Saint Paul's Epistles (2 Cor. vi. 10; Phil. iv. 4), and the *Lives* of the saints. It was said of the hermit

Anthony that he was always joyful—*semper hilarem faciens gerens.*[5]
No doubt the influence of the French troubadours then touring Italy
contributed to Francis's youthful love of bright colours, gay songs,
and natural beauty. All this was "baptized into Christ." His joy became spiritualized and vitalized as he perceived God's handiwork
in mountains and meadows, the songs of birds, flower fragrances,
sunlight and shadow. Gaiety and nature mysticism were inseparably
intertwined in his character. "He had learnt to marvel at the glorious
handiwork of the Creator even as seen in little things" (*Bon.* viii. 9).
All lovers of the countryside know the lifting of the heart which
comes with the sight of a lovely scene or brightly plumaged bird. In
their most intense form, experiences of this kind become rapture
such as the young Wordsworth knew; but when they are combined
with the consciousness of God as the source of beauty and the over-
whelmingly bounteous bestower of all good, a unique delight mingles
with the mystic ecstasy. The worship of nature as such is seldom or
never enough to generate this kind of joy because additional intensity
is contributed by the acknowledgement of a Power beyond things
seen which creates, sustains, and cares.

The life of the Little Poor Man of Assisi was a vindication of St.
Paul's triumphant claim: "Having nothing, yet possessing all things"
(2 Cor. vi. 10). His joy was the outcome of the abandonment of self
and the spiritual freedom thereby acquired. He used to encourage
his companions, saying, "Cast thy burden on the Lord and He shall
sustain thee" (*Bon.* iii. 7). His appreciation of nature was thus
intensified by his emancipation from worldliness. Like Thoreau he
was the richer by virtue of what he could do without.

Poverty

The early Franciscan wandering way of life, involving devotion to
poverty, enabled the friars to acquire a feeling for the outdoor world
unknown to most townsfolk of their time for whom nature was an
unfamiliar and sometimes disquieting background to their lives.
During the thirteenth century the majority of educated men lived

[5] Migne, *Patrologia Latinae* LXXIII, 156; *Vita Ant. c.* 40; *Hist. Laus: Vita abb. Apoll.*

enclosed inside town or monastery walls and, intellectually, remained within modes of thought and frameworks of doctrine formulated with scarcely any reference to, or observation of, wild nature. This "return to nature" may have nurtured in the companions of Saint Francis an independence which rendered some of them less amenable to authoritarian direction. Francesco Bernardone's original inspiration had been to gather together an itinerant brotherhood to serve the Church. When, not long after their founder's death, the friars were increasingly drawn to settle in towns and places of learning, their love of nature and compassion for animals declined.

So assimilated to their woodland haunts did Francis and his companions appear that women fled from them and folk spoke of them as if they were more like indigenous denizens of the forest than fully human beings—*quasi silvestres homines* (3 *Soc.* 34, 37). They lodged in caves such as may be seen at Greccio and the Carceri on Mount Subasio where a hollow in the rock is pointed out as the saint's bed, or in booths made of branches. Those who visited the friars described their sleeping places as like the lairs of wild beasts (2 *Cel.* 63). In the *Fioretti* we hear of them praying in the woods three times as often as in churches. Celano (1 *Cel.* 71) aptly applies to Francis a verse of the Song of Songs (ii. 14): "In the clefts of the rock he built his nest and in the hollow of the wall was his habitation."

Allegiance to destitution was, for Francis, so supremely important that his followers, after his death, were willing to endure torture and martyrdom rather than betray this ideal. In wedding Lady Poverty he was adopting a way of life which had always had an attraction for earnest Christians, inspired by the memory of John the Baptist and of Christ's sojourn in the wilderness. As we shall see presently, the renunciation of possessions was characteristic of many sects and communities before and during the time of Saint Francis, though he carried it to a length uncommon among such groups by repudiating communal as well as personal property. Francis's wish for his men was that "poverty should sing out to them of their pilgrimage and exile" (*Spec. Perf.* 5). It is extremely unlikely that he ever envisaged his movement in terms of the existing monastic Orders or wished his followers to live enclosed. When he found that a house had been built in which to hold a chapter meeting, he was so incensed that the brethren should be involved in holding property that he clambered up to the roof and began ripping off the tiles, only stopping when it was pointed out to him that the house did not belong to the friars (2 *Cel.* 57; cf. *Spec. Perf.* 6–7). He said: "One ascends to heaven quicker from a hovel than from a palace" (1 *Cel.* 42). Celano mentions that he vacated a cell because someone referred to it as belonging to him (2 *Cel.* 59). The tradition that a monk should not call anything his own goes back to Cassian and Saint Columcille. Saint Benedict set in his Rule: "Let no one own any property."

A story relates that on one occasion Lady Poverty asked to see the brethren's cloister. Francis and his companions led her to the summit of a neighbouring hill and showed her the countryside, saying: "Madam, there is our cloister." At Erfurt the citizens offered to build a cloister for the friars, but Giordano di Giano replied: "A cloister! In our Order we don't know what that is. Just build a house near the water where we can go down to wash our feet."[6] Jacques de Vitry remarked of the friars: "They live after the manner of the primitive Church . . . By day they go into the towns and villages in order to win others by setting them an example. At night they return to some hermitage or lonely place and give themselves to meditation."[7] Only in England did the first friars establish themselves in towns, perhaps partly for climatic reasons. Their chapel in Cambridge was so flimsy that a carpenter was able to construct it in one day.[8]

The origins of some monastic Orders were not very different. The Carthusians came into being in 1084 when Bruno, a Cologne nobleman's son, settled with a small group of followers in a rocky wilderness outside Grenoble. Their régime combined the ideals of Western

[6] E. d'Alençon, *Sacrum Commercium S. Francisci cum Domina Paupertate* (London, 1904), p. 36; H. Boehmer, *Chronica fratris Jordani* (Paris, 1908), p. 39.
[7] G. Golubovich, *Bibilioteca della Terra Santa e dell'Oriente Francescano* I (Florence, 1906), 5.
[8] Thomas of Eccleston, *De adventu fratrum minorum in Angliam*, ed. R. Howlett, in *Monumenta Franc.* II (Rolls series, London, 1882), 1–28; *Analecta Franc.* I (1885); Fr. Cuthbert, *The Chronicle of Thomas of Eccleston* (Edinburgh, 1909), p. 28; *Tractatus de adventu fratrum minorum in Angliam*, ed. A. G. Little (Manchester, 1951).

monasticism with the practices of Eastern anchorites in a manner
reminiscent of Irish asceticism—which long retained traces of its
derivation from the way of life of the Desert Fathers. Like the Irish
monks, they devoted themselves to transcribing books. In view of
these similarities and the powerful influence of the Irish in Cologne
during Bruno's youth, we cannot escape the inference that his ideas
may have been moulded by what he knew of Irish beliefs and
practices.[9] The movement spread rapidly, but Bruno migrated to
join the hermits occupying the caverns of Della Torre in Calabria.
One of his letters expressing his delight on viewing a beautiful landscape is reminiscent of St. Basil's appreciation of the scenery around
his hermitage on the river Iris.[10] It foreshadows the similar enjoyment of the countryside felt by Joachim of Fiore (p. 30).

   The Cistercians, too, evolved from a small community established
in a few huts on a densely forested hill at Molesme in 1075. Stephen
Harding, usually considered their founder, was reared in Sherborne
monastery of which the Irish-educated Saint Aldhelm had been abbot
for thirty years. His character and ideals closely resembled those of
Saint Francis. Less well known is the Order founded by Blessed
Robert of Arbrissel (1117) who sought solitude in the forest of
Craon, living at first in a hollow tree with forest creatures as his only
companions until his sanctity attracted men and women to his
retreat. He may have influenced the *Humiliati* from whom Francis
drew some inspiration.[11] Thus Francis, in adopting the rustic way of

---

   [9] In Cologne the church of Saint Brigid adjoined the abbey of Saint Martin
which, together with the abbey of Saint Pantaleon, became Irish during the
tenth and eleventh centuries. The church of Saint Martin still treasures relics
of Saint Brigid. Four other parish churches and seven chapels in the diocese of
Cologne are dedicated to the saint of Kildare, and local farmers placed their
animals under her protection well into the twentieth century and perhaps do so
still. Cf. L. Gougaud, *Gaelic Pioneers of Christianity* (Dublin, 1923), p. 107.
   [10] *Ep.* XIV. Cf. R. J. Deferrari, *St. Basil, the Letters* I (London and New
York, 1926), 106–110.
   [11] E. S. Davison, *Forerunners of St. Francis and other Studies* (London,
1928), pp. 51, 172; E. Gilliat-Smith, *St. Clare of Assisi* (London, 1914), p. 21;
Orlando of Chiusi had a cell under a beech tree (*Fioretti, 2nd consid. of stigmata*), and Saint Anthony of Padua retired from time to time to a cell in a

life as an aid to greater devotion, was continuing an ancient tradition.

In addition to these monastic and anchoritic movements, the eleventh and twelfth centuries had seen the rise of many sects and communities led by laymen, some orthodox but the majority adjudged heretical, seeking a different way of life from that which the Church, as they saw it, seemed to represent. The rapid spread of unorthodox views, especially in the south of France, had been stimulated by the Church's failure in its two primary functions, pastoral care and teaching. These Catharist heresies were dualist, revivals of eastern Manichaean beliefs based on the principle of two equal powers at war in the world, one good, the other evil. The way was thus opened for extreme doctrines that led on the one hand to ascetic austerities, and on the other to immorality. There were swarms of such sects: *Reclusi, Humiliati,* Beghards, Apostolic Brethren, Brothers of the Free Spirit, Brothers and Sisters of Penitence, *Continentes,* and so forth. The lives of the members of some of these contrasted favourably with the self-seeking, indolence, and corruption of many of the clergy. They exalted poverty but held learning in contempt. The Apostolics, believing that Christ possessed nothing, lived in destitution. Some groups were pacifist, celibate, and vegetarian. Thus among these sectarians were precedents for the pacifism, repudiation of property, and tenderness toward animals characteristic of Francis. In 1052 some folk in Gosslar were declared heretics because they would not kill a chicken.[12]

The best known of the leaders of such movements was a wealthy merchant and usurer, Peter Waldo of Lyons. Inspired by a troubadour singing of the heavenly bliss attained by a young nobleman who renounced great possessions for a life of cheerful poverty, he sought

---

walnut tree. Cf. L. de Kerval, *S. Antonii de Padua Vitae Duae* (Paris, 1904), pp. 47–52; *St. Anthony of Padua according to his Contemporaries* (London, 1926).

12 Davison, *op. cit.,* pp. 208, 255–259. Manichaean motivation for avoiding injury to animals differed widely from Christian principles. Their concern was primarily with things while Christian sympathy for animals was an extension of concern for individuals. Cf. F. C. Burkitt, *The Religion of the Manichees* (Cambridge, 1925), pp. 59–60.

the counsel of a spiritual guide. He quoted: "If thou wilt be perfect sell all that thou hast and give to the poor and follow me" (Matt. xix. 21); and, acting on this advice, Waldo devoted himself to ministering to the sick and poverty-stricken.[13] Eventually he and his followers, the Poor Men of Lyons, fell foul of the Church mainly because the permission to preach granted them by the Lateran Council (1179) was so framed that they could not exercise it effectively. The Poor Catholics (*Pauperes Catholici*), an orthodox branch of the Waldenses, established two communities, one in Catalonia, the other in Lombardy. Their Rules were approved by Innocent III in 1208 and 1210, respectively. For them the acceptance of poverty meant, as it did for Saint Francis, a hand-to-mouth existence. The Rule of the Humiliants (*Humiliati*), was approved in 1201 and some of them eventually joined the Franciscans. There were three grades or Orders: husband and wife living a family life, men and women living together in separate cloisters, and priests as well as lay folk dedicated to the life of religion. Because the Humiliants dominated the wool industry of northern Italy, Pietro Bernardone must have had dealings with them, and his son is likely to have been aware of their principles.

Some historians have sought to point out details in which the Franciscan Order differed from all others,[14] but plainly it embodied much from these earlier movements and from another to be commented upon presently, the Irish *peregrini*. It has been suggested that

[13] Few texts have influenced history more than this. Saint Augustine states in his *Confessions* that it was because he knew that Anthony the Hermit, hearing it by chance, had acted upon it that he opened the Bible and read Romans xiii. 13-14. All his doubt was dispelled. By an odd, and perhaps suspicious, coincidence Francis found and was influenced by the same text as Peter Waldo (3 *Soc.* 29). According to the *Fioretti* (2) he opened the Bible thrice. The other texts he lighted upon were Luke ix. 3 and Matt. xvi. 24. (Cf. Mark viii; Luke ix. 23). Following Celano (1 *Cel.* 22) and Bonaventura (iii. 1) the crucial Gospel text that Francis, like Anthony, heard being read at Mass was Mark vi. 8. The biographers identified Francis with the ancient tradition of the divine election of reformers, conflating Augustinian tradition in different ways. It has been suggested that Celano (1 *Cel.* 1) was influenced by Saint Augustine's *Confessions* in stressing the dissolute youth of Saint Francis.

[14] P. Gratien, *Histoire de la Fondation et de l'Évolution de l'Ordre des Frères Mineurs au XIII* *Siècle* (Paris, 1928), pp. 59-60.

Francis himself was influenced by ideas current among heretics, especially their attitude toward animals. He cannot have been entirely unacquainted with such teaching. During the latter half of the twelfth century, there was a heterodox community of about 100 persons in the valley of Spoleto; and in 1203, Assisi elected a heretic, Giraldo di Giberto, as podestà. A Catharist bishop at Florence exercised authority in Lombardy, Tuscany, and the March of Ancona.[15] But the period was one of great ideological ferment, and sympathy for nature was manifested alike by some heretics; by Joachim of Fiore, whose opinions disquieted the authorities but did not involve him in being declared heretical; and by Francis.

By the time Francis came on the scene, the ecclesiastical authorities realized that efforts to suppress communities which, whatever their aberrations, were basically Christian, had often been ineffective; and they were ready to welcome a man and a movement that could be moulded to conform to the views of the papacy. Cardinal Ugolino, Francis's friend and confidant, when he became pope as Gregory IX, declared the saint's Testament invalid, thereby setting in motion disputes on the interpretation of the vow of poverty which rent the Order until a belated compromise was reached in 1517 with the division of the sons of Saint Francis into Observants and Conventuals. Occasionally the biographers, concerned to portray Francis as the authorities of the Church wished him to appear, almost inadvertently depict him in more human terms, as when, starting up from his sick bed, he shouted: "Who are they who snatch my Order and my brethren from my hands?" (Spec. Perf. 41). Paul Sabatier enumerated seven major principles in regard to which his disciples "vied with one another to misunderstand his thought" and on which infidelity to his will was complete less than twenty-five years after his death.[16] The Order became something other than Francis had envisaged in his pioneering days, but he was not equipped to deal

15 L. Salvatorelli, "Movimenti Francescano e Gioachismo," in Relazione del X Congressa Internazionale di Scienze Storiche, III (Florence), 463–498; D. Waley, The Papal State in the Thirteenth Century (London and New York, 1961), pp. 47–48.
16 Sabatier, The Life of St. Francis of Assisi (London, 1920), pp. 185–186.

with the administrative problems that success brought in its train. No more today than in the thirteenth century do seer and administrator see eye to eye.

If we are to point to one person in particular who may have influenced Saint Francis and who undoubtedly prepared the way for and influenced the Order, he is the Cistercian already mentioned, Joachim of Fiore (1145–1202). A recent biographer comments: "Certainly it seems unlikely that Francis had not heard of Joachim de Flore and of Pierre Valdez since all the world were talking of them."[17] And in one of the most sceptical critiques the author says: "It is possible that Joachim influenced to some extent Francis himself, although I must say the parallels so far adduced are not completely convincing."[18] From his mountain eyrie in Calabria, the resort of visionaries, Joachim promulgated mystical ideas, including a prophecy of a World Order following a sequence of three epochs represented by nettles, roses, and lilies. His views could be described as both evolutionary and apocalyptic. Voluntary poverty would be one of the characteristics of this culminating age which, later on, the Franciscan Spirituals assumed to be the time in which they were living. His saying that the true monk owned nothing but a lyre reminds us of Francis accompanying himself on a make-believe viol. His pacifist opinions anticipated the convictions that led the saint to seek the conversion of the Saracens.[19] It was typical of his love for nature that when clouds cleared away from above the church in which he was officiating he saluted the sun, sang the Veni Creator, and led the congregation forth to view the shining landscape.[20] Joachim had scant regard for learned argument, holding that: "Dialectic hides what is clear, is the cause of vain argument, rivalry and blasphemy, as is proved by those arrogant scribes who by their

[17] O. Englebert, Saint Francis of Assisi (London, 1950), pp. 88–96.
[18] M. W. Bloomfield, "Joachim of Flora," Traditio XIII (1957), 249–251. Cf. E. Gebhart, Mystics and Heretics in Italy at the End of the Middle Ages, trans. E. M. Hulme (London, 1922), pp. 70–93.
[19] Expos. In Apoc. (164). Cf. G. La Piana, "Joachim of Flora: A Critical Study," Speculum VII (1932), 256–282.
[20] Sabatier, op. cit., p. 51.

reasoning fall into blasphemy." [21] The saintly John of Parma, Minister General of the Order before Bonaventura, was powerfully influenced by Joachim's teaching, and his ideas coloured the friars opinions for a long time. His writings were condemned by the Pope in 1256, and adherence to his views was partly responsible for one of the Spirituals, John of Rupescissa, being sentenced in 1349 to seven years imprisonment in the papal jail.[22]

Interest in nature

A common assumption is that Saint Francis's regard for nature was almost without antecedents in his age. But, apart from centuries-old traditions to be discussed later, interest in nature was beginning to stir, and in the West men's minds were tentatively reaching out beyond the symbolisms and conventions that, due to an outlook influenced by Pliny and the *Physiologus*—that strange product of Alexandrian apologetics in which imaginary peculiarities of animals were set forth as disclosing divine truths—had for so long distracted attention from any interest in how organisms actually behave.

In the British Isles the first indications of pleasurable interest in nature come to us from Celtic circles. This is not fortuitous. The early mythology and poetry of the Irish and Welsh exhibits such sensitivity. Writing of Lindisfarne, where the memory of the Irish saints and their disciples was treasured, Geoffrey, a monk of Coldingham, described how the eider ducks nested all round the island and were not disturbed by noise or people passing to and fro. Another twelfth-century monk of Durham, Reginald, a friend of Saint Ailred of Rievaulx and biographer of Saint Godric of Finchale, went out of

---

21 *Commentarium in Apocalypsim* (Venice, 1527), p. 70.

22 Among the many writers who have commented on the relationship between Joachism and Franciscanism may be mentioned: E. Renan, "St. François d'Assise," in *Nouvelles Études d'Histoire religieuse* (Paris, 1884), pp. 217–233; P. Fournier, *Études sur J. de Flore et ses Doctrines* (Paris, 1909). E. Gebhart, *op. cit.*, pp. 70–93; L. Salvatorelli, *op. cit.*, pp. 403–418; M. W. Bloomfield and M. E. Reeves, "The Penetration of Joachism into Northern Europe," *Speculum* XXIX (1954), 772–793; E. R. Daniel, "A Re-examination of the Origins of Franciscan Joachitism," *Speculum* XLIII (1968), 671–676.

his way to mention that in Saint Cuthbert's time the Farne eiders nested in houses and allowed themselves to be stroked. They would make their nests under beds or even among the blankets. Only saints would have tolerated such intrusions! [23]

Giraldus Cambrensis (ca. 1146–1220), in his accounts of Ireland and Wales, mentions that no nightingales sang in these countries.[24] He refers to the clear note of the golden oriole, a rare visitor to the British Isles, and describes the feeding behaviour of crossbills which arrive in flocks at irregular intervals.

In the visual arts, bright-eyed observation was beginning to oust adherence to convention. Early in the twelfth century, an unknown monk of St. Edmundsbury painted ivy and bramble leaves freshly gathered in the abbey grounds. Toward the end of that century, Gothic sculptors fashioned the buds and uncurling leaves of early spring. In the thirteenth century the buds burst into bloom and the leaves unfolded. A realistic lizard, carved shortly before 1215, clambers over foliage in Wells Cathedral. The capitals of Southwell, decorated somewhat later, are gay with the foliage of forest trees and blossoms of buttercup and potentilla. Here, too, are birds, pigs, hares, and lizards, Jack-in-the-Green garbed with leaves for a rite dating from pre-Christian times, as well as heads depicting the gamut of emotions from gaiety to lasciviousness.[25] Naturalism has not completely ousted symbolism. Thus the sun-loving lizard represents illumination of the soul and the resurrection, and the pig, Saint

[23] The Monk of Farne, translated by a Benedictine of Stanbrook (Helicon Press, Inc., Baltimore, 1961, p. 13. Eider ducks still nest in derelict buildings on the Farne Islands and allow themselves to be stroked. Cf. Reginaldi monachi Dunelmensis libellus de admirandis beati Cuthberti, ed. J. Raine (Surtees Socy., 1835), I. xxvii, 60.

[24] Topographia Hiberniae (1188) and Itinerarium Cambriae (1191). The Topographia was edited by J. F. Dimock in the Rolls series (1867). Cf. also the edition by J. J. O'Meara (Dundalk, 1951).

[25] MS Bodley 130. Cf. R. T. Gunther, Early British Botanists (Oxford, 1925); E. Mâle, Religious Art from the Twelfth to the Eighteenth Century (London, 1949), p. 66; N. Pevsner, The Leaves of Southwell (Penguin Books, 1945); A. C. Seward, "The Foliage, Flowers and Fruit of Southwell Chapter House," Camb. Antiq. Soc. Comm. XXV.

Anthony's emblem, is a warning against sensuality. It is indicative of the more candid outlook of the age that Christian artists and craftsmen began to represent nude figures in the decoration of ecclesiastical buildings.

Not only did the details inside churches and cathedrals imitate what was to be seen outside, but the structures themselves, supported by soaring columns terminated by ribbed vaults, later to evolve into fan-vaulting, increasingly resembled the aisles of a forest and the windows rivalled the sunset in splendour. It has been said: "In the Gothic style there is not only the movement of the human spirit upwards towards God, but outwards to all created things." [26]

In the period with which we are concerned, observational and artistic interest in the natural world was awakening not only in northern Europe but here and there throughout the Continent. At the court of Frederick II (1194–1250), Roman emperor, king of Sicily and Jerusalem, a crafty magnifico so accomplished in many fields that he was called *stupor mundi et immutator mirabilis*, there assembled an extraordinary galaxy of talent. The emperor himself had scientific interests coupled with brutality and lust which prompted him to have criminals vivisected and to keep a harem guarded by eunuchs. He wrote a pioneer work on falconry, *De arte venandi cum avibus*,[27] in which he included observational notes such as a reference to what is now called "distraction display" or "injury-feigning" by nesting birds, an adaptation to deflect attention from their eggs or young. He dissected barnacles in the attempt to disprove the belief that they developed into barnacle geese. Christian, Jewish, and Moslem intellectuals rubbed shoulders at his capital Palermo, then a superb and well-ordered city, twice the size of Paris. The Irishman, Michael the Scot, astrologer and translator of Averroes and Aristotle, was one of the emperor's advisers, and Pier della Vigna († 1249) was another. The latter initiated verse in sonnet form expressing the intense love of nature which became characteristic of Sicilian

[26] E. Newton and W. Neil, *The Christian Faith in Art* (London, 1966), p. 122.

[27] Augsburg, 1596.

poetry of the period and was probably mainly inspired by Moslem and Provençal literature. Other literatures of this period illustrate the awakening delight in nature.[28]

It is not to minimize the achievement of Saint Francis but to place it within its setting to recognize that the intellectual and aesthetic milieu was at last such that his example of gaiety, asceticism, single-minded devotion to Christ, and sensitivity to Creation could appeal to pious, enterprising, and intelligent people. He enlarged their outlook by revealing the lark and the wild flower as sacramental and all nature singing out to man to join in adoration of the Creator. Unfortunately, controversy soon concentrated on the degree of honour due to Lady Poverty—to the neglect of the fair maiden Gaiety and bounteous Dame Nature.

The Irish tradition

As a prelude to comments on certain natural history allusions in the Franciscan Legend introduced later, some reference may here be made to the possibility that Irish ideas and practices influenced Francis and the Order. Suggestions to this effect have hitherto been dismissed, despite the well-known achievements of the islanders in penetrating deep into the Continent, making pilgrimages to Rome, founding monasteries, and doing evangelistic work. This is the more strange as in no movement other than the Franciscan do we find reproduced so conspicuously the characteristics of Irish Christianity —complete dedication to Christ, blithe acceptance of poverty, loose organization, adventurous missionary enterprise, and love of nature. We shall notice later the evidence of Irish influence provided by the occurrence of Hibernian motifs in the Franciscan Legend, but here we may briefly consider the general grounds for regarding Irish sources as providing inspiration for the Franciscans.

Throughout centuries before Francis, the Irish had been traversing the roads of Europe, living in the open air and doing missionary work

[28] At first references in Provençal poetry to nature tended to be conventional allusions to the pleasure in being with a pretty girl in springtime woods when the nightingale was singing. Cf. J. Anglade, *Anthologie des Troubadours* (Paris, 1927), p. 42; M. Raynouard, *Choix des Poésies Originales des Troubadours* III (Paris, 1818), 53.

as he and his companions were to do.[29] Because travel was so much slower in those days, it is easy to underestimate the comings and goings on medieval roads. Never before had there been such opportunities for contacts between people from different environments as at this time. In an age when all roads led to Rome, Irishmen were constantly passing through northern and central Italy. They had many ports of call where they could receive hospitality from their countrymen on their way. It was not until 1418 that the abbeys of Nuremberg and Vienna ceased to be exclusively Irish and only later did other such foundations follow suit. Incidental evidence of the commerce in thought and culture between Ireland and the Continent is provided by the influence of continental designs on Irish art during the tenth and eleventh centuries.[30] The most important Irish foundation abroad, at Ratisbon, founded in 1090, had a very wide influence. During the twelfth century it established a number of daughter houses in Allemania, Bavaria, and Austria. The group of Franciscan friars sent on the mission to Germany in 1221, which included Caesar of Spires, John of Pian de Carpini (who later travelled to the Far East), and Thomas of Celano, stayed at Ratisbon. They could hardly have failed to become acquainted with some Irish traditions. But it is of much greater significance that as Ludwig Bieler has pointed out, "Ratisbon was probably the last link in the transmission of numerous *Lives* of Irish saints, which sometime after 1181 were incorporated in the *Magnum Legendarium Austriacum.*" [31] This is sufficient explanation of the diffusion of stories from the *Lives* in Italy and their influence on the Franciscan Legend.

29 E. Duckett, *The Wandering Saints* (London, 1959); L. Gougaud, "L'Oeuvre des Scotti dans l'Europe continentale," *Rev. d'hist. eccl.* IX (1908), 21–37, 255–277; Gougaud, *Gaelic Pioneers of Christianity* (Dublin, 1923); Gougaud, *Christianity in Celtic Lands* (London, 1932); Gougaud, *Les Saints Irlandais hors d'Irlande* (Louvain, 1936); J. Ryan, *Irish Monasticism and Early Development* (London, 1931); Ryan, ed., *Irish Monks in the Golden Age* (Dublin, 1963).

30 J. Guilmain, "Zoomorphic Decoration and the Problem of Mozarabic Illustration," *Speculum* XXXV (1960), 17–38; F. Henry, *Irish Art in the Romanesque Age* (London, 1970).

31 Ludwig Bieler, *Ireland: Harbinger of the Middle Ages* (London, 1963), p. 141.

Although during Francis's youth few Irish pilgrims may have visited or lodged in Assisi, its citizens and the inhabitants of other towns in the area are likely to have been familiar with such folk, and to some extent, with the heritage they represented. Indeed, Giordano of Giano in his Chronicle [31a] reports Elias as saying at the Chapter of the Mats concerning Germany: "There dwell there many pious Christians, whom we often see here coming through the valley with long staves and great travelling bottles, singing the praises of God and His saints, and in spite of the sun and sweat they go on to the graves of the Apostles." Irishmen must have been among these pilgrims. We have an account of the journey of Symon Semeonis who left Clonmel in Ireland in 1323 and travelled by way of Italy to the Holy Land. He was exceptional only in the extent of his travels and in his leaving such an informative narrative.[32] After traversing mountains and dense forests, in places infested by robbers, he came to Bobbio. There he saw much to remind him of Saint Columban. Thence via Piacenza and Parma he reached Venice and set sail for the East. Many an earlier pilgrim paused at Bobbio where memories of the famous Irish saint were constantly revived and the stories of other Irish saints recalled—to be shared with fellow-travellers later on. Salimbene, who visited Bobbio in 1249, reported seeing many relics of the saint.[33]

Columban lived six hundred years before Francis; but the centuries had added lustre to his fame and vigour to memories of this great man, for he was exemplar and paragon to innumerable wandering saints and other Christians in Italy. Reverence for him was so continuous and fervent that, at least as late as the middle of the nineteenth century, sufferers from various ills sought healing by visiting the cave at La Spanna, northeast of Bobbio, reputed to have been his retreat. Erysipelas victims laid their heads where he had laid his, nursing mothers visiting the grotto sought a plentiful flow of milk, and those afflicted with ills of one kind or another placed a hand on the imprint of his hand on a stone there. The renown

[31a] *Analecta Franc.* I (1885); Boehmer, *op. cit.*, p. 18.

[32] M. Esposito, ed., *Itinerarus Symonis Semeonis ab Hybernia ad Terram Sanctam. Scriptores Latini Hiberniae* IV (Dublin, 1960).

[33] C. G. Coulton, *From St. Francis to Dante* (London, 1906), p. 184.

of his beneficence and love of nature lived on in the legend that a
pretty and useful plant (of the pea family, Leguminosae) sprang up
in his footsteps.[34] Nor were his amicable associations with animals
forgotten. On his sarcophagus at Bobbio may still be seen the bas-
relief, carved in 1480, of a bear and ox yoked together drawing a
wagon, commemorating the occasion when Columban ordered a bear
that had killed one of the oxen dragging stones for his church to
take its victim's place.[35]

Columban and Francis both modelled their lives on an austere
interpretation of the Gospels, as, indeed, Columcille had done before them. Both had followed the Gospel injunction to "go out into
the highways and hedges" to seek the needy. "Let us live in Christ,
that Christ may live in us," said Columban, and the Poverello could
have said the same. The similarities between Adamnan's *Life of
Columcille* and the *Fioretti* are so great that a scholar, choosing his
words carefully, commented on "a certain kinship between them." [36]
The statement of Francis, "If at any time prelates and clergy, regular
or secular, come to their dwellings; the poor little houses, the little
cells, and tiny churches will preach to them" (*Spec. Perf.* 11), may
be compared with Bede's testimony to the frugality of the Irish missionaries to Northumbria. When they went back over the mountains
to Iona as a sad sequel to the acceptance of Roman rather than
Celtic usages, "there were very few houses besides the church found at
their departure; indeed, no more than were necessary for their day to
day existence; they had also no money . . . for if they received any
money from rich persons, they immediately gave it to the poor." [37]

---

[34] M. Stokes, *Six Months in the Apennines* (London, 1892), pp. 14, 144, 158,
187–190. There are strong traditions of particular plants being associated with
Irish saints: in Ireland the shamrock with Saint Patrick, in the Hebrides the
St. John's wort with Saint Columcille. He is said to have carried it on his
preaching tours. Cf. A. Carmichael, *Carmina Gadelica* II, 96 ff., IV, 117 (Edinburgh and London, 1928–1941). In Welsh betony is known as St. Brigid's
comb.

[35] Stokes, *op. cit.*, p. 130. There is a chapel in Saint Columban's honour in
the crypt of St. Peter's at Rome.

[36] C. S. Boswell, *An Irish Precursor of Dante* (London, 1908), p. 11.

[37] *Ecclesiastical History* III. xxvi. Probably because of such sentiments, exalting spirituality and simplicity, Dante places Bede in Paradise (x. 131). In
one of his Latin letters he reproaches the Italian cardinals for neglecting him

Sir Arthur Bryant remarked of the Franciscans who first began coming to England in 1224: "The all-embracing charity, cheerfulness and courtesy of these humble evangelists made a profound impression on the English. They revived memories of Aidan and the Celtic saints." [38] It was said of Francis and his companions: "They went about the world as pilgrims and strangers, bearing naught with them but Christ crucified" (*Fioretti* 5). Such, too, were the Irish *peregrini*. It has been claimed that the Franciscan Rule, which required the brethren to "live the life of the Gospel," was a "great and entire novelty." [39] How questionable this is will be apparent to all who have studied the Rule and practice of Columban, or indeed the lives of other saints—though who among us is entitled to judge between saints?

The Irish and Franciscan disciplines were very similar. Detailed comparison of the Rules is impossible as the Franciscan *Regula primitiva* exists only in a reconstructed form,[40] but it differed in spirit hardly at all from Columban's Rule: "Nakedness and disdain of riches are the first perfection of monks, but the second is the purging of vices, the third the most perfect and perpetual love of God and increasing affection for things divine, which follows on forgetfulness of earthly things." [41] Of course it is not necessary to suppose that Francis modelled his life on Columban's or consciously followed in the footsteps of the Irish saints. Their teaching and example were a *praeparatio evangelium* for his message and had so permeated the age and area which gave birth to the Franciscan Order that, as we shall see, in the stories about the saint's treatment of animals there are frequent reminiscences of Irish tales. As it can be

and other great Christian writers in order to concentrate on reading designed to further their temporal interests. Cf. P. Toynbee, *The Letters of Dante* (Oxford, 1920), p. 145.

[38] *The Medieval Foundation* (London, 1966), p. 97.

[39] Englebert, *op. cit.*, pp. 94, 124.

[40] Gratien, *op cit.*, pp. 29, 30, 98–100; J. R. H. Moorman *Sources for the Life of S. Francis of Assisi* (Manchester, 1940), pp. 38–54; P. A. Quaglia, *L'Originalitá della Regola Francescana* (Sassoferrato, 1943).

[41] G. S. M. Walker, *Sancti Columbani Opera. Scriptores Hiberniae* II (Dublin, 1957), 127.

argued that the lives of men trying to follow Gospel injunctions exactly in whatever century are bound to show similarities, apparently trivial details in common between Irish traditions and the Franciscan Legend, which will be pointed out as we proceed, have importance as evidence of the influence of one on the other. When the authenticity of an Old Master is in question, the decision may turn upon the resemblance of the brush strokes in a corner of the canvas to those in pictures known to have been painted by him; similarly, details inserted casually or even inadvertently in a saint's Legend may have evidential importance. So, too, the ancient character of many of the Lives of the Irish saints extant only in comparatively late written sources, is revealed by the incidental allusions to pagan beliefs which they retain.[42]

Only in two respects were there appreciable differences between the Irish and the Franciscan ideals. The gaiety of the Poverello is less evident in what has been recorded concerning the great Hibernian saints though the Irish were noted for their love of poetry, music, and song. Columban composed songs; Francis sang them. Certainly Irish monks and *peregrini* abroad inherited the devotional feeling, pleasure in poetry, and joy in nature characteristic of their famous forbears. Some of the comments in the Lives would make it appear that Francis despised learning whereas the Irish held it in high esteem. Indeed, to the Irish mind an illiterate monk was a contradiction in terms.[43] Celano remarks in his *Vita Secunda* (195) that Francis taught the brethren not to be over-anxious to learn and so become dabblers in research because he foresaw that times were approaching in which learning would be an occasion of falling; but in his *Vita Prima* (82) he had declared that such was the saint's regard for any scrap of written matter, pagan or Christian, that he would reverently pick it up and put it aside—as the Chinese used to do. Francis, in his *Testament*, mentioned that, whenever he found writings bearing the name of God or His Word, he was careful to set them in a safe place. He also advocated respect and honour for all theologians. The divergent opinions expressed by the hagiographers

---

[42] C. Plummer, *Vitae Sanctae Hiberniae* I (Oxford, 1910), cxxix–cxlv.
[43] Walker, *op cit.*, p. xiv.

must be seen in the light of the disagreements in regard to priorities which soon beset the Order. On the whole we may accept Saint Bernardino's clarification of the matter: "Fra Bonaventura . . . in reply to a friend who had said the friars were not to study, said that this was meant by Saint Francis for men who were not fit to learn, but not for the young who were able to do so. Those who are able to learn and to do honour to the Church of God and to our Order are following God's will." [44]

Whether the Irish tradition of scholarship could have had more than an indirect influence on the Friars Minor is uncertain though the visits of such Franciscans as Salimbene to Bobbio must have renewed memories of what the Irish had achieved. But in thirteenth-century Italy earnest men, believing that sophistication had led many into heresy, were not without grounds for being suspicious of learning. Saint Francis set himself in holy simplicity "to walk in the footprints of Christ" (2 *Cel.* 90, 210) and to attract others to do likewise; and it is by their example rather than their theology that the memory of the saints lives among the people. Through God's grace a great saint builds better than he can be aware. Francis could not have known what great profit the world was to gain from the stimulus given by his movement to art, literature, and science.

It might seem that the argument for Irish influence on Franciscanism is being unduly laboured, but it has had to be pressed because the only writer to have given detailed consideration to this possibility has ruled it out. [45] Surprisingly, after enumerating more parallels between the two movements than it has been possible to mention here and remarking that "similarities so numerous, so intimate and so substantial" demand explanation, Tommasini concluded: "The explanation may be found, in my opinion, in the ardour and force of expansion which follow every genuine and profound 'conversion.'" This is a *non-sequitur* because profound conversion experiences have often led, not to following in detail the ex-

[44] I. Origo, *The World of San Bernardino* (London, 1963), p. 218. For references to the differing opinions on Saint Francis's attitude toward learning, cf. Englebert, *op. cit.*, p. 241.

[45] A. N. Tommasini, *Irish Saints in Italy* (London, 1937), pp. 442–492.

ample and methods of predecessors, but to divergence from them. He stresses the loose organization of the Irish church as a major difference, ignoring the evidence that the Seraphic Father's original inspiration was to establish peregrinating evangelistic groups of the kind typical of the Irish church. He demolishes his own case by adducing evidence that more than 220 parish churches and hundreds of other smaller churches, chapels, and shrines in Italy were dedicated to Irish saints. In many of them their Feast Days are still observed.

Generation after generation of Irish *peregrini*, pilgrims, and monks had so effectively influenced and permeated with their ideas the outlook of some continental areas, not least northern and central Italy, that an anomalous situation has arisen in which modern writers are able to take the traces of Irishism in Franciscanism to be merely natural developments of Christian thought, specious coincidences, local idiosyncrasies, or the independent inventions or inspirations of Saint Francis. The wandering saints would not have been disconcerted to learn that their success had thus concealed their achievements, for like Saint Paul and Francis himself, they were concerned only that Christ be preached. As the flame of pioneering faith, with its emphasis on people and adventurous devotion rather than on organization and enclosure, which the Irish had borne into the heart of Europe diminished and flickered, sparks from it were among those that kindled another torch in Umbria. Passing from hand to hand it touched yet other brands to flame. Soon they were to be carried into the Far East and eventually to continents then unknown. The greatest city named after the Little Poor Man is in the New World.

Having considered the circumstances that contributed to Saint Francis's tender regard for nature, we may now scrutinize the Franciscan legends concerning birds and beasts in the expectation that we may gain further insight into the mind of the saint, the intellectual climate of his time, and the outlook of his biographers.

III

Saint Francis and the Birds

The Welcoming Birds

A delightful tale shows us saint and birds enjoying each other's company. With a few of his closest companions, Masseo, Angelo, and Leo, Francis set forth for La Verna, the wooded peak donated to Saint Francis by Orlando, Lord of Chiusi, where some huts and a small chapel served as a devotional centre for the Brothers. Here was the wilderness retreat most dear to Francis. Those aware of the sequel—the saint's ecstasy and stigmatization—will feel that the description of the little party's arrival has special poignancy:

> When they were come nigh to the foot of the very rock of La Verna, it pleased St. Francis to rest a while under the oak tree that stood by the way, and there standeth to this day; and resting beneath it St. Francis began to consider the lay of the place and of the country round about. And lo, while he was thus pondering there came a great multitude of birds from divers parts that, with singing and fluttering of their wings, showed forth great joy and gladness, and surrounded St. Francis, in such wise that some settled on his head, some on his shoulders, and some on his arms, some on his bosom, and some around his feet. His companions . . . beholding this, marvelled greatly, and St. Francis rejoiced in spirit, and spake thus: "I do believe, dearest brothers, that it is pleasing to our Lord Jesus Christ that we abide on this solitary mountain, since our sisters and brothers, the birds, show forth such great joy at our coming" (*Fioretti, 1st consid. of stigmata*).[1]

This is beautifully told and breathes the authentic spirit of the saint. Francis takes it for granted that, as the Lord Jesus Christ cared

[1] On the path up Mount La Verna is an inscription indicating the reputed spot where the birds bid Saint Francis welcome and at the monastery another inscription reads: *Non est in toto orbe sanctior mons.* Cf. J. Joergensen, *Pilgrim Walks in Franciscan Italy* (Edinburgh and London, 1908), pp. 151–152.

for and took pleasure in birds, so they, in welcoming the Brothers, were doing His will and thus indicating to Francis and his friends that, in making their temporary home there, they were acting as would please Him. The lively description should be viewed as we would a delicate water-colour of the scene. Some readers may prefer to let the imagination dwell thus on the incident and inquire no further; but if we are to be true to Saint Francis who, indeed, was a romantic but most certainly disliked dissembling, falsehood, and sham, we must probe deeper into the real significance of the incident. We should inquire, both as naturalists and as historians, what is its significance? In asking this question we are not treating a minor episode with undue seriousness. This and other such stories may not give us much information about birds, but they do provide insight into the setting that gave birth to the Franciscan Order.

Sabatier, in common with many writers since, treated the description as an authentic account of the incident, but some of his natural history allusions are in such exaggerated terms that he discredits himself. We are greatly indebted to him for his portrait of Saint Francis, but he was not a naturalist. Thus the vegetation by the Arno is said to be "thoroughly tropical" and the forest of La Verna is described as inhabited by "legions of birds" though mixed woods of conifer and beech such as clothed much of it do not provide a particularly favourable habitat. As evidence he mentions an ornithologist in Casentino, a few miles from La Verna, who had "begun" a collection of birds which already included more than five hundred and fifty varieties.[2] He thus implies that a small area in Italy harboured well over half the total number of species known from Europe, North Africa, and Asia north of the Himalayas. There are just over four hundred species that nest regularly in the whole of Europe. Writing when he did, he may be pardoned such exaggerations, but it is regrettable that since his time many admirers of the Umbrian saint who manifested exceptional interest in nature should have treated the natural history in the biographies with so little respect. Indeed, some have altered or added to the narratives in order to romanticize

---

[2] Sabatier, *The Life of St. Francis of Assisi* (London, 1920), pp. 287–290.

them or make their own accounts more picturesque, and others have been ignorant of or set aside elementary facts of animal behaviour. Perhaps the oddest example is a passage in the French translation of Johannes Joergensen's biography in which Francis is represented as advocating the scattering of grain to feed the swallows at Christmas! [3]

Clearly the writer of the description in the *Fioretti* has employed both poetic and hagiographical licence—the liberty of a saint's biographer to embroider and exaggerate—to which modern commentators are not entitled, whatever their sentimental reactions may be. Some social birds may twitter in flocks, but very few European species sing socially, for full song is normally a warning to other males to keep away. Although mixed parties of small birds feed together in tropical forests, such associations seldom occur in the temperate zone. [4] Even in remote places where birds have suffered little disturbance from man and are therefore relatively "tame" (that is, do not recognize him as dangerous), a mixed flock of wild birds would not settle on a human being. There are still some isolated areas, such as the Galapagos Islands and remote parts of Australia, where birds have had so little experience of man as a predator that individuals may perch on a person's head seeking hair to line the nest, but the notion of a flock of birds greeting a man by alighting on him and singing is a poetic fiction belonging to the Orphean and Earthly Paradise way of thought and reflects the intense longing of the human spirit to find responsiveness in nature. It portrays the outgoing nature of the saint rather than the tameness of birds.

Claims of such intimacy with wild birds have seldom been made for persons other than saints, though sagas tell of heroes such as Cú Chúlainn being greeted, accompanied, or warned by a bird or birds. When, however, we find that similar stories were told of a series of Irish saints before the time of Saint Francis, it is reasonable, in view of the discrepancies in the Franciscan story and the indications of Irish influence in Italy already noted, to consider whether they could have inspired it.

Columban's disciple, Chemnoald, described seeing birds and small

[3] *Saint François d'Assise*, trans. T. de Wyzewa (Paris, 1922), p. 390.
[4] E. A. Armstrong, A *Study of Bird Song* (London and Oxford, 1963*a*), pp. 185–187. (New edition, Dover, New York, 1973.)

beasts from the woods perching on the saint, frolicking around and being fondled by him.[5] Bobbio, some 190 miles distant from Assisi, where Columban founded his last abbey and finished his earthly pilgrimage, was the place in northern Italy where the saint's memory was held most dear, though he was honoured in many other localities.[6] Thus the possibility that the motif of the Welcoming Birds may have been borrowed and attributed to Saint Francis deserves to be taken seriously. In the *Fioretti* (47) the same borrowed motif appears elsewhere. We are told of a friar who, while he was "on a time wholly lifted up and ravished in God, for he had notably the grace of contemplation, certain birds of divers kinds came to him and settled themselves tamely upon his shoulders, upon his head, and in his arms, and in his hands, and sang wonderfully." Comparable stories were told of St. Remedius and other holy men.

Earlier saints than Francis or even Columban were reputed to have enjoyed the company and music-making of birds. The biographers cannot have been unaware of this tradition, as we shall see in further detail later, but here we may mention some other Irish stories of birds perching on saints.

The hunter Brandubh, son of Eatach, in pursuit of wild boar came unexpectedly on Saint Kevin (Coemghen) beneath the greenwood trees with birds fluttering around, settling on his hands and shoulders, and singing sweet songs to God. The description of the episode closely resembles what was related of Saint Francis: *Et erat ibi sub arbore sanctus Coemganus orans, et aves plures super manus eius et humeros stabant, et volabant circa eum, carmina suavia sancto Dei canentes.*[7] According to other legends Saint Kevin was even more closely associated with birds during his sojourn in the hermitage at Glendalough. Blackbirds nested in his outstretched hand:

> He would stand on a rough bare flag-stone
> Though the cold hurt his feet;

---

[5] Jonas, *Vita S. Columbani,* c. 15–30; Migne, *Patrologia Latina* LXXXVII (Paris, 1851), 1013–1046.

[6] A. N. Tommasini, *Irish Saints in Italy* (London, 1937), pp. 289–314.

[7] C. Plummer, *Vitae Sanctae Hiberniae* I (Oxford, 1910), 244. He suggests that parallels might be found in Indian literature, but the *Motif-Index of Folk-literature* by Stith Thompson (Copenhagen, 1958) does not mention any.

The chant of angels was round about him
To him in his strong pen it was refection.

A fortnight and a month without food,
Or somewhat longer, was he, great the effort;
Suddenly a blackbird hopped from a branch,
And made a nest in the hand of the saint.

Coemgen (Kevin) remained in the pen
Alone, though great was the pain,
And the nest of the blackbird on his palm,
Till her birds were hatched.[8]

So the Irish poet told the story. Giraldus Cambrensis, who gives another version, mentions that "all the images of St. Kevin throughout Ireland show a blackbird in his outstretched hand." [9] The biographers of Irish saints, seeking to outdo each other, succumbed to the temptation to add prodigy to prodigy. If friendly birds were said to have perched on one saint's hands, why should they not have nested in the hand of another?

We need not look far among the biographies of the Irish ascetics to discover examples of this incremental exaggeration. When St. Finnian of Clonard sent Bishop Senach to observe how his pupils were occupied, he reported: "Different, in sooth, that at which each of them was found with his hands stretched forth and his mind contemplative of God, and birds resting on his hands and head." Colomb, it should be noted, was standing in a special posture while he meditated, holding out his arms so that with his body they formed a cross. This prayer posture was so commonly adopted by ascetics in Ireland that there was a term to describe it in Irish: *crossfigell*. It was practised by Irish saints on the Continent.[10] The motif

[8] C. Plummer, *Bethada Náem nÉrenni: Lives of the Irish Saints* II (Oxford, 1922), 137. This may be regarded as a combination of two motifs, the Welcoming Birds and the Saint Providing Nesting Site.

[9] *Topographia Hiberniae* (Frankfort, 1603). Cf. J. J. O'Meara, *The First Version of the Topography of Ireland by Giraldus Cambrensis* (Dundalk, 1951), pp. 60–61.

[10] L. Gougaud, *Devotional and Ascetic Practices in the Middle Ages*, trans. C. C. Bateman (London, 1927), pp. 10–17. Colum Mac Crimthann stood enraptured in *crossfigell* with birds perching on his head and hands. Cf. *Life of*

reached its culmination when some scribe, not content with the stories of blackbirds nesting in Saint Kevin's hand as he stretched it forth from his hermitage, thought to do him honour by describing him as maintaining this devotional posture for a marvellous length of time. As a gloss on the *Liber Hymnorum* he wrote that the saint remained seven years standing "with a board under him merely and he without sleeping during that time in *crossfigell* so that the birds made their nests in his hands." [11]

St. Findian of Clonard in *Lives of Saints from the Book of Lismore*, ed. and trans. W. Stokes (Oxford, 1890), pp. 79, 226. Saint Peter Damian and his followers used this devotional posture, and it is mentioned in the *Chansons de Geste*.

The other most distinctive Irish penitential exercise, evidently derived from the Near East (p. 132), was exposure to cold or icy water. Cf. L. Gougaud, "La mortification par les bains froids," *Bull. d'anc. Litt. et d'Archéologie chrét.* (1914), pp. 96–108. We are told that Francis and his companions practised very similar austerities, exposing themselves to snow and plunging into cold water, but these tales should be viewed with suspicion.

A fourteenth-century manuscript recording Francis's avoidance of friendships with women states that he cursed one of the brethren for maintaining contact with a nunnery and reproved another, Brother Stephen, who had been involved. "Blessed Francis upbraided him harshly and bade him by way of penance cast himself into a stream by which they were passing, just as he was with all his clothes on, although it was in the month of December, and dripping wet and trembling from head to foot with cold he accompanied Blessed Francis to the home of the brethren, which was two miles from the place where this happened." Cf. Fr. Oliger, *De Origine Regularum Ordinis S. Clarae* (Quaracchi, 1912). This is not the only occasion on which a chronicler's anxiety to make a fabricated story plausible introduces exact details; in this instance the name of the friar, the month of the year, the low temperature, and the length of the journey. Above all, we are told that Brother Stephen was of "such transparent honesty that one would hardly believe him capable of lying." The chronicler protests too much. This is evidently a rehash of Celano's incredible tale (2 *Cel.* 206) (p. 130). The Franciscan stories appear to be derived from the tradition of Celtic aquatic austerities elaborated in the light of thirteenth-century sexual obsessions.

[11] The nearest non-European parallel to these stories is an Indian tale relating that a man doing penance remained rooted to the spot for ten months while birds built in his hair. Cf. Stith Thompson, *op. cit.* V. 246. We cannot assume this influenced the Irish motif because this seems to have grown by accretion from the *Liber Hymnorum* version. The Indian story may be an extrapolation from the actual practices of fakirs. Some held up an arm until it became fixed in this position. In G. Smith's *Life of John Wilson* (London, 1878), p. 246, an Indian yogi is said to have been seen lying motionless in the sun in the

Thus we have evidence that, with Saint Columban and Saint Gall, this theme, which had attained its most elaborate formulation in Ireland, was carried deep into the Continent. By the time it had reached the Franciscan hagiographers it had become modified and in their hands was romanticized and pruned of its more extreme embellishments. Some further internal evidence from the *Fioretti* adds confirmation of the story's history and negates the supposition that it was the independent invention of some Franciscan friar.

The writer had in the back of his mind, if not the forefront, some knowledge of the Irish threefold association: saint, cross-vigil, and birds. Shortly before the passage describing the welcoming birds at La Verna and in the same section, we read: "And in the selfsame night they saw him (Francis) praying with his arms held in the form of a cross. . . . And thus he passed all that night in these holy exercises, without sleep." Moreover, this is not the only chapter of the *Fioretti* in which this threefold association is found. A few lines before the accounts of Francis stilling the swallows and preaching to the birds, it is explained (16): "St. Francis called Friar Masseo, after he had eaten, into the wood, and there knelt down before him, drew back his cowl, and making a cross with his arms, asked of him, 'What doth my Lord Jesus Christ command?' " The motif, having diffused so far into a strange environment, has become somewhat disjointed, but is still recognizable. As we might expect, in Bonaventura's sophisticated narrative (x. 4; xi. 14) the association between cross-vigil and birds has disappeared.[12]

Thus, whether they realized it or not, the Franciscans were influenced directly or indirectly by Irish traditions. So important did the

---

street with the nails of his hands grown into his cheek and a bird's nest on his head. It is more likely that the nest had been placed there or that it was an accumulation of dried grass than that a bird had built in such a situation. There is a Chinese proverb: "You can't prevent the birds of trouble flying over your head but you needn't let them nest in your hair." According to some critics there have been times in the history of the House of Commons when birds nested in the Speaker's wig!

[12] The significance of such recurring associations or "image-clusters" in authenticating the work of writers and indicating borrowings is discussed in Armstrong, *Shakespeare's Imagination* (Lincoln: University of Nebraska Press, 1963b).

cross-vigil posture become that in the *Caeremoniale romano-seraphi-cum* O.F.M. down to the edition of 1908 it was enjoined *ex ordinis consuetudine* that the friar serving Mass should recite, between the Elevation and the Pater Noster, a number of prayers *genuflectus, brachiis per modum crucis extensis*.[13]

Before we leave the theme Cross-vigil and the Birds, we may return to the story of Saint Kevin and the Blackbird to notice that the cumulative exaggeration which led from birds perching on saints to birds nesting on them may have been prompted by an earlier well-known story concerning Saint Malo. A ninth-century Life of this saint, who was born in Wales but settled in Brittany, tells of a wren's laying in the cowl of the habit he had laid aside while working in the vineyard of the monastery. He took compassion on the bird and deprived himself of the use of the garment until the young had been reared. Some versions, in accordance with the embellishment principle just mentioned, state that no rain fell upon it while the birds were busy incubating and rearing their chicks.[14]

The original story is not far from being authentic natural history,

---

[13] Devotional cross-vigil may be among the many indications of contacts between Ireland and the eastern Mediterranean though the original inspiration was biblical. The themes that appear on the Irish high crosses are Old Testament motifs which occur in the Byzantine ritual on the Festival of the Holy Cross. On these crosses Moses is represented with arms outstretched in the form of a cross praying for victory over the Amalekites (Exodus xvii. 8–12). Scenes recalling the Desert Fathers are also depicted, notably the hermits Anthony and Paul with the bird bringing bread to them and the Temptation of St. Anthony. Cf. F. Henry, *Irish High Crosses* (Dublin, 1964), pp. 40–42; D. D. C. Mould, "The Sign of Victory," *Sobornost*, ser. 5., no. 3 (1966), pp. 187–195.

[14] F. Plaine and A. de la Borderie, *Deux vies inédites de Saint Malo* (Paris, 1884). A similar story is told of Saint Avitus. Cf. Plummer, *op. cit.*, I (1910) cxlvi n. 14.

The theme of an object, person, or place being exempt from rain, hail, or snow is a common and ancient motif in hagiography. It occurs in the Lives of a number of Irish saints and reappears in the Franciscan Legend in the form of stories that hail ceased to plague countrysides associated with Saint Francis (*Bon.* viii. 11, xiii. 7). A related motif describes how some valuable object, such as a book, falls into water but is rescued miraculously undamaged. Cf. Sister Donatus, *Beasts and Birds in the Lives of the Early Irish Saints* (Philadelphia, 1934), *passim*; C. G. Loomis, *White Magic: An Introduction to the Folklore of Christian Legend* (Cambridge, Mass., 1948), pp. 39–40, 158; Plummer, *op. cit.* I (1910), cxxviii. Cf. Judges vi. 36–40.

for there is no other European bird about which it could so plausibly be told. Wrens' nests have been found in such sites as an old bonnet on a hedge, a scarecrow's pocket, and a nook in a punt. Also, a wren can construct the framework of the nest quickly. An American house wren, a closely related species, built in a boy's swimming trunks hung out to dry and was allowed to continue and rear the brood.[15] There are modern Saint Malos who, on finding a robin's nest in a cycle bag, become pedestrians for a few weeks. It is less credible that the saint's bird laid an egg, for only after the cock has built the nest does the hen line it and lay. But what saint's biographer can be blamed for adding one egg so small? If a version of this story of Saint Malo reached Saint Kevin's biographer, as it well might, it would account for the development of the legend. He had only to link the motif of Birds Perching on Saint with the motif of Saint Providing Nesting Site to produce a piquant story emphasizing both the extraordinary persistence in devotion of St. Kevin and his marvellous compassion for living creatures.[16] The history of this legend thus illustrates the process of growth by accretion which often contributed to incremental exaggeration, items from one legend being detached and added to another. In connexion with an episode in the Voyage of Maeldune, we shall presently note a passage so replete with accretions that it is difficult to detect the original theme (p. 65).

That the story of Saint Kevin and the Blackbird was designed to emphasize pity and love for God's Creation is apparent from another story in which the saint's affection for the Irish countryside is poignantly described. An angel, making lavish promises, tried to persuade him to found a monastery among the mountains. Kings

---

[15] E. A. Armstrong, The Wren (London, 1955), pp. 134–135.

[16] It may have been to illustrate the kindliness of John of Parma, Minister General of the Order from 1247 to 1257, and how closely he followed Saint Francis that Salimbene commented on the pair of birds which came in from the woods and built their nest and hatched their brood under his desk. They were as big as geese and allowed him to fondle them. Cf. O. Holder-Egger, Mon. Germ. Hist. Scriptores XXXIII, 310. No woodland species indigenous to Italy fits the description. Pheasants may become relatively tame, and Francis made friends with one (p. 85); but they are not as large as medieval geese, and the cock does not concern himself with the nest.

would render the place splendid and the monks' lives would be of great sanctity. Amazing miracles would be performed in order that all this might be done: "And verily if thou shouldst will that these four mountains which close this valley in should be levelled into rich and gentle meadow lands, beyond question thy God will do it for thee." But Kevin would not be tempted. He liked the mountains as they were; and who, knowing the Wicklow hills, would disagree? He replied: "I have no wish that the creatures of God should be moved because of me: my God can help that place in some other fashion. And moreover, all the wild creatures on these mountains are my house mates, gentle and familiar with me, and they would be sad of this that thou hast said." [17]

Similar love for mountains which had served as a retreat for prayer and contemplation was expressed in Francis's moving farewell to La Verna: "Addio, Addio, Monte la Verna. Addio, mountain of Angels. Addio, beloved mountain. Addio, brother falcon, I thank thee once more for thy kindness to me. Addio, towering rock, we shall see one another no more. Addio, St. Mary of the Angels. I commend to thee my children here, Mother of the Eternal World." The Brother reporting the farewell concludes: "We wept warm tears. He, weeping too, left us bearing our hearts with him." This kind of affection for, or at least interest in, hills and woods appears in later Italian painting, but a mystical regard for mountains developed much earlier in the Far East than in Europe.[18]

[17] Plummer op. cit. I (1910), 245–247; H. Waddell, *Beasts and Saints* (London, 1934), pp. 134–136.

[18] *Codice diplomatico della Verna: Fioretti, 3rd consid. of the stigmata.* Cf. O. Englebert, *Saint Francis of Assisi* (London, 1950), p. 285. Johannes Joergensen, in *St. Francis of Assisi*, trans. T. O'C Sloane (London, 1912). p. 304, gives a slightly different rendering based on the *Addio di S. Francesco alla Verna* attributed to Brother Masseo. The only existing manuscript dates from the sixteenth century. He remarks that internal evidence points to the authenticity of the document and quotes from Amoni's translation of Celano's *Vita Secunda* (Rome, 1880), pp. 314–315, Francis's blessing of the mountain as a place wherein God is well pleased to dwell, concluding: "Peace be to the beloved mountain. We shall not meet any more." Sabatier (*op. cit.*, p. 298) regretted that Amoni did not give his source. Englebert considers it an apocrypha.

The Turtle-Doves

One day Saint Francis met a lad who had snared a number of turtle-doves.[19] He "who ever had singular compassion for gentle creatures, gazed upon those doves with a pitying eye, and said to the youth, 'O good youth, prithee give them to me, lest birds so gentle that chaste, humble and faithful souls are compared to them in the scriptures, fall into the hands of cruel men who would kill them.'" Immediately the young man gave them to the Poverello who gathered the birds to him and spoke thus: "O my little sisters, ye simple doves, innocent and chaste, wherefore suffer yourselves to be caught? Now will I rescue you from death, and make nests for you, that ye may be fruitful and multiply according to the commandments of our Creator." He constructed nests for them, and the birds reared their young, feeding from the hands of the friars "nor did they depart until St. Francis gave them his blessing." The youth became a friar, renowned for his sanctity (*Fioretti* 22). As with other creatures with which Francis had to do, a measure of human understanding is attributed to the doves so that his power could be made apparent in eliciting their obedience. They waited to receive his blessing before flying away.

This is a much more plausible story than that a saint's hand provided a foundation for a bird's nest, but the motif Saint Providing Nesting Site has a pedigree comparable to the wren-blackbird legends and parallel with them but documented earlier. The Celtic practice of establishing hermitages and communities of monks on marine islands brought ascetics into close touch with birds which have always resorted in great numbers to such comparatively safe breeding sites. On the Farne Islands off the Northumberland coast, the centre of

[19] Celano (2 *Cel.* 207) comments on the "snaring of full-fledged birds" and refers to a misguided friar's acting like a bird hastening to a snare (2 *Cel.* 32). From early times the setting of snares for birds was customary in Italy. In countries where Roman influence was strong, great numbers of birds are still slaughtered on migration. Estimates of those destroyed annually in Italy vary from ten million (K. Curry Lindahl, *Bird Study* XVII [1970], 74) to 150 million (*The Times*, 22 October 1969).

Irish tradition in northern England, the eider ducks availed themselves of facilities unintentionally provided for them by the hermitage
buildings, as has already been mentioned (p. 32). Saint Cuthbert and
the anchorite Bartholomew were on friendly terms with them.[20]

Felix, the author of the eighth-century Life of Saint Guthlac (†
714), was acquainted with northern traditions, including the details
of Saint Cuthbert's life, as his references to birds indicate, and
modified what he wrote accordingly. Guthlac was the son of a
Mercian nobleman who, after seeing military service on the Welsh
border, during which he learned the language, entered the abbey of
Repton where he came into contact with Celtic lore and customs.
(It was a double abbey of men and women, such as were found in
Ireland and Gaul—a tradition going back to Saint Patrick and Saint
Columcille.) He migrated to Croyland in the East Anglian fens,
establishing his hermitage on an island. We are told that "ravens"
—more probably jackdaws—tormented the saint of the Farnes by
plucking the thatch from his hut. They repented, showing their
contrition by bringing him a year's supply of lard wherewith to
smear his footwear to keep out the damp. Similarly "ravens" pestered
Saint Guthlac, entering his hermitage, despoiling it and his possessions. They stole and dropped a document, but it fell among the
reeds and was miraculously preserved from damage by the water—
again a motif from Irish hagiography. Following Irish and Scottish
precedent, birds—in this instance swallows—rested twittering on his
shoulders, arms, and breast. In commenting on this prodigy, Felix
quotes almost verbatim a remark in Bede's Life of Saint Cuthbert:
"Not only, indeed, did the creatures of the earth and sky obey his
commands, but also even the very water and the air obeyed the true
servant of the true God." Saint Francis's biographers comment in
very similar terms (*Bon.* viii. 11; *Spec. Perf.* 115). Anticipating the
Umbrian saint, Guthlac provided nesting sites, including a basket,

---

[20] Geoffrey, *Vita, c.* 24, 25, in appendix to *Historia Dunelmensis Ecclesiae*
by Symeon of Durham; B. Colgrave, *Two Lives of St. Cuthbert* (Cambridge,
1940). D. J. Hall's *English Mediaeval Pilgrimage* (London, 1966) includes a
useful bibliography of Saint Cuthbert.

for the birds that frequented his hermitage. Thus he might be adopted as the patron saint of those who put up nesting boxes.[21]

The basic truth of the story of Saint Francis and the turtle-doves is not in doubt, for it further illustrates his compassion for all life, men and birds, worms and wolves; but discrepancies in the anecdote indicate that we are concerned with tradition and parable rather than natural history. Imagination has been enlisted to drive home in a picturesque way the importance of pity. Since turtle-doves snared and handled after their spring migration would not breed where released, as domesticated doves might be expected to do, we can be sure birds of this species are mentioned because they had symbolical and allegorical significance. In his account Celano emphasizes the symbolism of doves—emblems of chastity, innocence, humility, and faithfulness. He was expressing conventional medieval ideas derived from scriptural references such as Matthew x. 16, "Be wise as serpents, harmless as doves," and allusions in the Song of Songs (i. 11–15, v. 2, 12), especially vi. 9, "my dove, my perfect one." This collection of love poems had long been allegorized to refer to Christ and the Church. Such references inspired Francis's allusions to doves as "innocent and chaste." Perhaps, also, they account for the tolerance shown by the monks on Mount Athos toward the doves which may be seen courting on the roofs of the monasteries, despite the centuries-old interdiction on the presence of females of all kinds. For Celano, however, the relevant text was Psalm lxxiv. 19: "O deliver not the soul of thy turtle-dove unto the multitude of the wicked." Thus he considered this bird the most suitable species to figure in an anecdote concerning deliverance. The allegorical significance of the parable is subtly carried beyond the freeing of the birds to the release of the lad into the glorious liberty of Christian dedication and fulfilment as a friar.

The stress on symbolism and sacramentalism is greater in this story than in most of the Irish nature legends which generally keep closer to nature and savour more of the woods and mountains and less of the library.

[21] *Acta Sanctorum*, O.S.B., III, pt. i; B. Colgrave, *Felix's Life of Saint Guthlac* (Cambridge, 1956), pp. 120–123.

In connexion with the statue of Saint Francis holding the turtle-doves which stands beneath the trees beside the rocky torrent at the Carceri, it is said there that a pair of these birds once nested in the figure's hands, but it is incredible that on such a small base where so many folk pass by they could have constructed a nest. Here we have one legend generating another.

The cooing of doves, one of the pleasantest sounds of summer and elegantly commented on by Virgil,[22] was particularly attractive to the Franciscans. Brother Masseo craved the grace of humility so fervently that he vowed he would give his eyes if he could but obtain it. He was granted the virtue without this sacrifice, and from hence-forth he was ever blithe and gay, "and many times he made a joyous sound like the cooing of a dove, coo, coo, coo. . . . and being asked by Brother James of Falterone wherefore he changed not his note in these jubilations, he answered with great joyfulness that when we find full contentment in one song there is no need to change the tune" (*Fioretti* 32). The innocence of the dove and merry naïveté of the friar go well together. Brother Sylvester and Brother Leo were also described in the same words Caesarius Heisterbacensis had used of Brother Ensfrid, the well-intentioned buffoon, when he spoke of him as being "of dovelike simplicity" (*Bon.* vi. 8; *Fioretti* 9). There is similar artlessness in a tale of Brother Giles.[23] Hearing a turtle-

---

[22] *Eclogue* I. 58.

[23] The personality of Brother Giles, uneducated and conservative but spiritu-ally minded, of penetrating insight and pawky humour comes before us vividly. He constantly pilloried the brethren who, in his opinion, betrayed their founder's teaching and example, devoting themselves to study and a semi-collegiate life. He compared them to sheep, bleating fruitlessly, and insisted that it was better to teach oneself to lead a holy life than to set about teaching the whole wide world. When one of the friars asked a blessing on his project to preach in the piazza at Perugia, he agreed on condition that he said: *Bo, bo, molto dico e poco fo!* "Blah, blah, much talk and little done." In the same vein was his comment when he was shown proudly the great Sacro Convento: "Truly all you need now are some women." Cf. *Chronicle of the XXIV Generals, Ana-lecta Franc.* III, 74–114; *Fioretti; Doctrines and sayings of Friar Giles;* O. En-glebert, *Les Propos du frère Égide* (Paris, 1930). Giles was a stalwart upholder of the old order and would have agreed with the Franciscan poet Jacopone da Todi: "O cursed Paris, thou hast destroyed our Assisi." Cf. *Poesi Spirituali,* ed. Tresatti, I (Venice, 1717,) Satira. 10.

dove in the garden he addressed it: "Sister Turtle-dove, may I tell
you how to serve the Lord. You repeat *Qua, qua* and not *La, la,* that
is, 'Here, here on earth' and not 'There in heaven.' Oh, my Sister
Turtle-dove, how rightly you coo. But you, man-child, why do you
not learn from the example of Sister Turtle-dove." His little sermon
to the birds had a moral for himself as well as for them. In such
moods the aged friar was overwhelmed by nostalgia for the good old
days when he and Francis, God's troubadours, roamed the flower-
decked meadows, singing the praises of Lady Poverty and Fair Maid
Chastity, accompanying himself as Saint Francis had done on a
make-believe fiddle and bow of two sticks, recalling those joyful, carefree times.[24]

The Sermon to the Birds

Few, if any, incidents in the Life of Saint Francis have caught popular imagination more effectively than the Sermon to the Birds. An

---

It is said that Giles, when an old man, approached Bonaventura and put to
him a series of queries: Could ignorant folk as well as scholars be saved? Could
an unlettered man love God as well as an educated man? "Certainly," replied
Bonaventura. "An old woman can love God better than a master of theology."
Immediately Giles ran to the balustrade of the garden and began to shout at the
top of his voice to all the world: "Everybody listen! An old woman who has
learned nothing and cannot read may love God more than Brother Bonaventura."
Cf. *Analecta Franc.* III, 101. Joergensen points out in *St. Francis of Assisi* (*op.
cit.,* p. 238) that in Bonaventura's *Collationes* we seem to have a reminiscence
of this conversation: "Thus an old woman with a tiny garden gathers finer fruit,
because she has charity, than a great master who owns a huge garden, and
understands the mystery and the nature of things." Cf. Bon. *Opera* (Quaracchi,
1891), p. 418. Another of his illustrations also seems to be a reflection of
Brother Giles's remark: "Which is the richer, he who has a little garden and
makes it fruitful or he who possesses the whole earth and derives no profit from
it? So plenty of knowledge is nothing worth for salvation but he who is truly
wise should work hard and keep his head bowed." Cf. *Analecta Franc.* III,
86. Perhaps, however, such phrases were common coin in Franciscan circles;
but they are of significance as indicating that, despite the feud in the Order
concerning the extent to which strict poverty should be observed, there was a
considerable measure of agreement between an eminent scholar such as Saint
Bonaventura and one of the simplest and saintliest survivors of the companions
of Saint Francis.

[24] *Analecta Franc.* III, 86, 101; Feo Balcari, *Vita di frate Egidio; Spec. Perf.*
93; 2 *Cel.* 127.

account of it is given in several sources (*Actus*, 17; *Fioretti* 16; 1 *Cel.* 58; *Bon.* xii. 3)—an indication of its appeal to the early followers of the saint. The scene was portrayed by a number of painters, the most notable being the fresco in the Upper Church of San Francesco attributed to Giotto.[25] Thus undoubtedly the incident was accepted by the early disciples of the saint as characteristic of him. Nature mystic as he was, his followers and biographers may not have been able adequately to comprehend his ecstatic experiences, but his sympathetic attitude toward Creation had been emphasized by his biographers and could be illustrated pictorially as well as described in word pictures. His mystical sense of affinity with birds and beasts may have induced him to respond to them in a personal way. It is common enough today for a pet owner to talk to his or her cat or budgerigar, and the tradition of telling news to the bees is not yet extinct. We may, therefore, accept and continue to cherish the picture of the little man talking to the birds in a roadside bush. He may have known that he was not the first to do so. If the documents merely suggested such a playful incident, we might well pass on to other matters, but since scrutiny of the Welcoming Birds revealed some tales as possessing more significance and a longer history than is apparent at a glance, we may inquire whether the Sermon to the Birds also embodies influences on Franciscanism which are not immediately apparent.

Examination of its content reveals that it has been expanded in the comparatively late *Fioretti* (16). In Celano's *Vita Prima* (58) the Sermon is quite brief: "My brother birds, much ought ye to praise your Creator, and ever to love Him who has given you feathers for clothing, wings for flight, and all that ye need of. God has made you noble among His creatures, for He has given you a habitation in the purity of the air, and, whereas ye neither sow nor reap, He Him-

[25] The extent to which Giotto was personally responsible for the frescoes in the nave of the Upper Church at Assisi representing the Legend of the saint is disputed. They may have been inspired by him. Cf. M. Meiss, *Giotto and Assisi* (New York University, 1960); P. Murray, "Notes on Some Early Giotto Sources," *Journ. of the Warburg and Courtauld Institutes* XVI (1953), 59–80; A. Martindale and E. Baccheschi, *The Complete Paintings of Giotto* (London, 1969). See Notes to Illustrations.

self doth still protect and govern you without any care of your own." Bonaventura (xii. 3) transcribes the passage with a few trivial altera-tions, apart from omitting the scriptural reference (Matt. vi. 26; cf. xii. 24). He, too, has Saint Francis call the birds "brothers." Torn between anxiety to point out the perspicuity of the birds in recog-nizing the saintly authority of Saint Francis and medieval doctrines concerning sub-human creatures, here, and again when he mentions the Stilling of the Swallows (xii. 4), he speaks of the birds acting "as if they shared human understanding." The writer of the *Fioretti* disclaims giving a verbatim report, remarking that his account is only "the substance of the sermon." The birds—an infinite multitude —are addressed as "little sisters," they are reminded that they should show gratitude for being endowed with "a triple vesture" and for being preserved in the Ark. Not only are they fed by God but they have rivers and fountains provided to satisfy their thirst, mountains to range over, and trees in which to nest. They need neither spin nor sow; and because God has dealt so bounteously with them, they should beware of ingratitude and constantly praise Him. This is compiled from biblical texts including the accounts of Creation (Gen. i. 20) and the Deluge (Gen. viii. 19), our Lord's teaching in Matthew vi. and Luke xii., and also Psalm civ. 10–12 and 16 f. The writer, Bible in hand, has extended Celano's account. For his part Celano, being a stylist who liked to embellish, may have built on Francis's well-known attitude toward Creation—that it was the privilege, duty, and pleasure of all things to praise the Lord—and thus put into his mouth words he might reasonably be supposed to have uttered.

Other details of the incident have been similarly expanded and adorned by Celano and those who followed him. He alone particu-larizes some of the species constituting the congregation—doves, rooks, and jackdaws—a selection of conspicuous and well-known species, strangely omitting passerine songsters. If his feeling for nature had been intense, he would surely have mentioned birds with pleasanter associations than the Corvidae. The writer of the *Fioretti* and Bonaventura wisely omitted mention of particular birds and left it to the painters to depict a great variety of species. Thus indirectly the artists were encouraged to observe and record nature. Celano concludes: "At length he blessed them, and having made the sign of the cross, gave them leave to fly away to another place." Bonaventura exaggerates somewhat less. He says: ". . . nor did one of them move from the spot until he made the sign of the cross over them and given them leave"; but the *Fioretti* states that, when Francis made the sign of the cross over them, "all those birds soared up into the air with wondrous songs and then divided themselves into four parts after the form of the cross Saint Francis had made over them." Here again we have the incremental exaggeration so characteristic of hagiography which may sometimes be used as a principle of interpretation. Often the version with least accretions is the earliest and most accurate, though in some circumstances a saint's biographer may decide to omit embellishments acquired by a legend and pare away major incredibilities (p. 155).

Celano's *Vita Prima* is obviously compiled with the scrupulous care of a scholar who pays regard not only to using language elegantly but to the effective arrangement of his material. It cannot be accidental that he placed the chapter, "Of his preaching to the birds and of the obedience of the creatures" as an auspicious prelude to the saint's evangelistic tour through Umbria and the Marches and immediately after his chronicle of the failure of his mission to the Saracens. Thus he shows that if Moslems rejected the saint's preaching, birds, although many thought them of little account, did not. They responded with alacrity to his loving concern.[26] Later, in the

---

[26] A later tale may indicate some scepticism concerning the Sermon. It begins: "Brother Masseo has said that he was present when the Blessed Francis preached to the birds." This story describes how, rapt in devotion, the saint noticed a flock of birds by the roadside and turned aside to preach to them as he had done on the previous occasion. They all flew away and he reproached himself bitterly: "What effrontery you have, you impertinent son of Pietra Bernardone!" He did so, it is explained, because he realized that he was expecting them to obey him as if he, and not God, were their Creator. Cf. *Archivum Franciscanum Historicum* XX, 546–547. Perhaps, while Francis's humility is thus emphasized, Brother Masseo's veracity is gently questioned. We may detect a tendency to correct some of the exaggerations of Celano and Bonaventura which stress Francis's miraculous power over nature rather than his compassion and obscure his nature mysticism with stories of prodigies.

same chapter, Celano seems to have the recalcitrant Moslems in mind when he remarks: "And it is wonderful how even the irrational creatures recognized his tender affection toward them and perceived beforehand the sweetness of his love." The compiler of the *Fioretti* (40), perhaps taking his cue from Celano, makes more obvious use of the same device, portraying the attentiveness and obedience of fish to St. Anthony's preaching as a contrast to the careless and stubborn behaviour of the citizens of Rimini. The saint "rebuked the folly of infidel heretics by means of creatures without reason, to wit, the fishes even as in days agone, in the Old Testament, he rebuked the ignorance of Balaam by the mouth of an ass." This famous ass provided a convenient precedent for those who humanized animals in order to draw moral teaching from their behaviour.

Francis's manner of addressing the birds as "sisters mine" (*Fioretti* 16) represents an attitude to nature of which we have noted traces already (p. 51), but here it has an intimacy and a depth of feeling unknown before. These words express the profound compassion for all Creation characteristic of the saint. The point of view is similar to that of the Irish and poles apart from the attitude that considers nature as created for man's exploitation. The birds are not looked on as merely provided for human use or even delectation. The earth with its resources and beauties, the mountains, valleys, and trees, is assumed to be for their use and pleasure as well as for ours; and they, as our sisters, are regarded as kin to us, members of God's family, sharing the world's riches. God deals bounteously with men and birds alike, and the duty and privilege of both, as of all Creation, is to offer praise and thanksgiving. These sentiments had been voiced from time to time throughout Christian history, but Francis was able to proclaim them with hitherto unattained clarity and vigour because "he discerned the hidden things of Creation with the eye of the heart, as one who had already escaped into the glorious liberty of the children of God" (1 *Cel.* 80).

St. Francis was by no means the first preacher to birds. The tradition may be traced to the book of Revelation (xix. 17): "And I saw an angel standing in the sun; and he cried with a loud voice, saying to all the fowls that fly in the midst of the heaven, Come and gather yourselves together unto the supper of the great God." This concept of birds perched on a tree being addressed by an angel entered the stream of Christian thought and iconography. As legend and in visual art it was borne onward for centuries.[27] Originally, in keeping with the apocalyptic context, the illustrations showed birds of prey perched on the tree above the angel; but later the theme mellowed, aesthetic considerations were given importance, and gaily plumaged, graceful, and realistic birds took the place of eagles and vultures.[28]

The history of this change is illuminating. The English writer Roger of Wendover took it upon himself to alter, and indeed, pervert the account of the Sermon to suit his own purpose. He placed it immediately after Francis's interview with Pope Innocent III in which, so it was said, Innocent told the dishevelled friar that he was only fit to consort with pigs. Afterwards he relented and granted him permission to preach. According to Roger's version the Little Poor Man began his evangelistic mission in Rome, but because its citizens treated him with contempt he addressed them thus: "Greatly do I deplore your abandoned state, for in spurning me, you are despising the Saviour of the World, whose disciple I am, and whose word I am bringing to you. I shall now leave your city, calling on the Lord of Heaven to witness your depravity; and for your confusion I shall carry the word of Christ to the brute beasts and the fowls of the air, that they may listen to the words of the Lord and obey them." This indicates that Roger accepted the literary setting of the Sermon in the earlier accounts as being designed to underscore the contrast between stiff-necked people and obedient birds.

[27] A sixth-century Irish saint, Fiacre, is said to have been represented preaching to the birds. Cf. G. Jobes, *Dictionary of Mythology, Folklore and Symbols* II (New York 1962), 1369. He established a hermitage and then a community at La Brie near Meaux on the Marne. Because he cultivated vegetables, he became the patron saint of gardeners with a spade as his emblem. His cult became popular with all classes in France during the seventeenth century, and his association with birds may date from this period or later. The vehicle called after him acquired its name from the cab that conveyed visitors to his shrine.

[28] In one of the Irish *immrama*, *The Voyage of Hui Curra*, the reverse occurs; the pleasant birds become birds of prey, tearing the flesh of sinners. Perhaps we may suspect the influence of the Prometheus myth. Cf. W. Y. Evans-Wentz, *The Fairy-Faith in Celtic Countries* (Oxford, 1911), p. 441.

He goes on to say that when Francis left Rome he "found crows, kites, magpies and many other fowls that fly in the midst of heaven sitting among carrion in the suburbs" and called out to them: "I command you in the name of Jesus Christ, whom the Jews crucified and whose sermon the miserable Romans despise, to gather around me and to listen to the Lord's word, in the name of Him who created you and saved you from the flood in Noah's ark." Thereupon the whole flock immediately surrounded the saint and rested, silent and motionless, attentively gazing at his face while he preached to them. When the news of this miracle reached Rome, clergy and people rushed out to witness the strange sight; and on being thus convinced, they repented and joyfully escorted Francis back into the city. From that time his fame spread throughout Italy.[29]

Emphasis is laid, not on the saint's love and compassion for the birds nor on the glory of praising God, but on the episode as thaumaturgic, a device by which proud and contemptuous people were brought to confusion and converted. The saint's humility and compassion have fallen into the background.

There were aspects of the contemporary situation which explain Roger of Wendover's tendentious treatment of the incident. He identified Rome with the Babylon of the Apocalypse which it was prophesied would receive power "one hour with the beast" and "make war with the Lamb" until the hour of its destruction (Rev. xvii. 13–18). King John of England had submitted to the papacy in 1213; and it seemed to Roger and to Matthew Paris, who reported his statements and illustrated the episode, that apocalyptic prophecies were about to be fulfilled. Therefore, he confounded the "doves, rooks and jackdaws" in Celano's report of the sermon and the song-birds of the *Fioretti* with the birds of prey which "eat the flesh of kings, and the flesh of captains" mentioned in the Apocalypse (Rev. xix. 17–18; cf. xviii. 1–2). Matthew Paris's illustration of the Sermon shows that he was ill at ease with Roger's interpretation, although

[29] M. Paris, *Chronica Majora* III (1876), 132–133, Rolls series; R. James, *The Drawings of Matthew Paris*, Walpole Society, XIV (1925–26); F. D. Klingender, "St. Francis and the Birds of the Apocalypse," *Journ. of the Warburg and Courtauld Institutes* XVI (1953), 13–23.

he sympathized with it, so he added a scroll reproducing the original sense of Francis's discourse in which the saint says: "Hail birds, praise your Creator, who feeds you and clothes you with feathers, although you toil not, neither do you spin, plough, sow or gather into barns." Underneath the drawing he wrote: "This happened while he was walking in the vale of Spoleto, and not only with doves, crows or daws, but with vultures and birds of prey." Thus, although correcting the record to some extent, he approves of the introduction of carrion-feeding birds as members of the congregation and clearly depicts a bird of prey, evidently an eagle, in his drawing. During the thirteenth century, English artists followed this tradition; but in the next century the illustrations were refined, as already mentioned, to show an angel holding forth to elegant, gaily plumaged birds of identifiable species perched on a tree (pls. 2a, b, c, 16, 17).[30]

The explanation of this change illustrates the difference between the medieval mentality and our own. Saint Francis had become approximated to an angel. As we have noted, Bonaventura, influenced by the teaching of Joachim of Fiore, was responsible for this. In his Prologue he wrote: "In like wise, he is thought to be not unmeetly set forth in the true prophecy of that other friend of the Bridegroom, the Apostle and Evangelist John, under the similitude of the Angel ascending from the sunrising and bearing the seal of the Living God. . . .

"Now that this Angel was indeed that messenger of God, beloved of Christ, our ensample and the world's wonder, Francis the servant of God, we may with full assurance conclude. . . ." Bonaventura emphasizes that his saintliness and stigmatization confirm this. It was during the "Lent of St. Michael" that the stigmatization occurred on Mount La Verna.

Thus the treatment of the Sermon to the Birds provides insight into the psychology of the men of the Middle Ages which must

---

30 Fourteen English illustrations of the scene are known from these centuries although few were executed on the Continent. Cf. Klingender, *op. cit.*; A. G. Little, *Franciscan History and Legend in Medieval Art* (Manchester Univ. Press, 1937), pp. 3–11, 37–76. Perhaps these may have helped to increase sympathy in England and English-speaking lands not only for Saint Francis but also for the birds. Cf. Armstrong, 1970, pl. 32.

influence our assessment of the whole Franciscan Legend and the lessons to be drawn from it. Even a rustic interlude in the saint's life could be skewed to serve political and ecclesiastical ends, and in the interest of exalting the humblest of men he could be approximated to an archangel. The medieval mind did not differentiate its concepts into the precise categories of our thinking. Birds and angels were not wholly different (p. 66). Francis could be more than human, and Saint Brigid could be assimilated to the Mother of God and even called "Mother of Jesus." [31]

The history of the Sermon to the Birds theme in England explains to some extent the popularity of its pictorial treatment, for in this country it achieved prominence beyond that attained elsewhere. But we must now retrace our steps and consider the evolution in Irish literature of apocalyptic biblical themes concerning birds. We shall find that a tradition was established long before Francis which culminated in his Sermon to the Birds.

About the ninth century Adamnan, writing of his Vision of Paradise, described the sermon Elias preached to the bird souls:

And these are the tidings which Elias declared continually unto the souls of the righteous, under the Tree of Life, which is in Paradise. As soon as Elias opens his book in order to instruct the spirits, the souls of the righteous, in the form of bright white birds, repair to him from every side. Then he tells them, first, of the wages of the righteous, the joys and delights of the Heavenly Realm, and right glad thereat are all the throng. After that he tells them of the pains and torments of Hell and the woes of Doomsday. . . . Then Elias shuts his book, and thereupon the birds make exceeding great lamentation. . . .[32]

In a later moral treatise, *The Two Sorrows of the Kingdom of Heaven*, Elias is described as standing in Paradise with the Gospels in his hand preaching to the birds perched on the Tree of Life. They are eating the berries. The *Félire Óenguso* also mentions Elias's

[31] L. Gougaud, *Gaelic Pioneers of Christianity* (Dublin, 1923), pp. 103–104.
[32] C. S. Boswell, *An Irish Precursor of Dante* (London, 1908), p. 46; J. D. Seymour, *Irish Visions of the Other World* (London, 1930).

addressing the flocks of birds while they eat the berries growing on the Tree.[33]

Birds have commonly been thought of as something more than winged creatures—as souls of the dead, angels, and so forth—and the birds of Irish mythology are often supernatural. In the Christian legends they may be part human or part angelic. Thus Maeldune and his fellow-voyagers, as they sailed, heard a resonant chanting like the singing of psalms and discovered that it proceeded from an island thronged by birds. Here, in this semi-pagan saga, we discover birds praising the Lord as Franciscan birds were to do later. In another episode a Great Bird and two eagles alight and feed on the berries covering a branch brought by the Great Bird. It then bathes in the lake waters, turned red by the berries falling into it.[34] It seems as if a number of tales had been cast into the well of imagination, and fragments had united in the magic waters to generate a composite legend—the birds of the Tree of Life, the great eagle of Ezekiel (xvii. 3–7) which plucked the branch of a cedar, the monstrous birds of Irish mythology with eastern affinities,[35] the birds of Revelation, and those to whom Elias preached, as well as the eagle of the *Physiologus* which periodically renews its youth—we seem to have reminiscences of them all. This passage is sufficient to remind us that we must not underestimate the traffic in oral and book lore which was constantly going on among folk during the Middle Ages. The compiler of the Voyage of Maeldune had picked up ideas and stories from the four corners of the earth.

In the Voyage of Bran, usually ascribed to the eighth century, birds sing the praises of God on a Blessed Isle and Earthly Paradise:

[33] The berry-eating birds have apparently flown to Ireland from the East. In the Vedas two birds perch on the top of the imperishable *açvattha*, one eating its figs, the other looking on. Two facing birds on the Tree of Life form an ancient and widespread motif in Asian art which was early taken over into Christian iconography and still persists. Moslem martyrs in the guise of exquisite green birds feast on the fruits of Paradise. The magical salmon which feed on the hazel "berries" falling into Connla's Well may be connected in mythology with the birds of the Tree of Life. Cf. Boswell, *op. cit.*, p. 174.

[34] Boswell, *op. cit.*, p. 154.

[35] T. P. Cross, *Motif-Index of Early Irish Literature*, Folk-lore series no. 7. (Bloomington, Indiana, 1936), pp. 55–56.

An ancient tree there is with blossoms,
On which birds call the Canonical Hours.
'Tis in harmony it is their wont
To call together every Hour.

Splendours of every colour glisten
Throughout the gentle-voiced plains.
Joy is known, ranked around music,
In southern White-Silver Plain.

Unknown is wailing or treachery
In the familiar cultivated land,
There is nothing rough or harsh,
But sweet music striking on the ear.[36]

Saint Brendan, too, discovered an island Paradise of Birds. Their singing was "like the music of heaven." The saint conversed with their spokesman and was informed that at one time they had all been angels but when Lucifer fell they were brought down with him. Their offence being trivial, they were permitted to make merry in their tree. Brendan and his companions kept Easter there and remained until after Whitsuntide "and the birds sang Matins and verses of the psalms, and sang all the Hours as is the habit of Christian men." [37]

We are reminded of Saint Francis: "Our sisters the birds are praising their Creator, let us go among them and sing unto the Lord praises and the Canonical Hours" (*Bon.* viii. 9; *Fioretti* 16).

Almost from the earliest days of the Church, Christians found

[36] T. P. Cross and C. H. Slover, *Ancient Irish Tales* (Bloomington, Ind. and London, 1952), p. 589.

[37] According to the *Navigatio* the little bird addressed Saint Brendan after he had ceased speaking, while Saint Francis bid the birds be silent and then spoke to them. Cf. W. Stokes, *op. cit.* (1890); Plummer, *op. cit.* (1910), I, 44–95; II, 44–92, 328–337. The Latin text of the *Navigatio* dates from the late ninth or early tenth century. Cf. A. Graf, *Miti, Leggende e Superstizioni del Medio Evo* (Florence and Rome, 1891–92) I, 184–185, 266; II, 395, for Italian and other texts; also E. G. R. Waters, *An Old Italian Version of the Navigatio Sancti Brendani* (Oxford, 1931) for a thirteenth-century version in Lucchese dialect.

delight in interpreting the songs and activities of birds as worship. Saint Ambrose and others among the Fathers of the Church thought of birds as offering prayer and praise to God, a tradition that has continued in poetry until the present time.[38]

Tundale's Vision, which receives further mention later, was in the succession of Irish Visions rather than the Voyages or *immrama* but, once again, we hear of flocks of pious birds. He beheld an immense tree, "the prop and stay of the Church," laden with blossoms as well as fruit. Perched on it were great flocks of birds singing all kinds of songs while around it multitudes of men and women had congregated to praise God.[39]

The earliest extant version of the legend of Saint Brendan, the *Navigatio Brendani*, dates from the eleventh century though the tale was probably current in the tenth. It became familiar to people throughout Europe and beyond. Versions appeared in Latin, French, Flemish, Saxon, English, Irish, Welsh, Scottish Gaelic, and Breton. Tundale's Vision was also widely read; Joachim of Fiore and the compiler of the *Fioretti* were acquainted with the story. It is improbable that these and other similar narratives were unknown to such scholarly men as Celano and Bonaventura, and we may reasonably assume that throughout Europe, including Italy, incidents from them were passed on by word of mouth. In view of the history of this theme, those who take for granted that the accounts of Francis's friendly dealings with birds may be adequately explained as slightly exaggerated accounts of their responsiveness to him as a nature mystic are making a considerable assumption.[40]

[38] E. A. Armstrong, "Some Aspects of the Evolution of Man's Appreciation of Bird Song," in *Bird Vocalizations: Their Relation to Current Problems in Biology and Psychology*, ed. R. A. Hinde (Cambridge, 1969), pp. 343–365.

[39] Boswell, *op. cit.*, pp. 212 ff., 224–229.

[40] The anxiety of many writers to stress Francis's originality while emphasizing his conformity to the doctrines of the Church has contributed to the neglect of the Celtic and other influences discussed here. A quotation from a modern biographer shows that such naïve interpretations are still current: "Just as the *Paternoster* was not the work of the Evangelists, so the Sermon to the Birds and the dialogue of Perfect Joy owe nothing to the compiler of the *Actus*, nor to the translator of the *Fioretti*." Cf. Englebert, *op. cit.* (1950), p. 238.

The Duet with the Nightingale

The motif of man and bird praising God together reached its highest refinement in a story that belongs to a time subsequent to Celano's biographies and may well be of later date than the *Fioretti*. While Saint Francis and Brother Leo were enjoying a meal together in the open air, they were delighted by the singing of a nightingale close by. Francis suggested: "Let us sing the praise of God antiphonally with this bird." Leo excused himself as he was no singer, but the saint lifted up his voice and phrase by phrase sang alternately with the nightingale. So they continued from Vespers to Lauds until Francis at last admitted defeat. Then the nightingale took wing and fluttered to his hand, where he fed it, praising it enthusiastically. He gave the small brown songster his blessing, and it flew off into the bushes.[41]

In this story we have the essence of Franciscanism, indeed Franciscanism idealized—its gaiety, humour, homeliness, piety, compassion, and sympathy for nature. A congregation of birds listened attentively to the saint, and another flock, as we shall see presently, ceased their twittering at his command; but in competition with the nightingale, he came off second best. We have already noted that birds could even disobey him (p. 59). The story is based on observation to the extent that a nightingale in full song could outsing saint

[41] L. Wadding, *Annales Minorum* II (1625–1648), 24–25; J. R. H. Moorman, *A New Fioretti* (London, 1946), pp. 67–68.
The incident is said to have occurred at the Carceri on Mount Subasio although there seems to be no conclusive evidence that Francis stayed there. Bartholomew of Pisa refers to Cardinal Ugolini's visiting the Carceri to seek out Francis and ask him whether he should join the Order; but it is very doubtful whether any such visit took place. Cf. *Liber de Conformitate Vitae Beati Francisci ad Vitam Nostri Jesu Christi*, in *Analecta Franc.* IV (1906), 342, 454, V (1912), *passim*. Other friars including Sylvester, almost certainly made use of these grottoes. His cave in the side of the ravine is still pointed out. Birds are plentiful at the Carceri. In spite of the evidence that the Sermon to the Birds was delivered elsewhere, an ancient ilex is pointed out as the tree on which they assembled. In June the wren, great tit, and chaffinch were still in song and a nightingale was singing in the valley below. The destruction of wild life in Italy which continues from September to May is not permitted here, but around Assisi, birds are still slaughtered.

or sinner.[42] (We must overlook some details, such as that to sing antiphonally for any length of time with such a bird would be impossible because the phrases could not be neatly intercalated, and no wild nightingale would feed from the hand.) In some other Franciscan tales there is the notion of nature as at man's service or obeying his instructions, but here the victory is conceded to the bird —and its triumph is in creating musical beauty. The saint enjoyed the contest as the emulation consisted in singing the praises of God. Thus we are given a glimpse of the Earthly Paradise, man and bird hymning the glory of the Creator. The episode is a realistic personal enactment of scenes in the Irish *immrama* and Visions in which men and birds engage in a colloquy or form a choir together. The tameness of the nightingale recalls other intimate relationships between birds and saints. Saint Brigid "blessed the frightened bird till she played with it in her hand," and Saint Servanus's pet robin perched on his head, on his shoulder, and in his bosom like the birds that were so friendly with Saint Guthlac.[43]

We need not allow our pleasure in Francis's Nightingale Duet and our appreciation of the anecdote as testifying to the spirit of delight in music and nature characteristic of the saint and his first followers to be dimmed by the realization that, in common with a number of the tales we are considering, this is probably a version of an earlier story. Apart from the legends already mentioned, our gossiping informant Salimbene mentions an episode that appears to be essentially the same tale without its fanciful features. He was a music lover and had many musical friends, among whom was Brother Vita of Lucca, a Friar Minor and a renowned singer. Salimbene tells us: "Whenever a nightingale sang in hedge or thicket it would cease at the voice of his song, listening most eagerly to him, as if rooted to the spot, and resuming its strain when he had ceased;

---

[42] P. Bond, "Timing the Nightingale," *The Field* CXCVIII (1951), 695.

[43] Lady Gregory, *A Book of Saints and Wonders* (London, 1920), p. 12. The robin used to call or sing as Saint Servanus prayed or read; and when it died after mischievous boys had played roughly with it, Saint Kentigern restored it to life. The Life of Saint Kentigern was written in 1125 by Joceline, a monk of Furness, but he used a much earlier source. Cf. A. P. Forbes, *Lives of St. Ninian and St. Kentigern* (Edinburgh, 1874), pp. 42–43.

so that bird and friar would sing in turn, each warbling his own sweet strains." [44] Not only was this put on record in writing before the story of Francis's duet was set down but, allowing for contemporary modes of thought and expression, it is completely credible. A nightingale would pause in its song on hearing a man singing close at hand; and, if he were to sing phrases in "a flute-like treble" like Brother Henry of Pisa, another of Salimbene's friends mentioned in the same context, the bird might reply to him. One may readily stimulate song from a nightingale by whistling a few notes close to where it is perched in a thicket as I have done beside Saint Mary of the Angels at Assisi. By interpolating a phrase now and then, a kind of antiphonal duet may result. [45]

Certainly nightingales sang around Assisi in Francis's lifetime as they do today. But we should not miss the real significance of these stories as illustrations of spontaneous Franciscan sympathy with all life and pleasure in participating in nature's exuberance. The creatures of God are felt to be man's brothers and sisters expressing *joie de vivre*, minstrels or jongleurs by the wayside, praising the Creator, heartening those who pass by and, perhaps, like earlier troubadours, drawing some of their hearers nearer to God. Saint Francis's nightingale announces the growth of that sense of affinity with nature which enabled art and science to set forth in search of territories hitherto unexplored. [46]

[44] C. G. Coulton, *From St. Francis to Dante* (London, 1906), p. 95.

[45] Primitive hunters imitate birds vocally, and at least as early as the fourteenth century attempts were made to imitate bird songs instrumentally (cf. J. Huizinga, *The Waning of the Middle Ages* [Penguin Books, 1955], p. 270); but apparently the Chinese did so much earlier. No doubt bird calls were thus imitated before bird songs. Cf. Armstrong, *op. cit.* (1969), pp. 343–347.

[46] There are similarities between this story and Saint Francis and the Cicada (2 *Cel.* 171), but in the latter "the man of God mingled his own praise with her songs" instead of singing antiphonally—which would have been difficult. Two swallows entered Saint Guthlac's hermitage "sharing every song of joy." Not only birds but also fish came at his call and obeyed his commands. The nature motifs in this Irish-influenced saint's Legend anticipate a number of those in the Franciscan Legend. Cf. Colgrave, *op. cit.* (1956), pp. 114–127.

The concept of the nightingale's praising God was not original. In verses of about A.D. 900 appearing with the poetry of Eugenius Vulgarius, the nightingale is described as perched with her young on a spray of myrtle singing so that they

The Stilling of the Swallows

Celano's account of the Stilling of the Swallows is elegantly told (1 *Cel.* 58):

One day (for instance) when he was come to the fortress of Alviano to set forth the word of God, he went up on an eminence where all could see him, and asked for silence. But though all the company held their peace and stood reverently by, a great number of swallows

in turn may learn to sing as she does, "songs worthy to offer to the Lord God, canticles divine." Cf. E. S. Duckett, *Death and Life in the Tenth Century* (Ann Arbor, Mich., 1967), pp. 225–243. John (or Nicholas) of Guildford in *The Owl and the Nightingale* (written 1189–1217) also describes the bird as joyously offering divine praises. The theme became secularized in *La Messe des Oisiaus* by Jean de Condé (ca. 1275–1340) in which the nightingale joins in a religious service in honour of Venus. Cf. T. P. Harrison, *They Tell of Birds* (Austin: University of Texas Press, 1956), pp. 26–31. A dialogue between man and nightingale is represented in a Middle English poem of the second half of the fifteenth century. Clericus and Philomena speak alternately. Cf. R. H. Robbins, *Secular Lyrics of the XIVth. and XVth. Centuries* (Oxford, 1952), pp. 172–179.

After the time of Saint Francis the theme of a duet between saint and singing bird reappears in South America. Saint Rose of Lima (1586–1617) sang antiphonally with a bird in praise of the Lord. She addressed it thus: "Thou dost praise thy Creator, I my sweet Saviour: thus we together bless the Deity. Open thy little beak, begin, and I will follow thee: and our voices shall blend in a song of holy joy." At once the little bird began to sing, running through the scale to the highest note. Then he ceased that the saint might sing in her turn . . . thus did they celebrate the greatness of God for a whole hour. . . . At last, towards the sixth hour, the saint dismissed him, saying, 'Go, my little chorister, go, fly far away. But blessed be my God who never leaves me!' " An interesting detail is that the bird is described as male at a period when it was customary to think of singing birds as female, but the voice of a male bird could be considered complementary to the voice of a female saint. Another detail, the incongruous command to the pious and obliging little songster to fly far away is reminiscent of Francis's dismissal of the nightingale and cicada. Moreover, we are told that birds alighted on St. Rose's head and shoulders as they did on his. He sang duets with a cicada; she ordered two groups of mosquitoes, buzzing alternately, to join her in saying her Office. At her command they flew away to return again at the appropriate hour. Francis saw a vision in which he was able to bend down the topmost branches of a lofty tree to the ground, indicating the stooping of the Apostolic See to his desire (*Bon.* iii. 8). When Saint Rose went forth, the trees bowed over her path. Francis, when dying, asked to be laid naked on the earth; Saint Rose asked to be laid on bare wood. The reason she did not enter

who were building their nests in that same place were chirping and chattering loudly. And as Francis could not be heard by the men for their chirping, he spoke to the birds and said: "My sisters, the swallows, it is now time for me to speak too, because you have been saying enough all this time. Listen to the word of God and be in silence, and quiet, until the sermon is finished!" And those little birds (to the amazement and wonder of all the bystanders) kept silence forthwith, and did not move from that place till the preaching was ended. So those men, when they had seen that sign, were filled with the greatest admiration, and said: "Truly this man is a Saint, and a friend of the Most High." And with the utmost devotion they hastened at least to touch his clothes, praising and blessing God.

This narrative may be regarded as combining the Sermon to the Birds motif with Stilling the Birds. The *Fioretti* (16) contains only a brief allusion to the incident shortly before the Sermon to the Birds, and it is located at Saburniano; whereas according to the *Actus*, it occurred at Cannara. Bonaventura (xii. 4, 5) as usual closely follows Celano, but he adds another swallow anecdote which provides a further instance of cumulative exaggeration and illustrates Bonaventura's unthrifty mythmaking. In Parma a scholar, irritated by a twittering swallow, identified it as one of those that had been silenced by Francis and commanded: "In the name of Francis, the servant of God, I bid thee come hither to me forthwith and keep silence." The swallow not only ceased twittering but, following long

---

a convent of Saint Clare was that the sight of a black and white butterfly—the Dominican colours—indicated that she should become one of their tertiaries. Cf. L. Hansen, *Rosa Peruana. Vita Mirabilis et Mors pretiosa S. Rosae a Sancta Maria* (Ulyssipone Occidentall, 1725); R. de Bussière, *Le Perou et Ste. Rose de Lima* (Paris, 1863); F. M. Capes, *The Flower of the New World: A Short History of St. Rose of Lima* (London, 1899). The Dominicans were not noted for their compassion for animals. It was said that Saint Dominic, exasperated by a sparrow, concluded that it was possessed by the devil and plucked it alive, rejoicing at its shrieks. Cf. Coulton, *op. cit.* (1906), p. 297. There can be little doubt that the story of St. Rose was influenced by the Franciscan Legend and that the duetting bird and insects of Lima are the successors of those of Umbria. So also the Wolf of Gubbio migrated to the New World (p. 216). It is regrettable that neither in Peru nor Italy did a famous saint's friendliness with birds and beasts create a tradition of compassion for them.

tradition, "gave herself up into his hands as though into safe keeping." He then released her and was troubled no more. The bird is represented as not only remembering St. Francis but recognizing and responding to his name. Such was the power emanating from the saint's holiness that it made a bird identifiable as having been in his company. Moreover, the invocation of his name could subdue its normal instincts.[47]

The Stilling of the Swallows by Francis may have been elaborated from a simple incident in which he called out to the birds to be quiet and so silenced them. Celano implies that they not only remained still but listened to the sermon, as, later on, Wadding described an ass listening to his preaching (p. 124). If we are to judge his account literally, the bystanders were little or not at all impressed by the sermon, although it seems that the swallows were, for it was the behaviour of the birds which called forth the admiration of the human congregation in words reminiscent of Scripture. The people sought to touch the saint's clothes as they had pressed around Christ to touch His garments (cf. Matt. ix. 21, xiv. 36; Mark v. 28, vi. 56). Evidently Celano was not content with illustrating Saint Francis's compassion by relating the account of the Sermon to the Birds. The saint's interest in birds had to be exaggerated into miraculous control of them so that in this indirect way the conversion of the bystanders could be said to have been achieved. Celano's credibility in other contexts must be assessed in terms of what he made of this incident. Could he have had in mind Elijah's docile ravens (1 Kings xvii. 4, 6) and perhaps a remark made by Sulpicius Severus, "*Qui etiam avibus imperaret*"? [48] The biographers tend to stress the impression made on spectators as proof of a prodigy. However, in the *Fioretti* the emphasis is rather different. Francis, with Friars Masseo and Agnolo, approaches Saburniano with ecstatic

[47] According to Caesarius Heisterbacensis (*Dial. Mir. X.* lvi), a pet bird that had heard a lady frequently say, "Holy Thomas, help me!" uttered these words when seized by a bird of prey. Immediately the hawk (or kite) fell dead. Thus the invocation of a saint by a bird was believed to be effective. In *The Golden Legend* Voragine gives another version. Cf. W. Caxton, *The Golden Legend*, ed. F. S. Ellis (London, 1900), IV, 59.

[48] *Ep.* III. 1478.

zeal, "taking heed neither of road nor path"; and when the crowd, enthused by the Sermon, wish to follow Francis immediately, he dissuades them, assuring them that he will ordain what they should do for the salvation of their souls. "And then he bethought him of the Third Order which he established for the universal salvation of all people." Flocking birds led to thoughts of flocking folk. The writer was not satisfied with Celano's giving prominence to the swallows' silence as a manifestation of miraculous power. He stresses the impression created on birds and people by his words and the prompt obedience they elicited. He rightly emphasizes obedience as a watchword of Franciscanism and presents Francis as one entitled to be granted it by birds, beasts, and people without delay or question.

Swallows appealed to the Franciscans as symbolic of spiritual activities. Friar Bernard was said to have a mind so "detached from earthly things, he, like the swallows soared high by contemplation." Friar Giles said of him, referring to his protracted vigils on the mountains, that "he was able to 'feed flying' as the swallows did" (*Fioretti* 28).[49]

Despite the persecution of birds in Italy, swallows are common, though children used to take them from the nest and may do so still (p. 117). Elsewhere, as in China, sentiment or superstition exempts them from interference. Their bright colours, glancing flight, and association with the joy and new life of spring explain the esteem in which they have long been held.[50] They still dart and twitter in the courtyard of San Damiano where their predecessors, one may believe, cheered the heart of Saint Clare, that enterprising

[49] Giovanni del Biondo represented a pair of nesting swallows in his Annunciation triptych. No doubt he introduced the birds in part as symbols of spring and new birth. In intentional contrast to the stiff and conventional dove, they are evidently painted from life. The nest, at which one of the birds is apparently feeding young—though it might be adding to the nest—is in an alcove above the Angel of the Annunciation. The picture is dated about 1385. Cf. H. Friedmann, "Giovanni del Biondo and the Iconography of the Annunciation," *Simiolus: Kunsthistorisch Tijdschrift* (1969), pp. 6–14. In ancient Greek art and modern folk ritual, the swallow is an emblem of spring.

San Bernardino mentions with displeasure the robbing of swallows' nests by children. Cf. I. Origo, *The World of San Bernardino* (London, 1963), p. 114.

[50] E. A. Armstrong, *The Folklore of Birds* (New York, 1970), pp. 179–185.

soul, confined there like a caged bird. When Francis welcomed her as sharing his ideals and aspirations, neither of them could have anticipated her lifelong incarceration. Antifeminist ecclesiastical prejudices and pressures thwarted her ambition to minister, like Francis, to the sick and needy.

We have assumed that Francis, on the impulse of the moment, called on the swallows to cease their twittering; but it must be acknowledged that, as we have found in regard to other incidents, the biographers may have been influenced by ancient traditions. Just as the *Fioretti* contains a parallel to the Sermon to the Birds, namely, Saint Anthony's Sermon to the Fish, so it includes a parallel to the Stilling of the Swallows: "One day as Friar Simon was in the wood at prayer, feeling great consolation in his soul, a flock of rooks began to do him much annoy by their cawing: whereat he commanded them in the name of Jesus to depart and return no more; and the said birds departing were no more seen or heard, neither in the wood nor in all the country round about" (*Fioretti* 12). We cannot be certain that, because Celano's *Vita Prima* was circulated before the *Fioretti*, the former cannot have been influenced by stories, perhaps transmitted orally, which eventually appeared in the latter, for it is acknowledged that some of the most authentic material, such as that which we owe to Brother Leo, was collected and put into circulation comparatively late. There is a further complication. Almost certainly the Friar Simon anecdote is adapted from an Irish legend.

Saint Cainnic, having sought out an island for prayer and meditation, was greatly vexed one Sunday by the clamour of the birds. He rebuked them, and forthwith they all became silent and settled with their breasts to the ground, remaining without movement (like Saint Francis's bird congregation) until Monday morning when the saint gave them permission (as Saint Francis also was to do) to go about their business.[51] Those familiar with what Dunbar called "the yammeris and the yowlis, and skrykking, screeking, skrymming scowlis, and meickle noyis and shoutis" of a large colony of seabirds such as breed on many Irish islands will recognize that Saint Cainnic had

[51] Plummer, *op. cit.*, I (1910), 161.

more cause for complaint than Friar Simon. Apart from the fact that the uproar made by a multitude of nesting seabirds is much greater than the noise of an average rookery and may be audible at a distance of two miles, the friar might have sought a quieter spot in the woods, but the Irish saint on his small island could not withdraw so easily.

The significance of these facts is that the motif Stilling the Birds is much less likely to have arisen in Italy than in Ireland, where many hermitages were within sight and hearing of noisy seabird colonies. It could be argued that the motif is so "natural" that it might have appeared independently in a number of different areas; but to students of mythology and folklore acquainted with the conservatism of the folk mind and the numerous impressive instances of artifacts, mythology, and ritual being preserved with little change for centuries and transmitted from area to area, this argument is not as plausible as it might appear at first glance. Stilling the Birds might seem an obvious motif, but so far as the writer is aware it is only characteristic of medieval Christian milieux. Unless the tradition can be found in other cultures it should be accepted that it came into the Franciscan Legend from Ireland.[52] It persisted after the time of Francis. There can be little doubt that the birds that ceased their singing at the command of Thomas of Florence did so because of the precedent set by Francis's bird congregation. Birds not only applauded and sang over the house of Francis the Confessor but ceased singing at his command. The mantle of his more famous namesake had fallen upon him. Other saints continued the tradition.[53]

[52] *Acta Sanctorum*, Oct., XIII, 880, col. 2; cf. Loomis, *op. cit.*, p. 180.

[53] Plummer, *op. cit.*, I (1910), 161.

In contrast to the Stilling the Birds motif, the Expulsion motif represented in the story of St. Cainnic and the Mice commonly occurs in non-Christian as well as Christian cultures. Both motifs are categories of The Obedient Animal. The Christian expulsion tradition involving animals begins with the Gadarene swine (Matt. viii. 30–32). The animals driven out include a wide range of creatures regarded as noxious, varying from dragons to fleas. Bonaventura (viii. 9), in his anxiety to impress his readers with the saint's superhuman power, spoils the delightful story of the duetting cicada by introducing the Expulsion motif: "And at once, his leave given, she flew away, nor was ever seen here again, as though she dared not in any wise transgress his command." Celano (2 *Cel.* 171)

Saint Bonaventura, as is apparent in his treatment of the fable of the scholar's swallow and other contexts, was not averse to gilding the lily—sometimes, in his zeal, doing so clumsily. In one of his sermons he tried to impress the congregation with Saint Francis's miraculous power over nature by framing an anecdote borrowing motifs from the stories we have been considering. He stated that during the saint's travels he came on many birds in a certain field making a great deal of noise with their songs. When he told them to be silent, they obeyed; and then when he told them to sing, they did so.[54] In the original stories the Stilling of the Birds was effected in order that Francis might make himself heard, but here he has become a wizard, dominating and controlling birds merely in order to manifest his power. We have already noticed that Brother Masseo's description of Saint Francis's reaction when the birds flew

contents himself with saying that "he gave her leave to depart so that she might not be the occasion of vainglory. He dismissed her and she never appeared there again." (Cf. p. 155.) In the Franciscan Legend there is a tendency, not so apparent in Irish legends but perhaps borrowed from Caesarius Heisterbacensis or some other hagiographer, for the saint to send a completely harmless and friendly creature away for ever, thus emphasizing the miraculous aspect of saints' dealings with animals.

The concept of God's will being manifested by wild creatures either remaining with a man or leaving him for ever appears in the stories of Caesarius Heisterbacensis (X. lvii, lviii). Cf. *The Dialogue on Miracles*, trans. H. von E. Scott and C. C. S. Bland, II (London, 1920), 218–219. In one of these a certain knight said to his doves that, if it was God's will, they should stay with him, but if not they might fly away. They did so and never returned. The other tale records that when storks flew around the monastery of Citeaux the prior concluded that they were awaiting his blessing. When he had bestowed it, "they flew off together with great cheerfulness." The motif of creatures departing after being blessed, which is so prominent in the Franciscan Legend, may have been adopted from such stories and perhaps influenced Francis. The account of the release of the doves concludes with a noteworthy question indicating that Saint Francis was not alone in the thirteenth century, outside Irish circles, in feeling compassion for birds: "Do you suppose it pleases God when sparrowhawks, falcons, cranes and other birds of the kind are reared for amusement?" It may not be without significance that, in the neighbourhood of Heisterbach, Irish influence, with its compassion for animals, was strong. Cf. Gougaud, *Devotional and Ascetic Practices* (1923), p. 107; Gougaud, *Les saints Irlandais hors d'Irlande* (Louwain and Oxford, 1936).

[54] Bonaventura, *Opera Omnia*, ed. Quaracchi, IX, 587.

away rather than waiting to hear his sermon may indicate a reluctance to depict the saint as wielding magic. In their zeal medieval hagiographers often failed to distinguish between the concept of divine power manifested through the saint and ·superhuman power exerted by him.

The Kindly Falcon

Saint Francis stilled the birds but a bird aroused the saint. Bonaventura (viii. 10) tells the story in his usual fine style:

> While, accordingly, he was sojourning in that place [La Verna], a falcon that had its nest there bound itself by close ties of friendship unto him. For alway at that hour of night wherein the holy man was wont to rise for the divine office, the falcon was beforehand with its song and cries. . . . But when the servant of Christ was weighed down beyond his wont by infirmity, the falcon would spare him, and would not mark for him so early an awakening. At such times, as though taught by God, he would about dawn strike the bell of his voice with a light touch. Verily, there would seem to have been a divine omen, alike in the gladness of the birds of a myriad species, and in the cries of the falcon, inasmuch as that praiser and worshipper of God, upborne on the wings of contemplation, was at that very place and time to be exalted by the vision of the Seraph.

Birds are thus endowed with supernatural intuition. The *Fioretti* (*2nd consid. of stigmata*) emphasizes that the falcon was not only an animated alarm clock but "she ofttimes dwelt familiarly with him." The bird had built her nest near by and awakened him at night for matins by "singing" and flapping her wings on his cell, making sure he had arisen before departing. Poetic, indeed, but unrealistic. Celano (2 *Cel.* 168), who does not mention La Verna as the scene of the friendly relationship, states that the bird was building its nest, while Bonaventura contents himself with stating that the nest was there. We can hardly give either of them credit for knowing that peregrine falcons and kestrels normally lay their eggs on ledges or occasionally in the disused nests of other birds, bringing no nest material. Bonaventura tells us that the incident occurred during the Lent of St. Michael (Michaelmas), and according to Sabatier's reckoning the saint did not reach La Verna until August,[55] by which time the young would have flown, although one or more of the birds might possibly be in the vicinity of the eyrie occasionally. The stigmatization is said to have occurred on Holy Cross Day, 14 September. The biographers, wishing to add authentication to the episode, have added details so carelessly as to counter their aim. Moreover Bonaventura by his embellishments has weakened Celano's point: the rapport and reciprocal friendliness between the Little Poor Man and all creatures, including the inanimate. "No wonder" says Celano "if the other creatures reverenced the chief lover of the Creator." The heading of the neighbouring section (125) is "How the creatures returned his love," and in it we are told that the surgeon's cauterizing iron, applied from ear to eyebrow, caused him no pain because he had pleaded with Brother Fire: "Be kind to me at this hour, be courteous, for I have loved thee of old in the Lord." Similarly Saint Kevin had thought of birds, beasts, and mountains as all alike "creatures of God." Brother Falcon, like Brother Fire, has respect for the Poverello's infirmities. The *Fioretti* (*2nd consid. of stigmata*) lays special emphasis on this: the falcon, when the saint was ill, sang later "after the manner of a discreet and compassionate person."

It is usual for those responsive to nature's moods to find their own feelings reflected in nature, their sorrows shared by the brooding mountains, their joys echoed in the birds' songs, their hearts dancing with the windswept blossoms. Among such was Saint Francis, as some of his biographers emphasized. The falcon "joined himself to him in a close alliance of friendship" (2 *Cel.* 168), but it would be more accurate to say that the saint allied himself in friendship with the falcon. The nesting bird uttered its sharp reiterated "kek, kek, kek" notes around dawn, and so acted as the saint's alarm clock. (Bonaventura has the bird call regularly at night which no falcon would do.) To use the term once customary in the north of England when a man made the rounds waking the factory workers, he was his "knocker-up." The saint and the bird being on such good terms, it was easy to imagine the sympathy between them to be so great that the falcon divined when Francis was infirm and with appropriate

[55] Sabatier, *op. cit.*, p. 289.

consideration rang his vocal bell "gently." It would be unnecessary to point out that this is poetry were it not that writers still like to suggest that the rapport between man and bird was of a supernatural character. Moreover, the motif of the creaturely "knocker-up" is traditional and reappears in the story of Lady Jacopa de' Settesoli's lamb (p. 112).

The allusion to the falcon's "song" as "bell-like" in the accounts is due, probably, to poetic licence. In the days when falconry was popular, the sharp staccato character of the bird's calling was well known, though rather more in courtly than ecclesiastical circles,[56] but in the Fioretti the story may have been intentionally placed preceding Francis's vision of the angel playing ravishing music on a viol. Birds and angels alike served and solaced him. The experience is described as a foretaste of the awakening to eternal bliss, hinting at an association between the falcon's call, cockcrow, and the resurrection. In a Church Order of the fourth century, Cockcrow is mentioned as the second of the night Hours when prayer is made "in hope of eternal Light in the resurrection of the dead." [57]

The basis of the tale is sound natural history to the extent that the Franciscan retreat on La Verna was situated in a habitat that could have been congenial to falcons—most probably—peregrines—which are sometimes very noisy when a human being is in the neighbourhood of the eyrie. The smaller falcon, the kestrel, is not so

[56] In likening the falcon's call incongruously to the sound of a bell, Bonaventura may have been influenced not only by the suitability of bell notes to awaken a saint but by a subconscious association with the bells attached to a falcon's jesses.

In England during the eleventh century the clergy were forbidden to engage in falconry, but this ruling was not always observed. Thirteenth-century church dignitaries were fond of the sport. Hawks were brought into church, and some canonries carried the right to do so. Cf. Coulton, op. cit. (1906), p. 339. A fourteenth-century Bishop of Ely excommunicated the thieves who stole his hawk which he had left in the cloister of a church while he was attending a service at Bermondsey. Cf. J. H. Gurney, Early Annals of Ornithology (London, 1921), pp. 32, 48, 64. Thus, as in the story of the Jackdaw of Rheims, persons unknown could be placed under a ban which could not be implemented unless they were found out.

[57] In Spain the Christmas midnight Mass is called the "Cockcrow Mass" (p. 138).

clamorous and has a weaker call, but my own experience when sleeping out beneath a nest was that it can be noisy at dawn. Peregrines finding a person near the eyrie in the early morning would be even more clamorous.[58]

The Cock and the Little Black Hen

References to people being awakened by birds, a fact of common experience, may be traced back for millennia. An Egyptian poem of the thirteenth century B.C. refers to a girl hearing a swallow at dawn inviting her to go out into the fields.[59] In Christian symbolism the cock constantly recurs not only as "the bird of dawning" (*Hamlet* I. i. 160) but also as the bird of warning which crowed when Saint Peter betrayed his Master (Matt. xxxvi. 34; Mark xiv. 30, 72; Luke xxii. 60; John xviii. 27). Prudentius (ca. A.D. 348–410) in "A Hymn for Cockcrow" alluded not only to the function of the cock's crowing in alerting the Christian but also to its alleged efficacy in banishing evil spirits. This belief was expanded into the notion that travellers in Libya taking a cock with them were immune from the attacks of lions and basilisks. In antiquity the cock and the lion were both regarded as types of courage. They appear together on ancient gems. The legend of Saint Colman and his Companions describes how the cock's "crowing awakened him at night to Lauds, as a bell might." [60] Similarly, as already mentioned, the falcon by ringing his "vocal bell" "always at night gave warning of the hour when the saint was wont to rise for Divine worship" (2 *Cel.* 127). We may call the motif of a bird or birds that arouse a person the Bird Awakener, a subsection of the more inclusive theme, the Animal Alerter.

The domestic fowl is referred to in a poignant passage in the *Legend of the Three Companions* (63). It describes an experience

---

[58] The factors that regulate the rising and first calling or singing of birds, such as the time of sunrise (or more exactly Civil Twilight, when the sun is 6 degrees below the horizon), cloud cover, the stage of the breeding cycle, and so forth, are well known as they have been the subject of much scientific research. Cf. Armstrong, *op. cit.* (1973), pp. 188–216.

[59] J. A. Wilson in *Eos*, ed. A. T. Hatto (The Hague, 1965), pp. 105–106.

[60] J. Colgan, *Vitae Sanctorum Hiberniae*, I (Louvain, 1645 and Dublin, 1948), 244a; Waddell, *op. cit.*, pp. 145–147.

that convinced the Poverello he must relinquish leadership of the Order as Minister General:

> The Blessed Francis had seen a vision that had availed to lead him to ask the Cardinal, and to commend his Order unto the Roman Church. For he beheld as it were a little hen that was black and had feathered legs with feet like a tame dove, and she had so many chicks that she was not able to gather them under her own wings, but they went about in a circle round the hen, beyond her wings.

Celano (2 Cel. 23) in recording the vision speaks of the chicks as "countless," a reference to the immense success of the Franciscan movement. On waking, the Holy Spirit revealed to Francis that this was a parable applying to himself. He reflected:

> I am that hen, small of stature, and by nature black, that ought to be simple as a dove, and on winged affection of the virtues to fly toward heaven. And unto me the Lord of His mercy hath given and will give many sons, whom I shall not be able in mine own strength to protect. Whence behoveth me to commend them unto Holy Church, the which under the shadow of her wings shall protect and govern them. [Cf. Psalms xxxvi. 7; lvii. 1; lxi. 4; xci. 4]

In view of the very ancient practice of using dreams to explain or predict the actions of important personages, as in the Bible, the possibility that Celano invented the dream to explain Francis's decision to relinquish control of the Order cannot be excluded. It would have carried more conviction if he had mentioned it in his *Vita Prima* in which efforts to placate the ecclesiastical authorities and idealize the saint are less apparent, but here it will be treated as an actual experience narrated by Francis to one of his companions.

The overt significance or manifest content of the dream is clear enough and was readily interpreted by the Little Poor Man himself, but it may have further meaning latent within it. The imagery is that of Christ's lamentation (Matt. xxiii. 37; Luke xiii. 34): "O Jerusalem, Jerusalem, thou that killest the prophets, and stonest them which are sent unto thee, how often would I have gathered thy children together, even as a hen gathereth her chickens under her wings, and ye would not!" At that time the Poverello's soul was torn between a consciousness of innocence and integrity in all that he had aimed to do for the advancement of Christ's Kingdom and qualms because his ideals and methods had not been found acceptable to the authorities of the Church. The dream expresses his "maternal affection" for his flock. Celano later spoke of his "maternal affection" for a small animal, a leveret (p. 190).

The extent to which maternal tenderness pervaded the thoughts of Francis and his first followers is noteworthy. In the short instruction, *De religiosa habitatione in eremo,* the term "mother" is used six times in this sense, and Francis encouraged his companions to address him thus. Celano (2 *Cel.* 137) twice reports Brother Pacifico as referring to him as *carissima mater,* and in his letter to Brother Leo he wrote: *dico tibi, fili mi, et sicut mater.* David Knowles in *The Religious Orders in England* points out that, while obedience in the Dominican Order was that of subject to lawgiver, Francis spoke of a "brother" and his "minister" or guardian. Few details in the records illustrate how widely Saint Francis's conception of the movement he founded differed from the legalistic, hierarchical, and authoritarian outlook characteristic of the Church at this time.

The dream of the Little Black Hen also expresses the saint's feeling of inadequacy and his anxiety that some of the brethren were wandering in what seemed to him aimless circles and away from care and control. Francis, seeking to fashion his own life in the image of Christ's, was too aware of his shortcomings to have consciously identified himself with his Master in this parable; but subconsciously he could have regarded his rejection as in some respects parallel to Christ's, and felt his anguish as a kind of crucifixion. Celano himself may have thought in these terms. A hen's black plumage contrasted with a dove's pink feet—thus we see in a dream-dramatization the conflict within the saint's soul, as well as imagery inspired by the strife in the Order to which the Franciscan annals bear witness. The innocence of the dove was characteristic of the saint in all that he sought to achieve. But whatever else the dream-vision represents it symbolizes Francis's realization that he could no longer care for the beloved, lively, but increasingly independent-minded brood around him. In this respect the parable of the Little Black Hen is relived to some extent by every woman who sees her children go out into the world and every man who, after bearing responsibility, especially if it be for the souls or bodily welfare of others, comes to that age or degree of frailty which forces him to relinquish his task.

The Duck and the Wolf, the Waterfowl, Crane and Pheasant

The Franciscan legend of the Duck and the Wolf is crude and artificial, interesting only as an illustration of how a group of legends may generate jejune offshoots. At Lugnano, on the borders of Lazio, it is said that Francis instructed a duck to rescue a child carried off by a wolf.[61] The concept is too far-fetched for the anecdote to be considered a natural product of the rustic imagination. We may regard it as a fabrication by folk wishing to believe in some special association between the saint and their locality. As with many highly derivative animal fables, the true nature of one of the creatures concerned is disregarded, and the duck is made to act completely out of character. Indeed, the rôles of the duck and the wolf in relationship to one another have been reversed, and we may suspect that the wolf appears because of the fame of the wolf of Gubbio. Francis acts as a magic-monger rather than a saint except that, from the tale-teller's point of view, the end justifies the means. The greater the prodigy —even to the reversing of the forces of nature—the greater the saint. We are in the realm of crude and elemental modes of thought.

While Francis was crossing the lake of Rieti on the way to the hermitage at Greccio, a waterfowl of an unspecified kind was brought to him. The assumption by a recent biographer that the bird was a kingfisher illustrates the gratuitous romanticization of episodes in which the saint was concerned.[62] It was probably a waterhen or duck which had become entangled in a net while feeding. On receiving the bird Francis invited it to fly away, but it crouched in his hands "as in a little nest" while the saint prayed and went into an ecstasy. After a long time and "as though coming back to himself from else-

[61] H. E. Goad, "The Dilemma of St. Francis and the Two Traditions," in *St. Francis of Assisi, 1226–1926: Essays in Commemoration,* ed. W. Seton (London, 1926), p. 160.
[62] Englebert, *op. cit.* (1950), p. 165.

where," he told the waterfowl to depart and gave it his blessing. Thereupon it flew joyously away. This may be the only instance in hagiography of a saint's falling into a mystic trance while holding a bird in his hands (2 *Cel.* 167; *Bon.* viii. 8) though Saint Kevin may have been thought by some to have been in a trance state while the blackbird was nesting.

In telling the story of the pheasant which became so attached to the Poverello that it hastened back on two occasions when taken to its usual haunts, Bonaventura (viii. 10) is more prosaic than Celano (2 *Cel.* 170). The latter describes how Francis rejoiced in such creatures for love of the Creator and said to it: "Praised be our Creator, Brother Pheasant." A vivid detail is his mention of the bird's forcing its way under the tunics of the brethren who were at the door. A later Franciscan, Saint Bernardino of Siena, elaborated the story picturesquely, describing the pheasant as holding up Saint Francis's cloak with its bill "as if he had been a bishop." [63] We are reminded of the birds that, according to Bonaventura (xii. 3), did not move when the Poverello's habit touched them, and of the flock that the saint "touched with the hem of his garment" (*Fioretti* 16). He caressed and talked to the pheasant. A medical man requested to be entrusted with the bird "out of reverence for the saint," but when he took it home it pincd and refused to feed. So the pheasant was brought back to "its father" and began to eat joyfully. Apart from some exaggeration and on the supposition that the bird, a present from a nobleman of Siena, had been hand-reared, the anecdote is plausible enough—though Bonaventura's statement that it was "fresh caught" weakens our confidence. It belongs to a group of tales in which Francis is depicted as loving rather than dominating wild creatures and they are described as reciprocating his affection. "He triumphed in all the works of the Lord's hands and through the sight of their joy was uplifted unto their life-giving cause and origin" (*Bon.* ix. 1).[64]

[63] Origo, *op. cit.*, p. 113.
[64] Irish legends tell of birds being attracted to saints or becoming pets. Ducks came to Saint Brigid to be caressed. Cf. Donatus, *op. cit.*, p. 180; Saint Molua's partridge lived with the Brethren. Cf. Plummer, *op. cit.* II (1910), 218.

One or two other birds mentioned in the Legend may be alluded to briefly. An incidental remark of Giles's (*Fioretti, Friar Giles,* 14), typical of his pawky wit, concerned the importance of avoiding garrulity. He said that it was as great a virtue to keep silence as to know how to speak acceptably, "therefore methinks a man hath need of a neck as long as a crane's so that when he would speak, his words should pass through many joints before they came to his mouth." In the *Hortus Sanitatis,*[65] a woodcut depicts a crane with an overhand knot in its neck. Whether any moral is implied is not clear. The crane was a familiar bird in Italy during the thirteenth and fourteenth centuries as the allusions by Dante indicate (*Purg.* xxvi. 43–44; *Inf.* v. 46–47).

Reference is made to the beauty of the peacock in connexion with the Cross as the sign tau, the last letter of the Hebrew alphabet. Its ancient form was a cross. (Cf. Ezekiel ix. 4. Vulgate.) [66] Brother Pacifico, the sometime troubadour, saw it displayed "with variegated circles" on Francis's forehead (2 *Cel.* 106; *Bon.* iv. 9). The suggestion seems to be of the glorious significance of this emblem. The peacock, taken over from Roman art, has a long history in Christian iconography as a symbol of the resurrection.[67] Francis used the tau cross on documents as equivalent to his signature. It may be seen on "The Benediction of Brother Leo" exhibited in the Sacro Convento at

---

As already noted (p. 53), Saint Cuthbert and the hermit Bartholomew were on friendly terms with the eider ducks of the Farne Islands. According to a Renaissance anecdote, Saint John was reproved by an archer for playing with his pet quail. He replied that as the string of a bow needed loosening from time to time so, for a man, relaxation preceded achievement. Cf. B. Fulgosus, *Factorum dictorumque memorabilium,* IX (Paris, 1578), 8. 8, f. 285v; cit. in E. Topsell, *The Fowles of Heauen,* ed. T. P.·Harrison and F. D. Hoeniger (Austin, Tex., 1972), p. 5.

[65] First dated edition, 1490.

[66] According to Saint Jerome, tau (T) was used in the Samaritan language to represent the Cross.

[67] The peacock was engraved on sarcophagi in the Roman catacombs as a symbol of the Resurrection. St. Augustine referred to its flesh as incorruptible. Its Christian symbolism may have been derived in a devious way from its status as the bird of Juno, representing the apotheosis of an empress, but the bird had religious importance in Persia. It is prominent in Byzantine art, and its symbolism became extended to include heavenly glory, the ever-vigilant church, and the grace of the Eucharist.

Assisi, still retaining the creases it acquired while carried in the friar's pouch. The *Fioretti* (*2nd consid. of stigmata*) gives a moving description of how carefully it was treasured by Leo, and mentions that by means of it the friars wrought miracles.

An anecdote about a greedy young robin that drove its companions away from the food provided by Francis is discussed later (p. 104), and references to the eagle are commented upon in connexion with its associate in mythology, the serpent (pp. 175–179).

The Cuckoo

According to accounts quoted by Sabatier, the saint made a playful reference to the cuckoo during his last days.[68] He had been severely ill, and after death had seemed imminent, he rallied—to the surprise of all around him. When a physician from Arezzo, a friend of his, visited him, Francis asked how long he might expect to live. The reply was: "Father, this will all pass away, if it pleases God." Smiling, Francis replied: "I am not a cuckoo to be afraid of death. By the grace of the Holy Spirit I am so closely united to God that I am content whether I live or die." Then the physician said: "In that case, Father, from the medical point of view your ailment is incurable, and I do not think you can last longer than the beginning of autumn." The saint stretched out his hands and said with great joy of mind and body, "Welcome, Sister Death!" (*Spec. Perf.* 122).

The phrase about the cuckoo was a popular saying. It was apparently connected with, or derived from, a story that was probably well known in the thirteenth century as more than one version has survived.[69] The daughter of a woman who was sick unto death wished

[68] In his *Life of St. Francis* (p. 330), Sabatier quotes the phrase as *Non sum cuculus*, but in English versions of the *Speculum Perfectionis* (122) the word in question is translated "faint-heart." In Sabatier's *Le Speculum Perfectionis ou mémoires de Frère Léon* (British Society of Franciscan Studies, XIII, 1928) it is cited variously as *corculus*, *torculus* or *tortulus*. Barthlomew of Pisa uses *corculus*. The translation "cuckoo" is accepted here because the account appears to have been influenced by the anecdotes concerning the cuckoo current in the thirteenth century. Moreover, this reading is in accordance with the cheerful, whimsical spirit of the saint.

[69] T. Wright, ed., *A Selection of Latin Stories from Manuscripts of the Thirteenth and Fourteenth Centuries* (London, 1842) pp. 42, 74. Caesarius

to fetch the priest, but the woman protested: "What's the use; I shall be better to-morrow or the day after." She grew worse, so her daughter brought in the neighbours to add their warnings, but she said: "I shall not die for twelve years. I have heard a cuckoo which told me so." At length, when she was near death and became dumb, her daughter decided she must call the priest. When he arrived he asked the mother if she wished to make her confession, but she only said, "Cuckoo." The priest then offered her the Sacrament, but still she said, "Cuckoo." He decided that nothing could be done and went home. Shortly afterward she died.

Saint Francis implied that he was not like the cuckoo-woman, deceiving himself or to be deceived by others, as to the seriousness of his illness.

The basis of the anecdote is the ancient and widespread playful belief or half-belief still current in some areas that, by counting the number of times the cuckoo calls when you first hear it, you may divine the future. A man or woman may thus learn how long he or she has to live or a girl how long it will be before she will get married. In Yorkshire children used to sing around a cherry tree:

Cuckoo, cherry tree
Come down and tell me
How many years afore I dee.

Similar rhymes have been current in most European countries. For example, in Germany (Lauenburg) the rhyme was:

Kukuk,	Cuckoo,
Spekbuk,	Fat-paunch,
Ik bir dy:	I pray thee:
Seg my doch,	Tell me now,
Wo vael Joer	How many years
Läw 'ik noch.	I yet shall live.[70]

Heisterbacensis (V. xvii) mentions a priest who, hearing a cuckoo call twenty-two times, decided to give himself to the pleasures of the world for twenty and spend the last two in penitence. But he was only vouchsafed two years.

[70] C. Swainson, *Provincial Names and Folklore of British Birds* (London, 1885), pp. 115–116.

In France (Franche Comté):

> *Cuccou,*
> *Bolotou,*
> *Regaide sur ton grand livre,*
> *Comben i a d'enées è vivre.*

Bolatou means a boy who robs nests and eats the eggs. A French version is as old as the Italian saying, for the belief is mentioned in one of the poems of the thirteenth-century "Roman du Renart." [71] Naturally and properly, country girls who addressed similar rhymed queries to the cuckoo concerning when they would be wedded regarded unduly reiterative cuckoos as crazy.

The Beloved Lark

The lark was Francis's favourite bird because he regarded it as symbolizing his ideals and exemplifying virtues the friars should emulate. In addition to the characteristics already commented upon which have caused birds from immemorial times to be endowed imaginatively with spiritual qualities, larks attract attention by their skyward song-flight so that Shakespeare thought of the skylark singing "at Heaven's gate" (*Cymbeline* II. iii. 21), and Shelley in "To a Skylark" imagined its song coming "from Heaven, or near it." Similar ideas were dwelt on by Christian writers very much earlier. As long ago as the third century, Tertullian wrote in *De oratione*: "Nay, the birds rising out of the nest upraise themselves and, instead of hands, extend the cross of their wings, and say somewhat to seem like prayer." He may have had larks in mind, as, living in North Africa, he must have seen and heard several species. The author of the *Fioretti* (16) also seems to have pictured larks when he wrote that, after Francis had given his avian congregation leave to depart, "all those birds soared up into the air in one flock with wondrous songs and then divided themselves into the form of the cross St. Francis had made over them."

In Christian circles an association arose between *alauda*, the Latin name, still in use as the generic scientific name for the skylark

[71] E. Rolland, *Faune Populaire de la France* II (Paris, 1879), 93.

(*Alauda arvensis*), and man's duty to give glory, laud, and honour to God. Isidore of Seville, writing in the seventh century, and Neckam in the twelfth derived *alauda* from *laus*, "praise," noting that the lark rises from the earth to greet the sun, but probably this etymology is incorrect, though it suits their moralizing aims.[72] Pliny in his *Natural History* (xi. 44 [37]) considered *alauda* a Celtic word, but he, too, was probably mistaken.[73] Goropius mentions the belief that the lark existed before the earth. It sings seven times a day high in the air, praising God, and thus prayer was the first thing that existed in the world. There is a curious twist to lark legends in France where it is said that the bird flies aloft uttering praise to God but when she has attained the height to which she aspires she becomes proud and begins to curse as she descends.[74]

Francis explained to his companions why he had a special regard for the lark (*Spec. Perf.* 113; *Leg. Ant.* 110). He said:

> Sister lark hath a cowl like a Religious; and she is a humble bird, because she likes to go along the road to forage and will even pick up food out of ordure and eat it. Flying she praises God most sweetly, like a good Religious, contemning earthly things, whose conversation is always in the heavens, always intent on praising God. Her garments—that is her plumage—resemble the earth, and so she sets an example to the Religious not to wear dainty and gaily coloured clothes, but cheap and dull as earth is meaner than the other elements.

The description has interest as indicating not only the contemporary cast of mind, active in reading symbolism into nature, but especially as an instance of direct observation of a bird—exceptional in that age

---

[72] In similar vein we are told that the dove's "moan" is an intimation that we should moan in this vale of tears until we attain the place of rejoicing. Cf. Migne, *Patrologia Latinae*, vol. LXXXII, bk. xii, chap. 7, pp. 459–470; A. Neckam, *De naturis rerum*, ed. T. Wright, II. lvi; *De laudibus divinae sapientiae* (London, 1863), p. 106.

[73] D'Arcy W. Thompson, *A Glossary of Greek Birds* (Oxford, 1936), pp. 164–168.

[74] A. de Gubernatis, *Zoological Mythology* II (London, 1872), 274; Swainson, *op. cit.*, p. 94. One of the poems of Charles d'Orléans represents the descending lark as saying farewell to God. Cf. Armstrong, *op. cit.* (1969), p. 348.

and an adumbration of the time when dissatisfaction would arise with reliance on merely traditional descriptions of the appearance and behaviour of animals.[75] We are told that the saint loved all creatures but especially those that, for him, were symbolic of God's being or attributes and of the ideals of the Franciscan Order, that is, could be regarded as sacramental, for he always looked through nature up to nature's God (*Bon.* viii. 6). In this he was a typical nature mystic. It has been said: "The true mysticism is the belief that everything, in being what it is, is symbolic of something more." [76]

The bird beloved more than all others by Francis was not the skylark but a species of lark common on the Continent which has never been found breeding in Great Britain—the crested, hooded, or "cowled" lark (*Galerida cristata*) *Lodola capuletta*, as it was called in the vernacular—the bird to which the description quoted refers. He said: "If I could speak to the Emperor, I would implore and persuade him, for the love of God (and my sake) to enact a law forbidding anyone to kill our sisters the larks, or do them any harm." He would ask for an ordinance that on Christmas Day those in authority should insist that people spread grain for the larks and other birds (*Spec. Perf.* 114; 2 *Cel.* 200). But still larks are caught, killed, or caged in Italy, although Italians honour Saint Francis as one of the two patron saints of their country, the other being Saint Catherine of Siena.

We have noted that in his wooded mountain retreat on La Verna where a crowing cock would have been out of place, a falcon aroused Francis in time to say the Office; but Saint Brigid, dwelling amid the extensive flower-strewn meadows and pastures of Ireland, was awakened each morning to another day of praise, prayer, and service

---

[75] As an illustration, taken almost at random, of what passed for natural history at this time, Jacques de Vitry's description of the capercaillie may be mentioned. He stated that it first lives on larks and partridges, then, in its second year, on sparrows and other small birds. Then it becomes so lazy that it dies of hunger. Cf. C. G. Coulton, *Life in the Middle Ages* II (Cambridge, 1929), 38. Apart from his suggestion that the bird eats some invertebrates, the description is nonsense. De Vitry's *Exempla* (ed. T. F. Crane, Folk-lore Soc., 1890) also includes a number of traditional fables.

[76] R. L. Nettleship, *Philosophical Remains* (London, 1901), p. 32.

by the skylark's song. Still, in Ireland, if a lark is heard singing on her day, February 1, it is regarded as forecasting fair weather. In Orkney and Shetland the lark is "Our Lady's Hen" and the nest is seldom molested. In Germany it is regarded as under the protection of the Blessed Virgin.[77] Great bird lover as St. Kevin was reputed to be, his compassion for birds was not allowed to exceed his consideration for his human helpers. When he found that the builders of his monastery at Glendalough, unlike some workmen today, were endangering their health by working too hard and taking too literally the injunction to "rise with the lark and lie down with the lamb," he forbade the larks to sing there.[78] The skylark's early song-flight has long been proverbial.[79] The legend may have arisen because the wooded surroundings of Glendalough were not a congenial habitat for skylarks. Enthusiastic as was the Irish concern for animals, it never became out of proportion as it did in some areas of India where the welfare of man has been subordinated to that of animals, monkeys and cows being permitted to roam in the streets and even commit depredations.

Several species of lark occur in Italy the wood lark, calandra, and short-toed, besides the skylark and crested lark—but we should not interpret "lark" narrowly. The allusion to the birds appearing in a great flock above where the saint lay dying is more appropriate to the skylark than the crested lark, which does not sing spiralling skyward, has an inferior, less sustained song, and assembles in smaller flocks. But although country folk could distinguish their cowled lark from others—for the crest is more conspicuous than the skylark's—we can assume that larks were spoken of in general terms and not as the taxonomist assesses them.

The larks that came to salute the dying saint were no ordinary birds. Birds and angels were sometimes confounded in legends, as we

---

[77] G. F. Black and N. W. Thomas, *County Folk-lore* III, *Orkney and Shetland* (London, 1903), p. 14; Donatus, *op. cit.*, p. 167; Swainson, *op. cit.*, p. 94.

[78] Giraldus Cambrensis, *Topographia Hiberniae*, trans. T. Wright (London, 1863), p. 89.

[79] Such sayings are soundly based. The skylark in northern England during mid-April is heard about 4:00 A.M. (sun time), earlier than any other bird. Cf. Armstrong, *op. cit.* (1973), p. 193.

have noted (p. 66). In some instances when they are mentioned as appearing on occasions such as the birth or death of saints, it is assumed that they should be understood to be in some sense spiritual beings expressing God's favour. The mind subconsciously makes this kind of association and becomes further conditioned to do so through symbolic language. Moreover, in Christian iconography and the art of some other cultures, pictorial or sculptural representations of supernatural beings show them with bird characteristics. At La Verna Francis received "many consolations from God, not only visits of angels, but likewise of wild birds" (*Fioretti, 2nd consid. of stigmata*). The underlying presupposition is that there is an affinity among angels, birds, and men of outstanding sanctity. From the Gospel account of the Spirit of God descending as a dove (Matt. iii. 16; Mark i. 10; Luke iii. 22; John i. 32) onward, such assimilations have been traditional in Christian literature and art. Dante called angels birds in the *Purgatorio* (ii. 38) but not in the *Paradiso*, wherein, however, the devil is once alluded to as a bird (xxix. 118). The association between angels, devils, and birds occurs in Revelation xviii. 1–2. In the *Inferno* (xxii. 96; xxxiv. 47), devils are called birds. Some early Italian frescoes show devils as grotesque and horrible beaked creatures, a tradition followed later by Bosch and other artists, such as Max Ernst, to the present day. This tradition of beings imagined as half bird and half human may be traced to the beginnings of pictorial art in the Palaeolithic. The gods of ancient civilizations and sometimes the Christian evangelist Saint John were represented as birdheaded.[80] Indeed there is a reference in the *Fioretti* (1) to Saint John as "the Eagle."

In the older Irish literature, both secular and religious, souls and other spiritual beings appear as birds: blessed saints and angels as doves or swans, lost souls as ravens. In Paradise birds appear among the angels.[81]

When Saint Fechan was born, angelic birds filled the glen from heaven to earth. There is mention of a bird appearing as the symbol

---

[80] Armstrong, *Encyclopaedia of Man, Myth and Magic* I (London, 1970), 259–263; Armstrong, *The Folklore of Birds* (New York, 1970), p. 21.

[81] Plummer, *op. cit.* I (1910), cxlvii.

of a saint at his birth, and angels appeared on the house where Saint Wilfrid was staying. When angels in the form of swans flew over the birthplace of Saint Colum da Tyre (Columba of Terryglass), the sweet music of their voices and wings lulled all those hearing them to sleep. Similarly, when a bird "more beautiful than all the birds of the world" sang three strains to Saint Mochaoi, abbot of Nendrum in Strangford Lough, it seemed that he listened to the heavenly music for an hour; but the bird was an angel and each of the three melodies represented the passing of fifty years. When he returned to the monastery, no one knew him and he found an oratory erected to his memory. This Monk and Bird motif, which is associated with two other Irish saints, reached the Continent from Ireland in the twelfth century and may well have influenced the Saint Francis Legend.[82]

Sir James Barrie, in his Rectorial address on "Courage" to St. Andrew's University in 1922, mentioned that Nansen had told him this, as he thought, Norwegian folktale. So, all over the world, stories from afar may become acclimatized and regarded as indigenous.

At Saint Malo's ordination, a white dove settled on his right shoulder; and while Saint Malachy was saying Mass, a similar bird settled on the cross above the altar.[83] No doubt these, as in so many paintings, represented the Holy Spirit rather than angels; but as the reader will realize, it is sometimes difficult to differentiate between appearances in avian form. The comment has been made concerning accounts of bird-spirit manifestations: "These are so familiar that we may miss what may be a special Irish influence giving an individual

[82] E. A. Armstrong, Birds of the Grey Wind (London, 1946), pp. 60–61; Donatus, op. cit., pp. 162–174; Klingender, op. cit., pp. 13–23; H. J. Lawlor, The Monastery of St. Mochaoi of Nendrum (Belfast, 1925).
The magical passage of time is a common theme in folktales. The concept underlying the account of the friar's visionary state which lasted from matins to prime but seemed many years (Fioretti 26) is rather different. Saint Catherine of Siena and other saints sustained trance states during which they were oblivious to the passage of time.

[83] Donatus, op. cit., p. 227. Although Saint Thomas Aquinas denied souls to birds this did not prevent their being regarded as representing the soul and the Holy Spirit.

turn or impress to the Christian tradition in some of its developments." [84]

The associations of birds with death go back to prehistoric times.
The belief took various forms in Egyptian thought. When Saint
Polycarp was martyred in A.D. 156, there were those who testified that
a dove issued from his body.[85] At the death of Saint Benedict's twin
sister Saint Scholastica, he saw her soul take wing as a white dove.
So well was this legend known in the fourteenth century that it
could be assumed a white dove in a painting would be interpreted as
representing this saint.[86] Angels in bird form are spoken of as as-
sembling around the body of a Christian saint or accompanying his
soul to heaven. Angelic guides, messengers, or portents in the guise of
birds are frequently mentioned in saints' Lives.[87] The same medieval
mental processes that enabled human and divine beings to be assimilated and mental, moral, and spiritual qualities to be attributed
to animals permitted souls to be thought of as birds. The symbol
could be envisaged as the reality.

The springs of such mental processes lie deep, and evidence of their
importance can be traced into the remote past. Belief in the bird-
soul or in a bird or birds accompanying the soul of the departed is
still found among shamanistic cultures in North America and
northern Asia, and traces of this conception still survive among the
Slavs, in the Faeroe Islands, and even among the seafaring folk of
the British Isles.[88]

The account of the death of St. Francis contained in the *Mirror
of Perfection* (113) records:

---

[84] Donatus, *op. cit.*, p. 226.

[85] K. Lake, *The Apostolic Fathers* II (London, 1912–13), 312–345.

[86] H. Friedmann, "The Iconography of an Altarpiece by Botticini," *Bull.
Metrop. Mus. Art* (Summer 1969), pp. 1–16. Saint Ulton dreamed of his
brother's soul flying away in the form of a dove. In the Franciscan Legend we
are told of the soul's being seen flying away, but in the two contexts its appearance is not described (*Fioretti* 25, 46).

[87] E. P. Evans, *Animal Symbolism in Ecclesiastical Architecture* (New York,
1896); Loomis, *op. cit.*, pp. 67, 180.

[88] Armstrong, *op. cit.* (New York, 1970), pp. 211–224.

It pleased the Lord that these most holy little birds should show some sign of affection towards him in the hour of his death. For late on the Sabbath day, after Vespers, before the night in which he passed away to the Lord, a great multitude of that kind of bird called larks came on the roof of the house where he was lying; and flying about, made a wheel like a circle round the roof, and sweetly singing, seemed likewise to praise the Lord.[89]

Bonaventura (xiv. 6) enlists the aid of imagination and symbolism in his version which lays stress on the birds' having a premonition of the saint's death. The differences between his description and that of the *Speculum* illustrate the subtleties of his style:

At the hour of the passing of the holy man, the larks—birds that love the light, and dread the shades of twilight—flocked in great numbers unto the roof of the house, albeit the shades of night were then falling, and, wheeling round it for a long while with songs even gladder than their wont, offered their witness, alike gracious and manifest, unto the glory of the Saint, who had been wont to call them unto the divine praises.[90]

Comparison of the two accounts serves to illustrate what is sometimes forgotten or neglected by historians, though it hardly needs emphasis in these pages, that Bonaventura's writing is imaginative

---

[89] Professor R. Vaughan, quoted in R. B. Brooke, *Scripta Leonis, Rufini et Angeli, sociorum S. Francisci* (Oxford, 1970), suggests that these valedictory birds may have been calandra larks (*Melanocorypha c. calandra*). This species performs a prolonged circular, solitary song-flight high in the sky. It would be exceptional for its song to be heard on 4 October (1226) when, according to the *Fioretti* Saint Francis died. The term *laude* indicates larks in general. The account is poetic and symbolic, not realistic. It may be compared with the description of how Francis received confirmation that he should stay at La Verna. As he was praying at dawn individual birds of various species arrived, sang and departed (*op. cit.*, p. 255). Although different species begin to sing at different light intensities this description also is unrealistic. Cf. Armstrong, *A Study of Bird Song* (New York, 1973), pp. 188–209. In both instances the narrator has caused the birds to act and sing in an abnormal way to suggest divine concern.

[90] The birds and beasts of the forest were similarly clairvoyant concerning Cellach's imminent death. Cf. Donatus, *op. cit.*, pp. 181–182. Clairvoyant birds could also carry a sinister message. According to Caesarius Heisterbacensis (*Dial. Mir.* I. xv), a flock of crows appeared above the house where a wicked knight lay dying.

when it diverges from his sources. We have to view some of his reports with critical minds or even with scepticism, and, as we have seen, he may lead astray modern readers who look for pure history and candid biography. We are in debt to him, not for accurate biography, but for giving us a poetic portrait of a poetic saint. This is true also of the other early biographers, as well as of many later. Sabatier appropriately referred to the dying saint as "the lark." [91] Bonaventura's moving description is appropriate to the passing of Christ's faithful disciple of whom it was said: *Mortem cantando suscepit* (2 *Cel.* 214).

The concept of a bird choir praising God rather than mourning at a saint's deathbed appears to be a Franciscan inspiration, but thoughts of angels ready to accompany the soul would naturally arise in the minds of the faithful—as, indeed, was the intention of the biographers. We have seen that the birds of the early Irish Voyages (*immrama*) became angels in *St. Brendan's Voyage*; and in other Irish stories there is ambiguity, no doubt intentional, for the ill-defined is most numinous, and that which activates the imagination stimulates the visionary sense which ministers to religious inspiration. Mystics and poets sometimes stir the waters of the well of the unconscious more deeply than they realize, and archetypal imagery with an emotional content arouses strange and significant harmonics.[92] In Christian literature birds and angels are often mentioned in close association, as in Dante's *Vita Nuova* where the poet describes the death of Beatrice:

> And birds dropped in mid-flight out of the sky;
>   And earth shook suddenly;
> And I was 'ware of one, hoarse and tired out,
> Who asked of me: "Hast thou not heard it said?
> Thy Lady, she that was so fair, is dead."

> Then lifting up my eyes as the tears came
>   I saw the Angels, like a rain of manna,
>   In a long flight, flying back heavenward;
> Having a little cloud in front of them,
> After the which they went and said "Hosanna" . . . .

[91] Sabatier, *op. cit.*, p. 317.   [92] Armstrong, *op. cit.* (1963*b*).

In poetry Dante could thus describe angels escorting the soul of Beatrice to Heaven; but writing the Life of a saint, Francis's biographers left it to their readers to interpret the birds as angels.

Thus the larks circling around where Saint Francis lay dying are symbolic of, or surrogates for, the angels that accompany the souls of the righteous, particularly appropriate to represent also the soberly clad, humble, singing saint, God's troubadour. The spirit of heaviness gives way to the garment of praise (Isaiah lxi. 3). Christian joy triumphs over sorrow, thankfulness and hope take the place of lamentation, death is swallowed up in victory. Francis, dying, had sung with the Brethren his Canticle of the Sun, praising and blessing God, for all Creation. Fittingly, as represented by the birds, Creation is depicted as joining in. The choir of larks sing the opening of heaven's gates, and beyond their torrent of music we hear the fanfare of distant trumpets. Before Saint Francis birds and beasts had mourned the death of saints, now they hymn the victory of the humblest of them.

The belief that other living things sorrow with suffering humanity is very ancient. The wild creatures gathered around grieving when the Buddha was dying and, in *The Iliad*, Achilles' horses wept tears for their dead master. At the Crucifixion, according to the Irish *Saltair na Rann*, "every creature wailed." [93] Most touching was the grief of the white horse on Iona, the animal that had plied with the milk skins between the byre and the monastery. Saint Columcille, weary with age, was sitting near the granary when

> he, coming up to the saint, wonderful to tell, lays his head against his breast—inspired, as I believe (so says Adamnan) by God, by whose dispensation every animal has sense to perceive things according as its Creator Himself has ordained—knowing that his master was soon to leave him, and that he would see him no more, began to whinny and shed copious tears into the lap of the saint as though

[93] *Saltair na Rann*, ed. W. Stokes (Oxford, 1883), p. v. In Friar Peter's vision (*Fioretti* 44), Saint John is heard saying: "Know thou that the Mother of Christ and I suffered above all other creatures at the Passion of Christ." The darkness that covered the earth at the time of the Crucifixion (Mark xv. 33) may have helped to suggest the mourning of all Creation.

he had been a man, and weeping and foaming at the mouth. And the attendant seeing this, began to drive away the weeping mourner, but the saint forbade him, saying, "Let him alone, let him alone, for he loves me. . . ." and so saying, he blessed his servant the horse as it sadly turned to go away from him.

It is scarcely possible that Bishop Arculf, shipwrecked on the wild shores of Scotland, who gave Adamnan details of the Holy Land, could have told him of the grief-stricken Xanthus, but Ulstermen on Iona are likely to have remembered how the Gray of Macha, realizing the doom overshadowing Cú Chúlainn, wept tears of blood upon him.[94]

The birds of Irish story also mourn their saintly heroes. A little bird grieved at the death of the gentle Saint Molua, of whom it was said he "never killed a bird or any other living thing" and "blithe will he be after arriving in heaven . . . the holy champion Molua MacOcha." Mael-an-faid saw a small bird wailing and lamenting. He reflected, "O my God, what has happened yonder! I will not partake of food till it is revealed to me." An angel appeared and said, "That is well, O cleric, let this grieve thee no longer. Molua MacOcha has died, and therefore all living creatures bewail him, for never has he killed any animal, little or big; so not more do men bewail him than the other animals, and the little bird thou beholdest." [95]

Man's sense of empathy with nature finds expression in such stories embodying the belief that nature reciprocates his feelings and that the Creator cares for his Creation; over Bethlehem a star, over Calvary, darkness. Because we are lonely and even human companionship has its limitations, we reach out not only to God but to our material environment, especially that which is endowed with life, for sympathy; and nature, our omnipresent companion, seldom fails those who are humble enough and have given her their love.

[94] Adamnan, *Vita* III. xxxiii; M. O'Donnell, *Betha Colaim Chille: Life of Columcille compiled in* 1592, ed. A. O'Kelleher and G. Schoepperle (*Illinois Univ. Bull.*, 1918); T. P. Cross and C. H. Slover, *Ancient Irish Tales* (London, n.d.), p. 334.

[95] *Calendar of Oengus*, trans. Whitley Stokes, *Trans Royal Irish Acad.*, MS, Ser. I (Dublin, 1880), pp. 57, 174, 183; Donatus, *op. cit.*, p. 162.

Coleridge in a later age experienced this sense of reciprocated love for nature and expressed it in imagery with religious nuances: "Even when all men have seemed to desert us, and the friend of our heart has passed on, with one glance from his 'cold, disliking eye'—yet even then the blue heaven spreads out and bends over us, and the little tree still shelters us under its plumage as a second cope, a domestic firmament, and the low-creeping gale will sigh in the heath-plant and soothe us by the sound of sympathy till the lulled grief lose itself in fixed gaze on the purple heath-blossom, till the present beauty becomes a vision of ecstasy." [96]

Unless the heart is cold or alienated, even the ragged rocks do not reply merely with a barren echo to those who seek a path through them. They are found to be more than granite or sandstone, and the birds that nest there, the plants that cling to their clefts are seen to be, not only fascinating objects for the ornithologist, botanist, or artist but, as Saint Francis perceived, immanent with the life of God. Communion with nature, which may sometimes rise to ecstatic experience, sustains us because, as a pagan poet proclaimed and a Christian prophet endorsed, "In Him we live and move and have our being" (Acts xvii. 28).

[96] S. T. Coleridge, *Animae Poetae*, ed. E. H. Coleridge (London, 1895), pp. 246–247. It is tempting to believe that Coleridge's imagery might have been influenced by a reminiscence of Saint Francis, to whom nature meant so much, sheltering beneath the bishop's cope on repudiating his father.

IV

Saint Francis and the Animals
of Household and Farm

Four-footed beasts, being without the endowments of flight and song
—which, as we have seen, were responsible for spiritual qualities
being attributed to birds—have less romantic associations in the
Franciscan Legend. A few, mentioned in the New Testament, are
introduced because of their symbolic connexion with Christian
virtues and effectiveness as illustrations of the power manifested by
saints; others represent unpleasant qualities to be avoided or condemned. As we might expect, these incidental anecdotes and references throw light on aspects of the Franciscan way of life and social
conditions of the time because the treatment of animals is important
in assessing the values of any culture. No discussion of Jain culture
would be complete without mention of the regard for animal life
which is so integral an element in it. Agricultural pursuits have thus
been inhibited and commercial interests stimulated, with the result
that sometimes tension has arisen between the adherents of this
faith and their neighbours. Nor can the mentality of the citizens of
imperial Rome be evaluated fairly by those who take no account
of their pleasure in witnessing pain and death being inflicted on men
and animals. In contrast, if a crowd of spectators at a football match
in Britain, however excited, were to see a man kicking a dog instead
of a ball they would regard it as an outrage.

The Dog

In order to avoid what might seem the ostentation involved in being
surrounded by an entourage of companions, Francis decided to leave
to the choice of individual friars whether or not they would accompany him from place to place. He commented, no doubt with a

smile: "I have seen before now a blind man with only a little dog to show him the way" (2 Cel. 144; Spec. Perf. 11)—a poignant comment in view of his own failing sight. Writing somewhat later William Langland (ca. 1331–ca. 1400) in Piers Plowman described a drunken character staggering to the door "like a blind singer's dog." Thus at this period the use of guide dogs by the blind was apparently not uncommon.[1] The degree of rapport thus established must have been unusual, for during the Middle Ages the dog was not looked upon as "man's best friend" although illuminated manuscripts depict pet dogs being fondled. The faithfulness of dogs to their owners was appreciated to the extent that they were represented in paintings and sculpture symbolizing fidelity, especially matrimonial, as in Van Eyck's "Arnolfini Marriage." The name "Fido" is a reminder of canine fidelity; but apart from some refined circles, dogs seem to have been held in low esteem throughout most of the medieval period. If we may judge by Shakespeare's allusions, they were commonly disliked at least as late as the seventeenth century. In Europe during much of the Middle Ages, the situation was rather like that which prevailed in the towns of the Near and Middle East until recently where dogs were tolerated as scavengers rather than valued for their companionship. The dogs that licked Lazarus's sores (Luke xvi. 21) were not friendly beasts.[2] It is presumably merely coincidence that the only reference in Scripture to the dog as a companionable animal is in a story about a blind man (Tobit vi. 1). Fear of rabies may have contributed to the dislike of dogs. In the Fioretti (4th consid. of stigmata), a woman "possessed by a devil" is said to have disturbed the whole countryside by barking like a dog. Perhaps, as in

[1] The first systematic effort to train dogs as guides for the blind was made during the eighteenth century at a hospital in Paris.

[2] E. A. Armstrong, Shakespeare's Imagination (Lincoln, Nebr., 1963b), pp. 168–171; Armstrong, The Gospel Parables (London, 1967), pp. 109, 212. For comments on faithful dogs mentioned in medieval tales and portrayed on sepulchral monuments cf. Gesta Romanorum, trans. C. Swan (London, 1905), pp. xlii–xliii. In one of these tales a falcon awakens a dog—as a similar bird awakened Saint Francis—so enabling it to kill a snake attacking a child. The child's father kills the dog, suspecting it of the attack, and on discovering his mistake goes on a penitential pilgrimage to the Holy Land. This motif has oriental antecedents.

Ireland up to the present time, there was a belief that a person bitten by a rabid dog barked like one. It is in keeping with what we are told elsewhere of Saint Francis's relationships with animals that his one recorded allusion to the dog refers to a situation of mutual rapport similar to that illustrated in the stories of his contacts with birds.

Salimbene's references to dogs show that, like many of his contemporaries, he thought of them as savage and disgusting. He quotes Proverbs (xxvi. 11), "as a dog that returneth to its vomit, so is a fool that repeateth his folly" (cf. Bon. xi. 5), and to illustrate how some individuals bring trouble upon themselves by provoking others, describes how a big dog, irritated by a smaller one, seizes it by the throat and drowns it in the river Po. Of the antipathies between Italian cities he wrote: "As there is a natural loathing between men and serpents, dogs and wolves, horses and gryphons, so there is between the Pisans and Genoese, Pisans and men of Lucca, Pisans and Florentines." The atrocities perpetrated during the conflicts between these cities bear witness to the truth of this statement except that there is little or no evidence that human animosities based on cultural differences are comparable with the innate attack reactions of some animals.[3] His attitude toward animals illustrates how little this Franciscan, whose life overlapped that of the Founder by five years, understood the saint's love of nature. He criticizes those of his own Order who, although "of excellent learning and great sanctity," had some "foul blemish." Their reprehensible fault was that "they love to play with a cat or a whelp or some small fowl but not as the Blessed Francis was wont to play with a pheasant and cicada, rejoicing the while in the Lord." [4] Salimbene was by no means alone in condemning the friar who might fondle a kitten or play with a puppy for, as we have seen, his attitude received the approval of the Order. We must find what consolation we can in recognizing that, in an age when men treated each other so savagely, at least the tradition of compassion for animals, if not the practice, should have survived.

[3] C. G. Coulton, From St. Francis to Dante (London, 1906) pp. 1, 28, 218, 237. Cf. H. A. Hyett, Florence: her History and Art (London, 1903), p. 210.
[4] Coulton, op. cit., p. 86.

The Cat

At this period cats were frequently kept because they were so useful in controlling mice. Rats were not then the serious pests they became later (p. 220). It was typical of the observant Salimbene to notice and record that, where some villages had been burnt down during the wars, twenty-seven fugitive cats had been snared.[5]

Celano (2 *Cel.* 18) mentions an incident in which a domestic cat was involved. While the saint and two of the brethren were enjoying a meal, two robins, cock and hen, came to the table to pick up crumbs.[6] He was delighted at the friendliness of "Brother Redbreast" and his mate and encouraged the birds to come each day, obtaining food specially for them. In due course the fledged brood accompanied their parents to the friars' board. When the cock and hen no longer appeared, the friars assumed this to imply that they had transferred the care of their brood to them. The birds became so tame that they would come to hand and went about the place "not as guests but as if they were at home"—like the robin with which Saint Kentigern's teacher had been so friendly. This confiding behaviour gave Francis and his companions much pleasure but they were sorry to observe the truculence shown by one of the youngsters. Not only did he gorge to repletion but he then kept the others away from the food—due, it might be supposed, to an assertion of dominance rather than a precocious development of the territorial instinct, though it is rather difficult to reconcile this behaviour with what we know of robins. "See what the greedy bird is doing" said the saint, "he grudges food to his brothers. He will come to a bad end." Sure enough he was found drowned in a basin of drinking water. Celano adds: "Nor was any cat or other beast found who durst touch the creature cursed by the saint." The interest of the story lies in the happy relationship

[5] *Ibid.* p. 56.
[6] A. Jameson, in *Legends of the Monastic Orders as Represented in the Fine Arts* (London, 1852), p. 263, refers to these birds as larks. Apart from this being a mistranslation of the Latin, it is inconceivable that larks would have acted as described. The error would not be worth mentioning but that it is representative of the misconceptions from which Franciscan natural history has not yet escaped.

between the friars and the robins, but Celano takes it seriously and inflates what seems to have been a playful remark into a prediction. A pleasant rustic episode is thus presented as of moral significance and a manifestation of supernatural power—but not of beneficent power as in the legend of Saint Kentigern who restored the dead robin to life. For good measure Celano introduces what is little short of a threat: "Horrible indeed is greed in men when it is thus punished in birds! Moreover, the sentence of the Saints should be feared, when punishment follows so soon upon it." He has led us from the countryside to the Hall of Judgement. But the tale is typical of the medieval tendency to discover esoteric significance in the behaviour of birds and beasts. Piety and superstition alike were nourished by such thinking.[7]

Celano noted that no cat would eat the carcass. Cats find robins unpalatable and if they eat one may disgorge it. Birds (and insects) with bright coloration tend to be distasteful, but it would be a mistake to regard the observation as evidence that Celano was in any sense a naturalist for a cat would be unlikely to eat a bird found drowned. Moreover, so young a robin would not yet have acquired the red breast, the features by which predators probably identify the adult as unpalatable.[8] No doubt the episode is founded on fact, but it has been dramatized. It gives an intimate glimpse of Francis and his friends eating out of doors and sharing their meal with the birds.

Robins were probably more plentiful in thirteenth-century Italy than they are today after centuries during which small birds have been regarded as gastronomic delicacies or suitable occupants of cages to solace city dwellers. To a visitor from Britain, Italy seems a birdless land. The very poor may be pardoned for killing small birds for

[7] During the Middle Ages the cat sometimes symbolized heresy. It was a familiar companion of witches, and according to folk belief, people could be transformed into cats. No such associations are involved here. The sinister qualities attached to the animal over a wide area appear to be more the result of inferences based on its nocturnal activities than the diffusion of beliefs. The Ainu connect it with witchcraft and demons. Cf. J. Batchelor, *The Ainu and Their Folklore* (London, 1901), pp. 294, 507.

[8] D. Lack, *The Life of the Robin* (London, 1943), pp. 124–125; *Robin Redbreast* (Oxford, 1953).

the pot and slum dwellers for trying to bring nature into their drab homes in the form of a caged bird, but Saint Francis, the lover of wild nature, has all too few disciples in Italy. My delight on hearing the mellow fluting of a blackbird close to my bedroom window in Assisi was tempered by finding the songster confined by a grating placed over a small space where a block of stone was missing from the house wall. Ironically, the pleasing and unusual fullness of his song was due to the sweet sounds being reflected from the prison in which he was immured.

The robin has long been more confiding in the British Isles than in Italy and elsewhere on the Continent where it is a bird of the woodland rather than the domestic scene. In England it is Donne's "household bird with the red stomacher" [9] and Thomson's "redbreast sacred to the household gods," [10] beloved of Cowper, Blake, Emily Brontë, and many another poet. In Italy, now or in the past, such friendliness between wild birds and men as that established between the Seraphic Father and the robins would seem so exceptional as to be almost, if not quite, miraculous. Even at the end of the nineteenth century, and probably later, piles of dead robins were exposed on the barrows of street vendors.[11]

The Good Shepherd and the Sheep

The religion of Saint Francis being essentially sacramental and based directly on Scripture, especially the Gospels, the sheep which figure so prominently in them had great symbolical significance for him. In this he was conforming to a continuous tradition; the concept of the sacrificial Lamb of God was of primary importance from the time of the primitive Church onward, and the symbol is still commonly represented in ecclesiastical art. Franciscan devotion to Christ's teaching and conformity to the outlook of the early Church is apparent in the imagery associated with sheep and lambs which appears in the Legend. For nearly five centuries the Good Shepherd was the principal Christian pictorial symbol, and not until the tenth century did

[9] "Epithalamium."
[10] "Winter."
[11] A. H. Macpherson, A History of Fowling (London, 1897).

the representation of Christ on the Cross become increasingly frequent. We may plausibly assume that Francis, visiting the Ravenna
churches, saw and was moved by the Good Shepherd depicted in
glittering mosaics in the Mausoleum of Galla Placidia and the flock
of sheep, representing the apostles, grazing in a spangled meadow
around the saint in San Apollinare in Classe.

When he found a dead new-born lamb, he was reminded of the
Lamb of God. He mourned for it, saying, "Alas, brother lamb,
innocent creature, who representest the everlasting advantage of
mankind" (2 Cel. 111). We may interpret his attitude to animals
in general in terms of the belief underlying this remark. For him
Creation in its multifarious variety, the heavenly bodies, elements,
birds, beasts, trees, and flowers, was the lettering in which God
spelled out His message of beneficent power and care for man. His
mind was thronged with Gospel imagery, and accordingly it translated trees, plants, and birds of the countryside into symbols. Com-
monplace objects became in his eyes sacramental and thus gained
additional interest and beauty. A sheep recalled biblical scenes,
parables, and similes, which, after his visit to the East must have
gained additional vividness. He was given to picture-thinking rather
than philosophic thought, and constant dwelling on Gospel symbolism reinforced its power. To Francis, his early followers and biographers, the Good Shepherd and His Flock represented an ideal the
prominence of which most modern biographers have failed to stress.

In the *Fioretti* Friar Leo is addressed as "little sheep of God" (10),
Saint Francis carries a boy "as the good shepherd doth his sheep"
(17) and prays "My Lord Jesus Christ, good Shepherd . . . grant to
me, Thy little sheep, such virtue and grace that for no sickness or
anguish or suffering I may depart from Thee" (19). We hear of his
snatching "so fair a prey from the world, and gathering so fair and
devout a flock to follow in the footprints of the true Shepherd,
Jesus Christ" (18) and reference is made to "the compassionate
and vigilant shepherd" watching over the flock to guard it from the
wolf (23), to edifying "Christ's little sheep by good example" (30),
and to Francis's being "like a good shepherd knowing his sheep"
(21). Friar John addresses Christ as "most gentle Lamb" and "most

compassionate Shepherd." In the *Mirror of Perfection* the Franciscans are mentioned as the Lord's "new and little flock" (26); and Francis, describing of what sort the Minister General of the Order should be, speaks of him as "the leader and shepherd of this family" (80). Words from the Gospel (Luke ii. 9) are borrowed to describe the awesome phenomena that accompanied the stigmatization: "Wherefore when the shepherds that were watching in that country saw the mountain aflame and so much brightness round about, they were sore afraid" (*Fioretti, 3rd consid. of stigmata*). When his companions saw that Francis was near his end, they lamented: "Father, what shall we do without thee? Thou wast ever our father and mother, begetting and bringing us forth in Christ. Thou wast a leader and a shepherd to us, a master and a corrector, teaching and correcting us more by example than by word. Whither shall we go, sheep without a shepherd, orphans without a father, rude and simple men without a leader . . ." (87).

Saint Bonaventura frequently uses shepherd imagery, referring to Jesus in biblical phraseology as "the crucified Lamb," "the Lamb without spot," and "the Lamb that was slain" (v. 8; ix. 2, 9). As Francis bought captured turtle doves, symbols of deliverance, so he purchased lambs, symbols of sacrifice. Both represented redemption. He reports the Lord as naming Francis "shepherd over My Religion" (viii. 3), and he is given the title of "Shepherd of the Church" (xv. 7). After his reputed journey to Morocco, he "returned to feed the sheep that had been committed to his care (ix. 6). On going forth to confront the Saracens, he and his companion sing a verse of the Shepherd Psalm (xxiii). When they come on two lambs, Francis quotes: "Behold I send you forth as sheep in the midst of wolves (ix. 8; Matt. x. 16). Later, when contemplating relinquishing the office of Minister General, he regrets that he sees no one sufficient to be "shepherd of a flock so large" (2 *Cel.* 184). In describing the saint's funeral, Celano (1 *Cel.* 116) says, "The flock followed their Shepherd hastening to the Shepherd of all".

The prominence in the Legend of sheep and lambs and of the figure of the Good Shepherd as symbols of gentleness and responsibility for the welfare of others indicates how strong was the Franciscan reaction against the cruelties and self-seeking of the age and, indeed, high-lights the essence of the Christian faith which condemns man's aggressive, domineering impulses and thus is committed to opposing and superseding the exaltation of power over love, whether in individuals or organizations. Not least, as the saint's own experience of life reminds us, has this struggle been evident within the Church itself. The shepherd, as symbolized by the episcopal hierarchy, has too often stood for the importance of the flock's implicit obedience rather than gaining the flock's allegiance by sacrificial love (John x. 11). The emphasis in the Irish church before the time of Saint Malachy was less on the hierarchy of power and more on compassion and sacrifice. We are told that, when Saint Cainnich heard that an *agnum amabilem* had been killed, he restored it to life; and in the Book of Lismore there is this gracious tribute to Saint Brigid: "She tended the sheep, she satisfied the birds, she fed the poor." She was presented with the gift of a miraculous white sheep.[12]

The frequency of shepherd imagery in the Legend emphasizes the essentially pastoral outlook of Francis and Franciscanism. The saint was concerned for the individual, the lost and straying sheep, human or animal. However we regard the disagreements which beset the Order, it is clear that in its conception and inspiration it was a movement that cared for people and animals as individuals. So long as the Church exemplifies this ideal it will win men's hearts. In so far as it fails, it is because it is in some degree inhuman and thus betraying its faith in the Incarnation, for godliness implies being truly humane.

The parable of the poor man's ewe lamb, which Nathan dared to tell King David to bring home to him his sin in conniving at Uriah's death in order to enjoy his wife (2 Sam. xii. 1–14), reminds us

[12] *Codex Salmanticensis*, ed. C. de Smedt and J. de Backer (London, 1888), pp. 246, 390. The motif of the animal restored to life appears in the Life of St. Molua, in the Legend of Nicholas of Tolentino with reference to a partridge, and in the Legends of other saints. Cf. T. P. Cross, *Motif-Index of Early Irish Literature*, Folk-lore series no. 7. (Bloomington, Ind., 1936), pp. 211–214; C. G. Loomis, *White Magic: An Introduction to the Folklore of Christian Legend* (Cambridge, Mass., 1948), pp. 84–85, 194.

that lambs were treated as pets some three thousand years ago. Sheep being very flock-conscious, a lamb in the absence of other sheep will follow a person and become fixated or "imprinted" on him or her. A lamb with its limpid eyes, "cuddly" coat, and confiding ways appeals to man's innate tender qualities, having some of a small child's attractiveness. In his attitude to sheep Francis doubtless responded to their innate appeal but more especially to their scriptural associations. When he came on a shepherd guarding a herd of goats with a little sheep in the midst, he took pity on it, comparing it to his Master, the Lord Jesus Christ, alone among the Pharisees and chief priests (cf. Acts viii. 32). Could he have thought of himself as being in a similar situation? There may be a reminiscence here of the parable of the Sheep and the Goats (Matt. xxv. 31–46).[13] Moreover, from ancient times the goat had a sinister reputation. With the help of a kindly merchant, he ransomed the lamb and impressed the bishop of Osimo by appearing before him with the little animal trotting at his heels. Francis, we are told, took the opportunity to expound the parable of the Lost Sheep at some length, and the good bishop, pricked to the heart, gave thanks for his innocence. The story is one of several in which high church dignitaries recognize the saintliness of the Little Poor Man. The lamb inevitably became an embarrassment to the itinerant preacher so he gave it to the nuns of San Severino. They were glad to accept it as a pet and later made a gift to the saint of a tunic woven from its wool (1 Cel. 78).

On another occasion Saint Francis met a man carrying two lambs on his shoulders to be slaughtered and forthwith bartered his cloak for them. Celano (1 Cel. 79) comments that the garment was worth much more than the lambs but, realizing the incongruity of representing the Little Poor Man as wearing so costly a cloak, naïvely comments that he had borrowed it that day to keep out the cold.

---

[13] It has long been the custom—still persisting in some Mediterranean countries, as in the south of France—to pasture sheep and goats together because association with the more active goats encourages the sheep to graze over a wider area, but the sheep largely outnumbered the goats. A single sheep among a herd of goats would be quite exceptional though a goatherd might make a pet of a lamb. Goats graze on herbage avoided by sheep.

Having rescued the lambs, Francis had again to face the problem of disposing of them, but this was solved by returning them to the man, at the same time cautioning him to take good care of them.[14]

Bonaventura, although content to tell extravagant stories, seems to have been unhappy about some of Celano's and substitutes his own (cf. p. 150), presenting, first a sheep anecdote which does not strain credulity and then two others which do (viii. 7). He changes the emphasis from compassion for men and beasts to stress on the symbolism, piety, and insight of sheep and the power inherent in saintliness. When Francis was in the neighbourhood of Siena, he came on a large flock of sheep at pasture. According to his custom, he greeted them "graciously." They ceased grazing, raised their heads, and gazed fixedly at him, as sheep in such circumstances are apt to do; but Bonaventura, who mentioned the bird congregation looking at the saint "in unwonted wise," is calling attention to the reverence he inspired. However, the brethren with Francis and the shepherds were amazed at what they construed to be such eager acclamation. Not only the lambs but even the staid rams were filled with delight. Obviously Bonaventura was painting a picture of the Earthly Paradise rather than Sienese pastures.

When a lamb was brought to the man of God at the Portiuncula, he welcomed it because of its guilelessness and exhorted it to be virtuous and to be instant in praising God. Accordingly it went to church when it heard chanting and, unbidden, would kneel and bleat

---

[14] Thomas of Celano again sits lightly to consistency and evidently is not writing for the critically minded who might query the morality of giving away property belonging to somebody else as, indeed, they have queried Francis's sale of his father's scarlet cloths to raise money for the repair of St. Damian's (1 Cel. 8; Bon. ii. 1). L. Wadding (Annales Minorum I [Lyons, 1625], 32), writing in the seventeenth century, found the incident embarrassing. Nevertheless, Celano had qualms about Francis's giving away what did not belong to him, for he sometimes shuffles clumsily when narrating such incidents. On meeting a poor man, he represents Francis as saying to his companion: "Brother, we must give this cloak back to the poor man to whom it belongs, for we have borrowed it until we should happen to meet someone poorer than ourselves." The friar expostulates but he replies: "I will not be a thief; it would be reckoned to us as theft if we gave not to one in greater need" (2 Cel. 87). Thus Francis is depicted in a rôle rather similar to that of Robin Hood.

before the altar. At the Elevation it would also kneel as if to reprove the irreverence of the undevout. Whether this tale played a part in stimulating story-tellers and painters to represent the animals at the Nativity as kneeling is doubtful.[15]

At one time Francis took a lamb with him to Rome, and having such reverence for the gentle Lamb of God, he entrusted it to the Lady Jacopa de' Settesoli. It accompanied her to and from church, and when she was tardy in getting up for Mass, it would bleat and butt her "admonishing her with gestures and nods to hasten to church." She cherished it as most loveworthy. Bonaventura probably recalled the tradition of the bird "knocker-up" and transferred it to a sheep, thus joining two motifs as he did on other occasions (*Bon.* viii. 7). These stories further illustrate the use of accretion and in-cremental exaggeration. The lengths to which Saint Bonaventura considered it legitimate to go appear in his final paragraph. He says of Francis "many dead have been miraculously raised through him." [16]

In spite of his adherence to medieval views concerning animals' lack of souls, Bonaventura attributes understanding and spirituality to sheep. He exhibits the inconsistency that enabled people of his time to deny a sense of morality to animals and yet hang them publicly as malefactors. Before allowing ourselves to be shocked at

[15] Caesarius Heisterbacensis (*Dial. Mir.* IV. xcviii) retailed an anecdote con-cerning asses which, after a brief exhortation from a priest, knelt before the Blessed Sacrament which he was carrying. In order to assuage the disputes between cities claiming that a miracle of Saint Anthony's was performed in their midst, namely, that a horse or mule knelt to adore the Host, hagiographers suggested that the saint "re-edited" his miracles, locating the portent successively at Rimini, Bourges, and Toulouse. Cf. L. de Kerval, "L'Évolution et le dévelop-pement du merveilleux dans les légendes de S. Antoine de Padoue," *Opuscules de Critiques Historiques* XII, XIII, XIV (1906), 221–288. A comparison between the evolution of these legends and the elaboration undergone by the Franciscan legends is illuminating. Horses knelt as Francis of Giralamo preached. Cf. Loomis, *op. cit.*, pp. 61, 178. Saint Colette, the reformer of the Poor Clares, had a pet lamb which, like Lady Jacopa's, knelt at the Elevation of the Sacrament. She was on friendly terms with the birds beloved by Saint Francis, turtle doves and especially the lark. Cf. Père Ch. Cahier, *Caracteristiques des Saints dans l'Art Populaire* II (Paris, 1867), 589. Thus earlier Franciscan traditions were attached to her in a modified form.

[16] O. Englebert, *Saint Francis of Assisi* (London, 1950), p. 32, says of Bona-ventura's *Life*: "It was exact in that it said nothing which was untrue."

such inconsistency, we would do well to take stock of our own society in which advertisers are so successful in exploiting the credulity of the public and the cheaper press purveys horoscopes as well as details of moon flights. We may reflect also that, if this tendency to endow animals with something akin to personality had followed a different course and instead of regarding them as caricatures of humanity or the embodiments of human vices (and less frequently, virtues) the men of the Middle Ages had been able to view them sympathetically as in some respects comparable with children, a more Christian attitude would have prevailed. It was integral to the Franciscans' protest against violence that they should lay stress on the gentler Christian virtues of mercy, humility, self-restraint, and renunciation by giving prominence to the animal that symbolizes innocence; but the difficulties in assuaging man's greed and brutality remained, as they do still. The medieval artists had recourse to the animal world to warn and deter the faithful. Devils were depicted in lurid colours equipped with claws, beaks, and tails, thus unintentionally calumniating the animals. Franciscan animal imagery and representation of angels with bird wings helped to redress the balance.

Saint Francis and the Pigs

By noticing the idiosyncrasies of the biographers and making allowance for the bias they gave to their narratives, we may come closer to the saint and in some instances discount stories that, in our eyes, are unworthy of him. Because Celano and Bonaventura told farfetched anecdotes about sheep is no reason to doubt that Francis showed special tenderness for them; but when we read that, moved with pity for a lamb killed by a sow, Francis uttered a malediction, "Cursed be the pitiless one that slew thee, and let no beast eat of her," we remember how Celano exaggerated Francis's comment about the greedy young robin into a curse. The lamb's body was avoided by all predators as if they wished to dissociate themselves thereby from an unholy deed—a curious instance of moral intuition and compunction being attributed to animals. The sow sickened and died. The corpse was cast into the monastery ditch where it also was spurned by other animals as the cat spurned the body of the wicked robin. It lay there until it became desiccated—an incidental glimpse of the unhygienic conditions tolerated at that time (2 *Cel.* 111). But did any such incident take place? Celano seems to be engaged in his ploy of spinning yarns from any hagiographical threads which came his way. According to one of the most widely known stories told in connexion with Saint Cuthbert's Sanctuary at Durham, a stag took refuge in a Lothian church on the festival of the saint's Translation in September 1155. The hunters paused, and the congregation poured out of the church to watch. When a man instigated his son to tease the distressed animal, it gored him to death but was itself slain after it had leapt over the churchyard wall. Because it had murdered the boy, the body was left where it lay. No one would eat of it.[17]

The story may well be based on an actual incident. Its kernel is Saint Cuthbert's love for animals, a living tradition which has survived to the present time. However, the theme is designed to show that even an animal such as the saint loved may become a criminal and transgress the rules of sanctuary. The medieval mind persisted in regarding animals as bound by the principles of Christian morality. The basic belief was that there should be no place in ordered society for the criminal who flouts the laws of God and man.

Celano's tortuous efforts in adapting the story of the sow to show that divine justice was administered led him to represent the preservation of the bodies both of the assassin and of her victim as a vindication of God's rule. Whatever the truth may have been, he was conforming to a motif so designed that the reader's compassion for one animal was to be enhanced by the condemnation of another. Celano's concern was to point a moral rather then to report accurately. Pigs had long been symbolic of greed, filth, and evil impulses, not merely on account of the muck in their sties but because they scavenged in the ordure of villages and towns. Also, people familiar with the Gospel associated them with the Gadarene swine (Matt. viii. 30; Mark v. 11; Luke viii. 32).

Celano's account reflects the materialistic attitude that prompted

---

[17] *Reginaldi monachi Dunelmensis libellus de admirandis Beati Cuthberti,* ed. J. Raine (London, 1835). Surtees Society, I, 180–185.

indignities to be heaped on the corpses of enemies and the ashes of heretics burned at the stake to be scattered—an expression of hatred, vindictiveness, and fear allied with the assumption that a man's opinions could be eliminated with his body. Frederick II is said to have tried to disprove the existence of the soul by enclosing a man in a barrel to die there. Celano thought that the evil deeds of an animal should be visited on its body after death—if only by other animals disdaining to eat it. Thus moral endowments were attributed to animals although they were denied souls. This mingling of materialistic and moralistic ideas led to confusion which not even the genius of St. Thomas Aquinas could dissipate. Indeed, his logic led to dogmas which did little to discourage the ill-treatment of animals. He taught that animals could be possessed by the devil and used as instruments of the powers of hell. Legal action taken against such creatures was directed against Satan. As Canon Law was God's law and all creatures were subject to God, they could be excommunicated or executed as criminals. The ambivalent medieval attitude to animals arose from the belief that they could be used by, or be manifestations of, supremely good or utterly evil powers. This preconception stood in the way of any objective evaluation of the behaviour of animals.[18]

Another tale in which pigs figure must be viewed with reservations although it comes from a contemporary of Saint Francis's, Matthew Paris.[19] When Francis and his apostolic group of twelve companions reached Rome, he made his way to the Lateran Palace and without any introduction appeared before the Pope. He was so dishevelled that Innocent III treated him as if he were a swineherd and told him not to talk about his Rule for the Friars: "Go and find your pigs," he said, "and preach to them as much as you like." Francis rushed off, went to a pigsty, smeared the mire over himself, and returned to the Pope. Innocent was not offended; on the contrary his heart was touched, and telling Francis to go and wash, he promised him an-

[18] G. Carson, "Bugs and Beasts before the Law," *Nat. Hist.* LXXVII, 4 (1968), 6–19.
[19] *Chronica* in *Archivum* I (Quaracchi, 1908), 81–82.

other audience. This story's truth, in so far as it has any, resides in its illustrating the lengths to which it was believed Francis's ardour would take him, as well as his naïveté and abject obedience to authority. But it has significance for us as indicating that Francis could be represented as known in papal circles to be one who did not disdain to preach to birds and beasts. Perhaps it shows that in some quarters this was regarded as a ridiculous, if pardonable, eccentricity. The anecdote is consistent with the strong language sometimes used by this Pope. In a letter to Tignosi, administrator of Viterbo, he wrote: "You fear neither God nor men; wallowing in your sins like the ass in its mire." [20]

One of Celano's anecdotes (2 Cel. 121) in which pigs are mentioned illustrates the extent of the divisions in the Order which were creating serious problems at the time he wrote his Vita Secunda. He relates that, after a friar had noticed "brethren abiding in a certain Court," he felt an attraction for their way of life and wanted to join them. While his mind was dwelling on this prospect, he had a dream in which he saw these friars separated from the fellowship and feeding out of a pigs' trough. Thus he was cured of any desire to join them. The reference is to the betrayal of the saint's principles by Elias who was eventually deposed from the office of Minister General in 1239 and excommunicated (2 Cel. 216). In an earlier passage Celano (1 Cel. 108) had recorded the blessing bestowed on him although alluding to the disquieting divisions in the Order in which he was later to be so deeply embroiled.

Herds of swine infested Florence and its environs at this period. They belonged to neighbouring monasteries and were under the patronage of the austere Saint Anthony who was represented in art with a pig lying at his feet symbolizing the power of sanctity to overcome gluttony and sensuality. Pigs were tolerated in Italian cities because of their value as scavengers and ultimately as pork. The tradition was ancient. Swine scavenged in Nebuchadnezzar's Babylon as they still do in Chinese villages. Dante (Paradiso xxix. 115–126) evidently had these Florentine pigs in mind when he alluded to monks growing fat by exploiting vain pardonings:

[20] A. Luchaire, Innocent III II (Paris, 1905), 93.

But nowadays men preach with jokes and japes,
  And if they raise a laugh, their cowls all swell
  With pride—they ask no more, the jackanapes.

Yet if the bird, which nestles in the tail
  Of all such hoods, the foolish crowd could see,
  What pardons they confide in they'd know well.

So gross has grown the world's credulity,
  No need is there the slightest proof to rig,
  At any promise men will rush with glee.

That's how St. Anthony doth feed his pig,
  And many others too, more pig-like still,
  Paying with currency not worth a fig.[21]

The sordid associations of swine did not prevent the distinguished
Franciscan preacher Saint Bernardino from drawing a moral from
their behaviour. He remarked: "Look at the pigs who have so much
compassion for each other that when one of them squeals, the others
will run to help him. . . . And you children when you steal the baby
swallows, what do the other swallows do? They all gather together
and try to help the fledglings. . . . Man is more evil than the
birds." [22] One of his incidental allusions gives some idea of the
squalor that accompanied magnificence in Italian cities. A thief
frequented the marketplace of Siena at night associating with the
pigs known as "St. Anthony's swine." Disguised as one of them with
a bell attached to his neck and a bag around his buttocks, he crawled
about with the animals in order to steal flour.[23]

In England there was a comparable tolerance of swine in city

[21] Translation by B. Reynolds in the completion of the version of the *Divina
Commedia* by D. Sayers (Penguin Books, Harmondsworth, 1962).

[22] L. Banchi, ed., *Le prediche vulgari de San Bernardino da Siena, dette
nella Piazza del Campo, Anno 1427* (Siena, 1880–1888), III, 341; II, 61–62.
Corporate activity that may be of advantage to the species is indeed characteristic of some herd animals and social birds. "Mobbing" of a predator by birds
calls attention to it and alerts neighbours.

[23] Banchi, *op. cit.*, III, 323. At this period a leper had to wear a bell around
his neck to give warning of his approach. He could be stoned or killed if found
within the walls of Assisi. Cf. I. Origo, *The World of San Bernardino* (London,
1963), p. 105.

streets at late as the second half of the sixteenth century. John Stow, who published his *Survey of London* in 1598, recorded:

> I remember that the officers charged with the oversight of the markets in this city, did divers times take from the market people, pigs starved, or otherwise unwholesome for man's sustenance; these they slit in the ear. One of the proctors for St. Anthonie's tied a bell about the neck and let it feed on the dunghills; no man would hurt or take them up, but if any gave to them bread, or other feeding, such would they know, to watch for, and daily follow, whining till they had somewhat given them; whereupon was raised a proverb, "Such an one will follow such an one, and whine as it were an Anthonie pig:" but if such a pig grew to be fat, and came to good liking (as oft times they did), then the proctor would take him up for the use of the hospital.

The pig was the most important protein provider during the thirteenth and fourteenth centuries in England and, no doubt, elsewhere in Europe.

The association between Saint Anthony and the pig began at the end of the fourteenth century. The cessation of an epidemic of swine fever was ascribed to the intercession of the saint, and a charitable organization originating in the Dauphinois, the Anthonines, having been permitted to let their pigs forage in the streets, artists represented the confraternity by a device depicting the saint together with a pig with a bell at its neck.

Because of the importance of symbolism to men of the Middle Ages, an animal could have ambivalent or contrary associations. Swine lived in such dirty conditions that they became by-words for what was abhorrent, physically and morally. A story told of John Parenti, who was a lawyer and the Minister General of the Franciscan Order from 1227 to 1232, relates that he joined because he heard a swineherd calling to his herd: "Get along pigs, return to your sty as judges go into hell." [24] Saint Anthony was the patron saint of swineherds, but this did not necessarily increase the esteem in which swine or swineherds were held. Nevertheless, pigs sometimes acquired a measure of sanctity through their association with

[24] L. Wadding, *Annales Minorum*, Ann. 1211, n. 21.

the saint; his sanctity rubbed off on the hog. Monks of Saint Anthony kept herds of swine which were allowed to forage at the public expense.[25] So, in the Italian *Novella* the connexion led to pigs under the protection of Saint Anthony being held sacred.[26] A shadowy Irishman, Saint Monus, was represented, like a number of other Irish saints, with a bell but also with a pig.[27] In Germany, where he is still revered, or was until recently, he is regarded locally as the patron saint of marriage and in common with another Irish saint, Fiacre, is invoked by those suffering from venereal disease. The association between Saint Monus and the pig evidently represents his ability to overcome the consequences of sensuality. (Saint Fiacre with his spade was connected with fertility.) Was it because Irish missionary saints were most active on the Continent before the introduction of syphilis by returning Crusaders that this curative power was attributed to them?

Saint Francis is associated with pigs indirectly in an ancient folk play *Saint Guillaume de Poitou,* the best surviving example of such a production not based on Scripture. This Breton versified drama in seven acts recounts the story of the wickedness and eventual reformation of the Troubadour Count. His sins are innumerable, yet one good deed is cited in his favour: he once gave two pilgrims a bed of straw in a pigsty. Saint Francis appears and throws this straw into the balance. The straw weighs it down in the Count's favour. Why should Saint Francis be involved unless those who composed the play remembered that he who had humbled himself by taking the Pope at his word by going to a pigsty was the most suitable person to act in this dramatically compassionate way? A more recent echo of the Franciscan and Breton theme occurs in Victor Hugo's play *Sultan Mourad.* This tyrannical scoundrel qualified for heaven because he was shown not to be unmitigatedly evil. He had once felt momentary

[25] A. Jameson, *Sacred and Legendary Art* (London, 1857), p. 750.
[26] D. P. Rotunda, *Motif-Index of the Italian Novello in Prose* (Bloomington, 1942), p. 3.
[27] L. Gougaud, *Gaelic Pioneers of Christianity* (Dublin, 1923), p. 142. St. Patrick herded swine on the hill of Slemish but the shamrock became the Irish emblem because he was reputed to have displayed it when expounding the doctrine of the Trinity.

compassion for a pig.[28] So legends survive and acquire further elements or additional motifs as they are transmitted down the centuries.

We have good reason to discount the story of Brother Juniper's
assault on a pig—which has embarrassed those who, regarding it as
factual, have not been able to reconcile it with the Franciscan compassion for animals. This friar, depicted as usual as a well-meaning
buffoon, is said to have cut off a living pig's trotter to provide a meal
for a sick man, arguing when he was reproved that God created
pigs for the use of men—the kind of plea which has often been used
to excuse cruelty. To cheer up the invalid the friar told him with
great glee of his assault on the pig (Fioretti. Friar Juniper 1).
Francis was scandalized, not, according to this report, on account of
the cruelty to the animal but because of the offence to the swineherd. Juniper went off obediently and in spite of the abuse rained on
him by the furious man embraced and kissed him to such good
effect that the swineherd burst into tears and, prostrating himself
on the ground, besought the friar's pardon. All ended happily, for
he then killed the porker, cooked it, and carried it piously to the
friars at the Portiuncula—and a right good feast they must have
had. Francis commented: "Would to God, my brethren, that I
had a whole forest of such junipers." [29]

[28] Countess Martinengo-Cesaresco, Essays in the Study of Folk-songs (London, 1914), pp. 20–21.
[29] Saint Clare is said to have named Friar Juniper Domine joculator or jacu-
lator. The latter is the reading in the oldest manuscript of the Legenda Sanctae
Clarae. There is disagreement as to the spelling and meaning of this word.
"Archer," "hurler," and "minstrel" have been suggested. Cf. E. Gilliat-Smith,
St. Clare of Assisi (London, 1914), p. 113. Perhaps in this context, "mountebank" interpreted in a humorous rather than a pejorative sense is as close as we
may get to the meaning. The translation of the Fioretti into French made in
1563 has "jongleur." Caesarius Heisterbacensus (Dial. Mir. VI. viii) applied
the term to the simple-minded. The tradition of the godly buffoon dates back
in Christian annals at least as far as St. Brendan's Voyage, but the belief that
men and women with mental abnormalities of various kinds are in a special
relationship to supernatural powers is very ancient and characteristic of many
primitive peoples. In the Voyage a simpleton who ventured on to an island infested by "sea-cats" and was devoured by them is called "a wonderful martyr."
Cf. Lives of Saints from the Book of Lismore, ed. and trans. W. Stokes (Oxford,
1890), p. 257.

Shocking as this episode appears to us it would scarcely have seemed so to Saint Francis's contemporaries in an age when "life bore the mixed smell of blood and roses." The brutality of the populace may be illustrated by reference to a public display in Paris in 1425. After a procession with drum and banner to assemble a crowd, four blind men armed with clubs were set to kill a pig, the entertainment consisting in seeing them belabour each other as well as the animal.[30]

We need not take Brother Juniper and his antics seriously. Apologists for the saint's attitude to him in this incident waste their ink. On the evidence it is very unlikely that he ever severed a pig's trotter. He clearly belongs to an established tradition of well-intentioned pious simpletons whose ridiculous activities made them figures of fun. The story is akin to one of the many anecdotes of a similar character told by the German hagiographer Caesarius Heisterbacensis, in which Brother Ensfrid surreptitiously cuts hams in two to give to the poor and chops up geese spitted for roasting. Suspicion that Brother Juniper is a scissors and paste character is confirmed when we note that Gregory of Tours described how a cook indiscriminately piled fish and beans into a pot to make a huge boiling. This story is evidently the ancestor of the anecdote in the *Fioretti* (*Friar Juniper* 1) which tells of the brethren's consternation on finding Juniper darting back and forth, red-faced, protected by a board in front of a raging fire on which were pots and pans into which he had heaped vegetables, eggs in their shells, unplucked fowl, and so forth.[31] Juniper, the simpleton, takes the place of a child on a see-saw, strips to his breeches as a sign of penitence when visiting a festival at Spoleto, and cuts off the silver bells on an altar cloth to give to a poor woman. The narrator of a number of stories in the *Fioretti* is heedless of what might seem to the reader incongruities and inconsistencies. We are not expected to ask ourselves how a Franciscan altar came to be furnished with "a hanging of gold, richly and sumptuously adorned" any more than to query the friars' feasting on pork nor to try to reconcile Saint Francis's austerities with his

---

[30] J. Huizinga, *The Waning of the Middle Ages* (Penguin Books, 1955), pp. 25–26.
[31] N. Tamassia, *St. Francis of Assisi and his Legend* (London, 1910), p. 195.

enjoying a meal provided by Lady Jacopa de' Settesoli including cray-
fish patties and marzipan (*Spec. Perf.* 110). In the recorded exploits
of Brother Juniper we have a monastic equivalent of the secular
"merry tale" of the Middle Ages. If we may judge by Salimbene's
chronicle, less printable tales circulated among the monks.

As we have noted, Francis's biographers were shy about stressing
his sense of humour, remarking that he encouraged spiritual gladness
but abhorred laughter (*Spec. Perf.* 96); yet he is recorded as laugh-
ing or smiling (*irridens*) when talking to a man from Ancona (2
Cel. 81). When referring to his light-heartedness, they became entangled in near contradictions as they did when dealing with his
relations with women (pp. 233–235). They felt impelled to mention
that, after singing French songs to the accompaniment of a make-
believe viol in the woods, he broke down and wept, remembering
Christ's Passion (*Spec. Perf.* 93), yet undoubtedly he and his companions combined gaiety with austerity. But it is not only in literature and below the surface of medieval monasticism that we find
humour. Carved conspicuously on Melrose Abbey is just such a one
as Brother Juniper, the cook with his ladle, and close to the solemn
saints of Chartres cathedral an ass rears up playing on a harp.
Grotesque gargoyles on many a church and cathedral contrast with
the austere statuary, and here and there on misericords or carved in
stone are humorous, facetious, or even erotic scenes.[32] There is a
story of a monk reproved for looking at a pretty girl. He replied that
a fasting man might look at a menu. Monks were human, too.

In early Franciscanism the vein of levity, sometimes becoming
ribaldry, which ran through medieval society found expression in
joy, delight in nature, and exuberant evangelistic fervour. Brother
Juniper is, of course, a caricature, but simple souls attracted to Saint
Francis and his friars, who needed all the tolerance their fellows
could give, must have added a touch of humour and variety to many
a community while straining their charity. We have a vivid example

---

[32] To attribute obscene intentions to the artists or their employers is unjustified. It must have seemed natural and reasonable to the designers of the Bayeux
tapestry, which depicts scenes of slaughter, that they should include in the
border a complementary erotic scene, suggesting the generation of life.

of one such in John the Simple (2 *Cel.* 190) who suffered from a mental disorder which impelled him to mimic every gesture made by Francis. The saint playfully called him Saint John. More recently, some of the eccentric clergy of Victorian times, such as Hawker of Morwenstow, made a valuable contribution to English social life, and still in Ireland priests with the characteristics of Father O'Flynn are beloved as well as respected. Nowadays Brother Simple appears more often as a character on television than in person, but his popularity throughout the centuries indicates a deep-seated realization that laughter has a place in the cloister as well as among Christian folk outside it. After Saint Francis, with stricter discipline of the Order and bureaucratic consolidation in Church affairs, gaiety, carefree discipleship, and humanity to animals diminished.

The Horse and the Ass

Naturally Francesco Bernardone as the son of a prosperous merchant rode a horse before his conversion. The selling of the steed at Foligno probably had a symbolic significance in Celano's eyes (1 *Cel.* 8) as representing the young man's renunciation of his accustomed ostentatious way of life, for thereafter we usually hear of his mount being the humbler ass. Celano is careful to mention that later when he went on horseback and was suffering from various infirmities he always dismounted to say the Hours (2 *Cel.* 96). We are told that "he went through the world to preach either on foot or on an ass (after he began to grow sick), or on a horse in the greatest and strictest necessity (because otherwise he would not ride) and this only a little before his death" (*Spec. Perf.* 35). Celano also states that on one of these journeys undertaken when he was ill the horse had been borrowed (1 *Cel.* 62). As we have noted, this biographer points out when he refers to any relatively valuable object in the saint's possession that it had been lent him. Bonaventura (vii. 12) also excuses his riding an ass borrowed from a poor man by mentioning that he was "weak in body." In choosing to go on foot when not hindered by infirmity, he was conforming to ancient apostolic tradition. Among the Irish wandering saints, to walk was considered an essential aspect of the mortification involved in a pilgrimage. A journey mounted or in a vehicle was not considered a valid pilgrimage. Saint Wilfrid at the age of 70 walked all the way to Rome.[33] Bede recorded of Saint Aidan that "he left the clergy a most salutary example of abstinence or continence . . . ; he neither sought nor loved any thing of this world. . . . He was wont to traverse both town and country on foot, never on horseback, unless compelled by some urgent necessity." [34] As we have noted, in other respects there were remarkable similarities between the disciplines of the Irish missionaries and the Franciscans.

In view of the evidence that the ecclesiastical encouragement of the Franciscan movement was based to some extent on its being regarded as offering an effective alternative ideal to the asceticism of some heretics, it is of interest that among the taunts levelled by the Catharist Perfectionists against the Catholic bishops was the accusation that they were "mounted ministers of a God who went on foot." This was hard to rebut as bishops were entitled to an equipage including thirty horses. As a counter-demonstration, in 1206 St. Dominic and the bishop of Osma undertook a preaching tour in Provence, travelling barefoot and begging their bread.[35]

Unlike some of the allusions to Francis's humility in riding an ass, another anecdote is evidently a whimsical invention. He was preaching one day at Trevi when a donkey stampeded noisily about the piazza. The bystanders were terrified, and all efforts to catch and calm the animal failed. Saint Francis then spoke to it, saying, "Brother ass, please be quiet and allow me to preach to the folk." On hearing this, the ass immediately bowed its head and, to everybody's astonishment, stood completely still. Blessed Francis, anxious lest the crowd should take too much notice of this amazing miracle, began saying funny things to make them laugh. So ends one version of the story; but the Irish historian Wadding thought this too flippant and amended it to read that the ass "listened with the utmost attention

---

[33] L. Gougaud, *Christianity in Celtic Lands* (London, 1932), p. 175.
[34] *Ecclesiastical History* III, v.
[35] *Acta Sanctorum*, 4 Aug. Cf. A. Boulanger, *Histoire Génerale de l'Église* II (Paris, 1935) v. 12. John Parenti, elected Minister General in 1227, travelled barefoot encouraging the friars at their settlements in Italy, France, and Germany.

to the rest of the sermon." [36] Thus in the seventeenth century as in the thirteenth biographers and annalists did not scruple to alter tales, even at the expense of credibility, in order to render them more edifying. The practice has not yet been abandoned.

The original story-teller can hardly have been completely serious, but the picture of Francis making jocular remarks agrees with what other writers tell us or allow us to infer about his character. On the one hand we are to understand that quieting a restive donkey with a few words was an astonishing miracle; on the other, that for Francis it was all in the day's work. The motif of dominating a beast is, of course, among the most ancient and recurrent in mythology as well as hagiography. This version may be regarded as a variation of the Stilling the Swallows theme and has affinities with the Wolf of Gubbio. It cannot be assumed when we are given circumstantial details of the exact place where an episode occurred, and even the name, Brother Tebaldo, of the eye-witness, that the facts are true, for even with far-fetched tales the biographers like to give incidents a local habitation.

Friar Giles regarded the horse as an object lesson of man's relationship to his superiors and to God. He remarked: "How useful is the nature of the horse! for how swiftly soever the horse runneth, he yet letteth himself be ruled and guided, and leapeth hither and thither, and forward and backward, according to the will of his rider: and so, likewise, ought the servant of God to do, to wit, he should let himself be ruled, guided, turned aside and bent, according to the will of his superior, or of any other man, for love of Christ" (*Fioretti. Sayings of Friar Giles* 5). The comment may have as its background James iii. 3.[37]

[36] *Archivum Franciscanum Historicum* XII, 389; Wadding, *op. cit.*, I, 153. H. E. Goad in *Franciscan Italy* (London, 1926), p. 7, states that the donkey came to listen on its knees.

The attentiveness of animals to preaching is a favourite Franciscan theme. Saint Bernardino declared that when Saint Francis was about to preach in the open air he gently bade the cocks and hens be still. They remained quietly roosting on ledges and roofs until he had finished his sermon. Cf. Origo, *op. cit.*, p. 115.

[37] Friar Giles (16) remarked that those entering the religious life should know how to endure its vicissitudes as a man riding a restive or vicious horse

From early times the horse has been symbolic of pride and power as biblical references indicate (Job xxxix. 19; Psalm xx. 7); but among Christians the ass had ambivalent or dual symbolism because, although it was treated as a lowly beast of burden, it had reproved Balaam (Numbers xxii. 22–30) and, more significantly, was associated with Palm Sunday (Matt. xxi. 5). It represented triumph as well as humility and therefore, in the eyes of Francis's companions its symbolism was particularly relevant to their leader. Bellini, in his lovely picture St. Francis in Ecstasy, appropriately placed Brother Ass as well as a bird in the background (pl. 12).

The Fioretti (1st consid. of stigmata) includes a revealing episode which has the ring of truth. As Francis made his way toward La Verna, he was so ill that his companions craved the loan of a poor man's ass—for the love of God. The rustic saddled the ass, invited Francis to mount, and followed behind for some time. Then he said: "Tell me, art thou that Friar Francis of Assisi?" And Saint Francis answered "Yea." "Now strive then," said the peasant, "to be as good as thou art held to be by all folk, for many have great faith in thee; therefore I admonish thee that thou betray not the hopes men cherish of thee." Saint Francis, we are told, "disdained not to be exhorted by a peasant nor said within himself, 'What beast is this that doth admonish me?' as many proud fellows that wear the cowl would say nowadays." He alighted, kissed the man's feet, and thanked him for his advice. The reference to Balaam's ass is covert, but the full significance of the episode's setting deserves emphasis. Just previously Francis had gone alone into a wood bewailing the Passion of Christ and was observed by the awestruck friars who had followed him standing in cross-vigil. After this incident he received the stigmata. Thus we see a sacred drama unfolding and are reminded of Palm Sunday and Good Friday, of Christ's humility and redemptive Passion. A little later in the narrative Francis, following Mosaic precedent and as earlier saints including Saint Cuthbert had done,

---

should know how to save himself from falling if it reared, and he pointed out (17) that the man of religion should, like the ox, bend his neck to the yoke of obedience.

makes water gush from a rock—an indication to the reader of his now highly exalted status.

As we have noted, after Francis returned from the Near East, he rode an ass because he was in an exhausted state and suffering from various ills. On a journey together Brother Leonard, walking behind, said to himself: "This man's parents and mine were not wont to play together as equals. But now he is riding and I am driving his ass." Divining his thought, Francis said: "No brother, it is not fitting that I should ride and thou be walking, because in the world thou wast nobler and mightier than I." Brother Leonard blushed, wept, and begged pardon (2 *Cel.* 31). The incident recalls the strength of class distinctions at the time and helps us to realize how Pietro Bernardone felt when his son threw in his lot with outcasts, and also the impact achieved by the Franciscans as a brotherhood in which distinctions of wealth and status were submerged. They were "all one in Christ Jesus" (Gal. iii. 28). In the light of these incidents we can appreciate the indignation among the friars when they found that Elias, who after the saint's death became Vicar-General, kept palfreys and pages. He would ride when he had to go only half a mile, breaking the rule that the Friars should walk except when infirm or in dire necessity. Friar Bernard used to run after him expostulating and pummeling the horse on the crupper.[38]

When Francis referred to his body as Brother Ass, he obviously meant that it should be strictly disciplined (2 *Cel.* 116). Celano informs us that while scourging himself he said: "Ah! Brother Ass, thus must thou be led, thus must thou submit unto the lash." He also spoke of Brother Body: "Let him know that a lazy beast wants the spur and that the goad awaits a sluggish ass" (2 *Cel.* 129). Such language, implying that animals sometimes deserved brutal treatment, seems out of character and is inconsistent with other statements by Celano; but it is in keeping with his anxiety to emphasize and, indeed, exaggerate the austerities the first Franciscans imposed on themselves. Knowing this we may assume that the somewhat milder language of the *Legenda Antiqua* (96) reports the Poverello

[38] Salimbene, *Chronica*, p. 157; cf. Coulton, *op. cit.*, pp. 82–83; *Chronicle of the XXIV Generals, in Analecta Franc.* III, 229.

more accurately: "When a well-fed ass refuses to carry his burden one must make the stick felt."

Passages in which the ass is mentioned by Celano and the other biographers might seem incidental and unimportant, but they constitute a touchstone by which the reliability of these writers may be judged and their methods discerned. If the argument that follows is sound, Celano and others following him invented incidents to depict the saint according to a preconceived pattern and manufactured anecdotes from selected portions of earlier hagiographical motifs. A consideration of these passages is therefore crucial for our estimate of the reliance to be placed on the stories scattered through the Lives.

It is odd that in some contexts the ass, snow, and nakedness should appear in association. There is no normal or archetypal connexion between them, yet they are linked in a cluster of ideas or images concerning humility and penance. The "Brother Ass" passage precedes the strange account of the saint's going out naked in deep snow to make seven mounds or "snowmen" representing a wife, two sons and two daughters, and a serving man and maid. (It is noticeable that the underlying conception is of a wealthy household.) The credibility of this incident is reduced rather than augmented when we notice Celano's comment (1 Cel. 40) that to subdue lust the friars flogged and tortured themselves, hanging from ropes, enclosing themselves in cages, sprawling amongst thorns, and stripping naked to roll in snow. This reads more like a catalogue of the austerities said to have been imposed on themselves by earlier ascetics such as Saint Benedict, who threw himself amongst briars, than the way of life of the little group of simple folk who companied with Francis in the Umbrian woods.[39] Moreover, it is clearly stated in the Fioretti

[39] A Benedictine monastery beyond Subiaco, in the Monti Simbruini, east of Rome, stands on the site of Saint Benedict's first hermitage. The rose garden maintained there is located where Saint Benedict, about the year 500, rolled in brambles to allay carnal longings. According to tradition, when Saint Francis visited the spot seven hundred years later he touched the brambles and transformed them into rose bushes. Cf. E. Wilkins, The Rose-garden Game (London, 1969), p. 125. In the precincts of the basilica of San Francesco at Assisi is a small enclosed garden of thornless roses, recalling the legend that when Francis sought to discipline himself by rolling among roses they lost their thorns.

(18, 19) that the saint forbade austerities such as wearing iron breast-plates and rings.[40]

Setting aside the difficulty of reconciling our picture of the gentle, modest Francis with the spectacle of a naked fakir making snow-men, other considerations arouse our suspicion that Celano is de-scribing him in terms of the extreme and sometimes grotesque asceticisms which were the stock in trade of hagiographers. Early in his First Life he makes us a little sceptical by informing us that Francis was beaten by robbers and hurled into a snow-filled ditch (1 Cel. 16; cf. Fioretti, 16). This episode is said to have happened in April when the Umbrian climate approximates to June in coun-tries farther north.[41] It would be unusual to find deep snow drifts close to Assisi at this season though they would linger in the moun-tains. Apart from this consideration, Celano in the previous sentence speaks of Francis wrestling "naked with his naked foe" and then refers to his being robbed of almost all his clothes. Thus at the beginning of his First Life the concepts of asceticism, humility, beat-ing, nakedness, and plunging into snow became connected. The ass was a natural addition to the linkage for it was the animal associated with beating and humility. Celano continued weaving these associa-tions into new patterns though sometimes omitting one of the com-

[40] Evidently Celano was trying to make sure that no one could claim for other men greater asceticism. It was, however, an age of excesses, as is shown by a quotation from Salimbene describing what he saw in 1260: "The Flagellants came through the whole world; and all men, both small and great, noble knights and men of the people, scourged themselves naked in procession through the cities, with the Bishops and men of Religion at their head; and peace was made in many places; and men restored what they had unlawfully taken away, and they confessed their sins so earnestly that the priests had scarce leisure to eat. And in their mouths sounded words of God and not of man, and their voice was as the voice of a multitude: and men walked in the way of salvation, and composed godly songs in honour of the Lord and the Blessed Virgin. . . ." Cf. Coulton, op. cit., p. 192. For a description of processional flagellation as witnessed in Persia in 1926, cf. H. Nicolson, Diaries and Letters, 1930–1939 (London, 1966), p. 31. In the glossary of an account of life in a convent of Poor Clares at the present day, there is the definition: "Discipline—a small scourge." Cf. Sister Mary Francis, A Right to be Merry (London, 1907), p. 212.

[41] Cf. J. Joergensen, Saint François d'Assise (Paris, 1922), p. 70; F. Rosen, Die Natur in der Kunst (Leipzig, 1903), p. 5.

A late tradition records that the encounter took place at Caprignone where a fresco shows Francis putting on a ragged garment.

ponents. Probably he was not fully aware of these mental processes. His narratives of icy austerities reach an extreme beyond all credibility (2 *Cel.* 206). He comments: "Another brother went in winter to a nunnery on some errand of compassion without being aware of the Saint's strong objection to such a visit. When the fact became known to the Saint, he made the brother walk several miles naked when the snow was deep on the ground." For a number of reasons we may dismiss this as a fabrication (pp. 47, 232). It is scarcely credible that a naked man could flounder for miles through deep snow and survive. Also, it is difficult to believe, however callous some Italian peasants may have been, that they would not have hounded from their midst a community that turned out one of their number stark naked to almost certain death in the snow. In the background of such stories was the medieval convention that as lust could be described in terms of heat its best antidote was cold. Thus Bonaventura (v. 3) remarks: "He was wont in the winter season to plunge into a ditch full of snow, that he might both utterly subdue the foe within him, and might preserve his white robe of chastity from the fire of lust. He would maintain that it was beyond compare more tolerable for a spiritual man to bear intense cold in his body, than to feel the heat of carnal lust, were it but a little, in his mind."

Frustrated eroticism colours these attitudes. The picture of Francis as a merciless and unjust disciplinarian is obviously a caricature of the man who, when he appeared among the crusading troops in Egypt, was thus described by an independent observer, Jacques de Vitry: "The leader of the Order is called Brother Francis, who is so lovable that he is held in reverence by all men." [42]

Celano was not alone among Francis's biographers in using this cluster of associations. The *Mirror of Perfection* (61) relates that Francis, as a penance for eating meat and while still suffering from an attack of malaria, had himself dragged naked with a rope round his neck to the market place in Assisi where he confessed his sin to the crowd. Bonaventura (vi. 2), anxious to temper the wind to the shorn lamb and in the interests of delicacy or prudery, remarks that he retained his breeches. We are to interpret the rope as a halter to

[42] G. Golubovich, *Bibilioteca della Terra Santa e dell'Oriente Francescano* I (Florence, 1906), 7.

lead Brother Ass (*Bon.* v. 4). Bizarre as this story is, some readers, aware of the lengths to which medieval ascetics sometimes went in mortifying the flesh, might be inclined to accept it as true were it not that emphasis is laid on its being a time of "very intense frost." The biographers vied with one another in exaggerating such austerities. Could a man even of the strongest constitution have survived such treatment? Clearly these writers are mythmaking, ringing changes on the theme, penance, nakedness, ice or snow, and the ass.

This image cluster appears also in the *Fioretti* (*4th consid. of stigmata*). We hear of Francis, benighted on a journey, sleeping in the snow with a man who had lent him an ass. By placing his hand on him as he lay by his side, the saint warmed him so that he felt as if he were a "fiery furnace." The owner of the ass was wont to declare afterward that he had never slept better in his life. This fable has its counterpart elsewhere in the *Fioretti* (24). Francis, instead of miraculously generating heat, is said to have been miraculously resistant to it. He strips himself naked and invites a prostitute to do likewise and lie with him on the "burning hearth" of a fierce fire. The happy outcome is her conversion.[43]

Saint Francis's biographers not only thought in terms of linked ideas and copied from each other but were strongly influenced by earlier hagiographers. The manufacturer of the fable concerning the saint, the temptress, and the fiery furnace remembered Daniel's ordeal (Dan. iii. 1–30) and probably also the tales told by Sulpicius Severus. It would seem that the compiler of the *Fioretti* probably knew of similar stories in the writings of Gregory the Great, Fredegar, and others, and had heard stories of the Irish saints who were able miraculously to create warmth—such legends as that told of St. Ciaran who warmed the water in which his frailer companion was keeping ascetic vigil with him and the saying about Saint Brigid that when she put her finger in the river "out went the hatching-mother of the cold." [44]

The prominence given to the endurance of cold in the Franciscan

[43] Tamassia, *op. cit.*, pp. 92, 110 for the sources of such stories.

[44] Lady Gregory, *A Book of Saints and Wonders* (London, 1920), p. 12; J. Pinkerton, *Lives of the Scottish Saints* I (Paisley, 1889) 136; W. J. Rees, *Lives of the Cambro-British Saints* (Llando-very, 1853), p. 105.

narratives is explicable in the light of the Irish tradition of immersion in river, lake, or sea as a devotional exercise, an ascetic discipline that arose in the Near East, was transferred to Ireland, and was observed by Celtic ascetics in England and on the Continent. Bede describes a monk in Northumbria breaking the ice in the river in order to do penance standing in it.[45] It cannot be coincidence that, in the Near East, Ireland, and Italy, saints reputed to have sustained these chilly ordeals were also famous for their friendships with animals. Nor can it be accidental that the conclusions to the stories of Saint Cuthbert's all-night vigil in the sea and Saint Francis's nocturnal figure-fashioning in the snow are so similar. In both narratives a member of the fraternity spies on the saint, sees him plunge into the sea or snow, and is detected by the saint and cautioned not to reveal what he has seen until after the saint is dead. As the account of Cuthbert being warmed and dried by otters after his vigil in the sea was included in *The Golden Legend*, we may assume that it was current on the Continent when the *Fioretti* was compiled.

In contrast with the peculiar inventions and compilations of those who so misguidedly thought to honour Saint Francis by narrating them, we have a down-to-earth account of what it was like to live with Francis which has a ring of truth not apparent in the stories we have been considering. The following is a deposition made to Thomas of Pavia, Provincial Minister of Tuscany, and is quoted by Wadding under the year 1258:

I, Brother Stephen, dwelt for a few months in a certain hermitage with Saint Francis and other brethren, to care for their beds and their kitchen; and this was our manner of life by command of the Founder. We spent the forenoon hours in prayer and silence, until the sound of a board called us to dinner. Now the Holy Master was wont to leave his cell about the third hour; and if he saw no fire in the kitchen he would go down into the garden and pluck a handful of herbs which he brought home, saying, "Cook these, and it will be well with the Brethren." And whereas at times I was wont to set before him eggs and milk and food which the faithful had sent us,

---

[45] Bede, *Ecclesiastical History* V. xii; E. Dawes and N. H. Baynes, *Three Byzantine Saints* (Oxford, 1948), pp. 88–185; L. Gougaud, *Devotional and Ascetic Practices in the Middle Ages*, trans. C. C. Bateman (London, 1927), pp. 159–178.

with some sort of gravy stew, then he would eat cheerfully with the rest and say, "Thou hast done too much, Brother; I will that thou prepare nought for the morrow, nor do aught in my kitchen." So I, following his precepts absolutely, in all points, cared for nothing so much as to obey that most holy man; when therefore he came, and saw the table laid with divers crusts of bread, he would begin to eat gaily thereof, but presently he would chide me that I brought no more, asking me why I had cooked nought. Whereto I answered, "for that thou, Father, badest me cook none." But he would say, "Dear son, discretion is a noble virtue, nor shouldst thou always fulfil all that thy Superior biddeth thee, especially when he is troubled by any passion."

This Saint Francis is a very human person expecting his companions not to take themselves or all he says too seriously. At his board there is gaiety and tolerance; around the hermitage is a vegetable garden and kindly neighbours see that the friars do not live in want. No man, it is said, is a hero to his valet, but Francis's cook spoke of him as his Holy Master all the more sincerely because he knew he had some frailties as well as great holiness.

The Christmas Crib

It is pleasant to turn from Celano's pious and well-intentioned but deplorable misrepresentations to the account of a delightful winter scene, the cave at Greccio where Francis arranged the Nativity tableau which has had so much influence in bringing the Christmas Crib into innumerable churches throughout Christendom. In every way this presentation was characteristic of him, for thus he expressed dramatically his devotion to Christ, his simplicity, gaiety and gentleness, love for men and animals, the imagination of a child together with the insight and ecstasy of the mystic. Possibly his own vivid recollections of the Holy Land helped to inspire the special character of this celebration.

A fortnight before Christmas he asked his friend the Lord of Greccio, Giovanni Velita, for his aid in making Greccio "a new Bethlehem." [46] The Crib was set up, lined with hay, and an ox and

[46] The Franciscan "Spirituals" who, contrary to the majority, adhered as closely as possible to the principles of Saint Francis, developed the parallels between their founder and Jesus Christ to such an extent that they came under

an ass led in. "The night was lit up as the day, and was delightsome to men and beasts . . . the woodland rang with voices, the rocks made answer to the jubilant throng." Francis was deeply moved, and Mass was celebrated above the Manger, beside which the two animals had been placed (1 *Cel.* 84; *Bon.* x. 7). The valorous knight Giovanni, who was in the congregation, declared that he beheld a beautiful Baby asleep in the manger. It seemed to him that He awakened when Francis took Him up in his arms. This representation of the Nativity created a great impression in the countryside. Celano reports that sick animals were cured by eating hay from the Crib, women in childbirth were relieved by placing some of it on themselves, and ailing folk were cured by visiting the grotto (pl. 18).[47]

The saint was interpreting in his own way a tradition of long standing which, indeed, may be traced to ancient observances at Bethlehem itself. When we try to determine the origin of a church custom, we often find that no precise point of origin in place or time can be located, and so it is with the Christmas Crib. From the ninth century the Introit in the Mass for Christmas (and Easter) was supplemented by a question sung by the choir answered by the congregation. This antiphonal singing evolved into drama as deacons and cantors impersonated shepherds and Magi with concealed boy choristers singing the Gloria in Excelsis.[48] Customs evolve and sometimes arise from the marriage of two or more traditions. Acted repre-

---

the condemnation of the Church. Bartholomew of Pisa in the *Book of the Conformities* approved by the Chapter General in 1399 set forward forty resemblances between them. Among geographical parallels besides Greccio as Bethlehem, Monte Colomba was regarded as a new Sinai because Francis had meditated there before going to Rome. He was thought of as receiving a new Decalogue from the hands of Jesus.

[47] He tells us that miracles were wrought with the parings of the saint's fingernails (2 *Cel.* 42), the reins of his horse and the cord with which he had girded himself (1 *Cel.* 63, 64). Bonaventura (vii. 11) refers to cracks in a wall being mended by placing some of his hairs in them. Such miracles had been conventional hagiography for centuries. Bede (*Eccl. Hist.* III. ii.) mentions a man's broken arm being cured by placing under it moss from a wooden cross erected by King Oswald before engaging the enemy.

[48] E. K. Chambers, *The Medieval Stage* II (Oxford, 1903), 8 ff; C. Davidson, *English Mystery Plays* (Yale, 1892); K. Young, *The Drama of the Medieval Church* (Oxford, 1935).

sentations of the events of the Nativity preceded the static Crib with Figures—for church celebrations, including the Eucharist, have always tended to be to some extent re-enactments of the event commemorated.

Francis must have seen the Praesepe, the *Bambino* in the Crib, in churches. In Rome there were cribs he might have visited in Santa Maria in Trastevere and the chapel of Santa Maria ad Praesepe.[49]

Bonaventura, who was apparently unaware of, or ignored, earlier Christmas Cribs, says that to avoid appearing to be an innovator Francis sought prior permission from the Pope for the presentation of the Crib scene; but Celano makes no mention of this, and we may assume Bonaventura to have inserted it in his anxiety to show that everything the Poverello did was approved and orthodox. Incidentally, his stated concern that "this might not seem an innovation" (*Bon.* x. 7) strengthens the case for believing that he and the other biographers who made no apology for introducing animal stories were aware that they were following tradition and had no fear that in showing Francis to have had special concern for animals he would be regarded as an innovator or unorthodox. Apart from the hagiographical tradition of friendliness toward animals, which we have seen to underlie stories in the Franciscan Legend, the saint's outlook might well have seemed, in contrast to the brutality of the age, a questionable eccentricity if not savouring of heresy. It was well known that the heretical Cathari had peculiar views about animals.[50]

[49] Father Cuthbert, *The Life of St. Francis* (London, 1912), p. 394; N. de Robeck, *The Christmas Crib* (London, 1938); E. Delaruelle, "La Pietà popolare alla fine del Medioevo," in *Relazione del X Congresso Internazionale di Scienze Storiche* III, 515–537. Cf. also in this volume (pp. 419–466) another essay by this writer in which he attributes devotion to the *Bambino* to the influence of the Greccio Crib, "L'influence de Saint François d'Assise sur la piété populaire."

[50] Tamassia's suggestion (*op. cit.*, pp. 103–106) that Celano's account of the Praesepe at Greccio is a story comparable with other medieval legends to counter aspects of heresy is, like some of his other suggestions, speculative and unconvincing. John of Parma, Minister General of this Order for nearly ten years, who is likely to have known the true traditions of the place, lived for some years at Greccio. But, in view of what we know of Celano's ability to embellish themes, J. R. H. Moorman's argument (*A New Fioretti* [London, 1946], p. 62) that

In staging the Nativity Tableau in a cave with living animals, Francis was indeed developing the Praesepe in a novel way and yet returning, as he had done in other ways, to the primitive Gospel. Just as he took the Gospel beyond the confines of church and monastery along the roads and hill-paths, across the sea and into the Egyptian wilderness, he brought the drama and romance of the Nativity from its ecclesiastical setting back to the countryside and into a cave such as he must have seen if he had visited Bethlehem.[51]

the detailed narrative indicates he is giving personal reminiscences is also uncon- vincing. Celano and Bonaventura romanticize the episode, but this is no reason to believe it to be unhistorical.

[51] This cave, still the goal of many thousands of pilgrims annually, was de- scribed by Bishop Arculf to Adamnan, Columcille's biographer, when his ship was driven by a tempest on to the western coast of Britain (*De Locis Sanctis*). Bede (*Eccl. Hist.* V. xvi) quotes his report. "There is a sort of natural half cave, the outward part whereof is said to have been the place where our Lord was born; the inner is called our Lord's manger. This cave is all covered with rich marble, over the place where our Lord is said particularly to have been born, and over it is the great church of St. Mary." The Cave of the Nativity is still as described. Nothing is known of Francis's itinerary in the Holy Land, but Paul Sabatier (*The Life of St. Francis of Assisi* [London, 1920], 231) pointed out that if he set out shortly after the fall of Damietta on 5 November 1219 he could easily have reached Bethlehem by Christmas.

Lo Spagna (Giovanni di Pietro) who died in 1528 depicted the Nativity scene set out of doors, the ox and ass sheltered by a flimsy straw roof supported on a rock in the lee of which two of the figures are kneeling. An extensive landscape is shown in the background. Probably the artist was motivated more by the desire to include a landscape than by the thought of a Christmas Crib in a grotto.

In connexion with Francis's visit to Egypt and the Holy Land there are discrepancies in the number of companions said to have accompanied him. According to the *Fioretti* (24; cf. 7, 13) and contrary to Celano (1 *Cel.* 55) and Bonaventura (ix. 8), who speak of one companion with him when he set out to try to convert the Soldan, Francis took twelve friars with him. In the *Legend of the Three Companions* (46) it is stated that he chose eleven men to go with him to see the Pope. Perhaps it was thought that one so humble as the saint would not be likely to form a group in which he might be misrepresented as appearing in the relationship of Christ to the Apostles. The writer of the *Fioretti* may be following Irish tradition as he does in regard to some other matters. Saint Columban set out from Ireland with twelve companions, and on the High Cross of Arboe thirteen figures appear, one with a crosier. Cf. R. Flower, "The Irish High Crosses," *Journ. of Warburg and Courtauld Institutes* XVII (1954), 94. The Irish referred to Christ as "the great abbot" and thought

The peasants' beasts of burden, too often harshly treated, were not regarded by him merely as animate accessories or spectators in the representation of the Incarnation. By virtue of participating in this sacramental act, they acquired status as living manifestations of the condescension and bounty of the Creator as, in his view, a flock of birds could symbolize, and in a sense actually be, an angelic choir, and a tree could inspire reverence because it expressed and participated in the sacredness of the Cross (p. 11). So he had a care for these beasts, recognized that they should have a share in Christmas jubilation, and declared that a special feed of corn should be provided for the farm animals and grain spread for the birds. Even when Christmas fell on a Friday, it should be kept with feasting; and no doubt with a twinkle in his eye he remarked that the very walls might eat flesh that day—or at least they could be greased! (2 Cel. 199–200; Spec. Perf. 114). Thus occasionally Celano lets us glimpse the humour and humanity of the Little Poor Man.

The Greccio Crib illustrates and emphasizes the saint's realism as well as his romanticism. He was not philosophic nor in the least inclined to abstract conceptions or theological niceties. He thought in pictures and set himself to realize them. Building up the Church meant for him setting stone upon stone with his own hands, tending the sick meant kissing lepers, contemplation of the Nativity was not allowed to remain an inward vision, the Crucifixion wounds were realized in his own body.

The romanticism of Francis, in harmony with that of his age, had the happy effect of stirring the imagination and inspiring quaint, edifying tales, such as some of those in the *Fioretti* and later Franciscan writings. Among these is an account of the Nativity con-

---

of Saint Patrick as judge of all Irishmen in the Judgement Day. Cf. Gougaud, *op. cit.* (1923), p. 103. Thus a missionary group of thirteen was not as incongruous in Irish circles as it evidently seemed to the author of *The Legend of the Three Companions*. However, there is at least one record from another Celtic area, Brittany (Armorica), of a Christian community of eleven men with another, Saint Guenolé, as leader. Cf. J. Decarreaux, *Monks and Civilization* (London, 1964), p. 183. In Greek and Roman religion, multiples of three, including twelve, were important.

tained in *Meditations on the Life of Christ*, at one time attributed to Saint Bonaventura but correctly assigned in the *Conformities* of Bartholomew of Pisa to a later Franciscan, Joannes de Caulibus.

When Mary and Joseph set out for Bethlehem, they went as poor cattle dealers. As they could not find suitable accommodation, they took refuge where they could in one of the covered ways of the city. (Bethlehem was thought of as built with arcades and covered ways like Italian cities.) Mary wrapped the Babe in her flimsy head veil and leaned against a pillar. When she laid Him down, "the ox and the ass bent their knees and stretched their heads over the manger, breathing through their nostrils as though they knew by the light of reason that the Babe, so miserably clad, needed their warmth at such a time of bitter cold." [52]

This lovely fancy of the beasts participating in the rejoicing at Christ's crude cradle became at an early date part of the Christian heritage and recurred in folklore, literature, and art down the centuries.[53] In Spain the Cockcrow Mass or Mass of the Cock (*Missa in Gallicantu*) at Christmas derives its title from a legend which relates that the cock proclaimed with flapping wings *Christus natus est*, the ox bellowed *Ubi*, the goats and sheep bleated *Bethlehem*, the crow cawed *Quando*, and the ass brayed *Eamus*. In England, too, there is a tradition that the cock announced the Holy Birth. From Brittany to Lithuania it is said that the animals acquire the power of speech at Christmas—a belief that has been transplanted to the United States. The bees are said to sing in their hives at Christmas time. English and Irish stories relate that the animals join in worship of the infant Christ, and an English legend, also known in the United States, describes how the animals may be found kneeling in their stables and byres at midnight of the Eve of Old Christmas (5 January). A Herefordshire farmer declared that on this night he saw his cattle kneeling with tears streaming down their faces. It was also said in some districts that the cattle acknowledged the sanctity of

---

[52] Coulton, *op. cit.* I (1928), 109–111.

[53] H. Thode, *Franz von Assisi in Italien* (Berlin, 1885), pp. 413–415. In Piero della Francesca's picture of the Nativity, a braying ass joins in the angel chorus.

Christmas by bowing three times to the east. In the well-known carol, "Good Christian Men, Rejoice," translated by J. M. Neale, there is the line: "Ox and ass before him bow." [54]

Thomas Hardy's poem was inspired by a local Dorsetshire folk tradition:

THE OXEN

Christmas Eve, and twelve of the clock.
"Now they are all on their knees,"
An elder said as we sat in a flock
By the embers in hearthside ease.

We pictured the meek mild creatures where
They dwelt in their strawy pen,
Nor did it occur to one of us there
To doubt they were kneeling then.

The Crib of Greccio may, perhaps, have had an effect in encouraging artists to portray the Nativity with the attendant animals, but the theme is much older than the thirteenth century and was introduced from the East, to be adopted in due course by Italian painters. The earliest representations are carved scenes on sarcophagi of the Visit of the Magi dating from the first half of the fourth century. This Byzantine Nativity convention lasted for some 1300 years. The ox and ass are represented in a fresco in the church of Santa Maria Antiqua at Rome which dates from the beginning of the eighth century, and they appear in an illustration of the ninth-century Sacramentary of Saint Géreon at Paris.[55] The Codex of Hitda, now at Darmstadt, dating from the beginning of the tenth century, depicts the animals, and a Greek ivory of the eleventh century shows the heads of the ox and ass leaning over the Infant, with underneath, *The Bath of the Infant*.

In eleventh-century miniatures the setting is a mountain cave. Particularly beautiful is the menologion of the Emperor Basileios

---

[54] E. and M. A. Radford, *Encyclopaedia of Superstitions*, ed. C. Hole (London, 1969), pp. 38, 88; Stith Thompson, *Motif-Index of Folk-literature, passim*.

[55] G. Cames, *Byzance et la peinture Romane de Germanie* (Paris, 1966), pls. 17, 35.

II in the Vatican Library, dating from about A.D. 1000. A shepherd with his sheep stands outside the cave with a tree near by and wild flowers at his feet. The ox and ass bend over the Holy Child. The practice of depicting the animals' heads appearing through an opening immediately above the manger may have encouraged the idea that they were kneeling—and, indeed, an ox in its usual resting posture could be imaginatively regarded as kneeling.

Byzantine influence is still apparent in fifteenth century representations in the West, but from the late thirteenth century onward increasing humanization and unconventionality is evident in the introduction of birds into Adoration scenes either of the Magi or shepherds. The goldfinch, symbolic of the soul, the Passion, the Crucifixion, and the Redemption, is most frequent, but the swallow, representing the Resurrection, or the titmouse, fertility, is sometimes depicted in the Child's hand. Occasionally the symbolic lamb is shown.[56]

No doubt there was a two-way relationship between painted and dramatic representations of the Nativity in some milieux. During the twelfth century mimes which sometimes became elaborated into one-act plays were performed in church by the clergy. The most usual themes were the Nativity and the Resurrection. An illustration in Harrad von Landsberg's *Hortus Deliciarum* (ca. 1180) depicting the visit of the Three Wise Men gives an idea of what such scenes were like. According to the *Ordinarium* of Amiens (1291), the visit of the Magi was symbolized by the movement of a Star across the choir. Evidently these performances lent themselves to disorder, for Innocent III, the Pope who had sanctioned preaching by Francis and his friends, forbade *ludi theatrales* in church. Nevertheless they continued in fourteenth-century France, embodying the various strands of tradition already mentioned. At Rouen the crib was set behind the altar, the shepherds entered by the great gates of the

[56] H. Friedmann, *The Symbolic Goldfinch* (Washington, 1946), *passim*; Friedmann, "The Iconography of an Altarpiece by Botticini," *Bull. Metrop. Mus. Art* (Summer 1969), p. 121; K. Kunstle, *Ikonographie der Christlichen Kunst*, III (Frieburg, i. B., 1926–28); E. Mâle, *Religious Art in France, XIII Century*, trans. D. Nussey (London, 1913); Mâle, *Religious Art from the Twelfth to the Eighteenth Century* (London, 1941); G. Ristow, *The Nativity* (Recklinghausen, 1967); trans. by H. H. Rosenwald of *Die Geburt Christi*.

choir, a child perched on a dais enacted the part of the angel, and two priests, robed in dalmatics, stood by the crib, representing midwives—as depicted in early paintings of the Nativity. The Magi entered in procession, then fell asleep and were warned by an angel to return another way. Earlier than this, religious plays were being performed elsewhere than in church. It should be noted, also, that Francis was not unique in arranging for living animals to feature in a representation of the Gospel narrative. Prior to the Crib of Greccio, dramatic church performances in France on the festival of the Holy Innocents included a procession of white-robed children preceded by a lamb with a cross attached to its back.[57]

Probably we have a reminiscence of the impression created by the Nativity presentation at Greccio in the story told in the *Vita e Fioretti di San Francesco* (1477) describing how Francis himself was born in a stable. Pica, we are told, was carried into the stable to give birth, and a chapel was erected to commemorate the event. Thus, in this way, as in many other respects, parallels were found between the saint and Christ. Sedulius, who published his *Historia Seraphica* at Antwerp in 1613 stated that he had seen the stable at Assisi transformed into a chapel. A fifteenth-century inscription over the door of this chapel of San Francesco il Piccolo at Assisi declares:

> *Hoc oratorium fuit bovis et asini stabulum*
> *In quo natus est Franciscus mundi speculum.*

Benozzo Gozzoli (1452) represented the scene on the walls of the church of San Francesco at Montefalco with the ox and ass beside the crib (pl. 15).[58]

Appropriately, Celano concludes the First Part of his *Vita Prima*

[57] Davidson, *op. cit.*, pp. 50 ff; Petit de Julleville, *Les Mystères*, I, *Histoire du Théatre en France en Moyen Age* (Paris, 1880), pp. 15, 52 ff. An early life of Saint Francis in French verse includes a description of the Christmas festivities at Greccio. It appears as an appendix to E. Chavin de Malan, *Histoire de Saint François d'Assise* (Paris, 1845), pp. 449–452.

[58] Thode, *op. cit.*, p. 413; cf. also p. 427 for a quotation from Bonaventura's *Meditationes vitae Christi* giving a description of the ox and ass kneeling at the manger and warming the Babe with their breath. Elaborate Neapolitan Crib groups including as many as thirty figures fetch £600 on the London market as antiques.

with the description of the Christmas festivities in the cave at Greccio. He leaves us with this vision of Francis enraptured among the joyful throng with the ox and ass standing by:

> The brethren sang, yielding due praises to the Lord, and all that night sounded with jubilation. The Saint of God stood before the manger, full of sighs, overcome with tenderness and filled with wondrous joy. . . . Then he preached to the people who stood around, and uttered mellifluous words concerning the birth of the poor King and the little town of Bethlehem. . . . Finally the place of the manger was hallowed as a temple to the Lord; and in honour of the most blessed Father Francis, over the manger an altar was reared and a church dedicated.[59]

[59] It has been said of Francis that he was "the precursor if not the parent of the carol." Cf. P. Dearmer, *The Oxford Book of Carols* (Oxford, 1928), p. vi. Perhaps the well-known carol by Bishop Phillips Brooks, "O Little Town of Bethlehem" may owe some inspiration to the phrase used by Celano.

❦ V ❦
The "Small Deer" of Saint Francis

Invertebrate animals are, on the whole, less interesting to man than birds and mammals, except, indeed, when they force his attention upon them as parasites or pests or can be used as food. The majority are relatively small; many remain under cover and are inconspicuous in coloration as well as secretive in behaviour. Moreover, it is much easier to feel some affinity with birds and some mammals than, for instance, molluscs, beetles, or spiders, though butterflies, being brightly coloured, dainty, quick-moving, sun-loving, aerial creatures have long attracted attention and been regarded by some peoples as disembodied souls. Those who have a deep regard for nature seldom lack interest in the smaller animals, and significantly, they have some importance in the Franciscan story, though, as we might expect, not nearly so much prominence as birds; but the references to "small deer" illuminate the character of Saint Francis, the outlook of his biographers, and the nature of early Franciscanism.

The Lowly Worm

Celano (1 *Cel.* 80) gives us a vivid picture of the Poverello striding along, probably through his beloved woods, noticing a worm on the path and placing it tenderly amid the vegetation by the wayside. Mention of the incident inspires the biographer to ask: "Who could ever express the height of the affection by which he was carried away as concerning all the things that are God's?"

> Who could tell the sweetness he enjoyed in contemplating in His creatures the wisdom, power and goodness of the Creator? Truly such thoughts often filled him with wondrous and unspeakable joy as he beheld the sun, or raised his eyes to the moon, or gazed on the stars and the firmament. O simple piety! O pious simplicity! Even towards little worms he glowed with exceeding love, because

he had read that word concerning the Saviour: "I am a worm and no man" [Psalm xxii. 6],[1] wherefore he used to pick them up in the way and put them in a safe place, that they might not be crushed by the feet of passers-by.

Voragine quoted this final sentence in *The Golden Legend* (*Vita Sancti Francisci*). Thus not only may we assume that he had read Celano, but we can be confident his widely read book was important in transmitting to later generations a realization of Francis's compassion for lowly, despised creatures.

In confessing his sins, Saint Francis referred to himself in the phraseology of the time, adopted from Scripture (Job xxiv. 20), as "the vilest of worms," so his care for creatures which he, and people in general, regarded as of a particularly base order of life is noteworthy. His sacramental attitude is thus evident. The Incarnation sanctified all life. As the Saviour had come manifesting God in human form, so God could and did represent Himself or symbolize His Nature to mankind in the creatures of His Creation—whether worms or birds, trees or flowers, fragrance or fire, water or rocks, sun or moon. They were all outward signs of divine grace. Francis, overwhelmed by God's goodness in manifesting Himself in innumerable ways to man, not only appreciated and gave thanks for the beauty, interest, and wonder of all the earth affords but felt that such beauty must naturally call forth tenderness and reverence. In the midst of natural beauty, he was on holiday with God. Only those who in some measure are nature mystics and know the ineffable delight of being surrounded by loveliness far beyond their capacity to appreciate can understand the joyousness of the saint's spirit. Every living thing shone with Divine radiance. God was revealing Himself, and man had but to look, listen, and worship to be carried to high heaven.

When Francis lifted worms from the path or spread grain for the birds in winter, he was very far from thinking in terms of the sentimental secularism that has appropriated to itself the ancient and honourable title of humanism. To him it was self-evident that animals possessed rights, notably the Divine dispensation of life. In his comments on living things, plants as well as animals, he accepted im-

1 A medieval interpretation of the text.

plicitly and proclaimed by word and action that they had dignity because of their value in the sight of God. It is man's privilege, as well as joy, to recognize that this is so. In accepting this point of view as axiomatic, Saint Francis followed Saint Ciaran of Clonmacnoise who included all Creation in his affections: *verum et in creaturarum irrationabilium necessitatibus infatigabilem ostenderet affectum.*[2]

It might seem that the Poverello's care for worms and insects sprang from motives similar to those that prompted Buddhist monks in pre-communist China to carry a staff fitted with jingling rings to warn small creatures to flee to safety and still influence Jain holy men to brush any spot before they sit down lest they should crush some insect or other organism; but Francis's motivation was quite different. The doctrine of *Ahimsā*, renunciation of the will to hurt or kill, dates from as early as the seventh century B.C., about the time when the Jains originated. It became prominent in their teaching as well as in Hinduism and Buddhism and led to animals being treated with consideration; but it was belief in reincarnation, not intensity of compassion, which provided the justification for avoiding the molestation or slaughter of animals. This Eastern tradition lived on among some of the Cathari of Saint Francis's time. No one who has observed how effectively the trees and herbage cherished by the monks in Chinese monasteries provided sanctuaries for wild life would wish to minimize the value for the conservation of nature of these doctrines, but there is a deep gulf between the motivation of the Franciscan friar sparing animals pain for the love of God and the Far Eastern monk inspired by fear lest, in injuring an insect, he may be inflicting suffering on such as he himself may become. Albert Schweitzer wrote of the Buddha: "He was no Francis of Assisi."[3] True, indeed, but outstanding scholar, musician, and exemplification of Christian compassion as he was, Schweitzer had no close personal experience of Buddhism in the Far East and failed to give adequate emphasis to the compassionate outlook generated as a secondary growth in many of its adherents by the doctrine of *Ahimsā*. To

[2] C. Plummer, *Vitae Sanctae Hiberniae* I (Oxford, 1910), 200.
[3] *Indian Thought and its Development* (London, 1936), pp. 99–104.

quote but one illustration: A story in the Jātakas relates that Gotama saw a starving tiger and "though composed in mind was shaken with compassion by the sufferings of his fellow-creature as Mount Meru is by an earthquake." [4]

It has been necessary to emphasize the distinction between the Eastern and Franciscan attitudes toward animals, especially in regard to minor organisms, yet Celano's account of the saint's concern for the worm savours of Eastern ideas. Certainly close parallels in prior Western thought are difficult to find, notwithstanding the sympathetic attitude of Celtic Christianity to animal life. The episode may best be regarded as evidence of such ideas pervading the ethos of the age and being assimilated unconsciously. It would be to go beyond the evidence—as some have been ready to do—to identify this vein of thought with the Catharist doctrines which, as we have seen, Francis and his biographers would have repudiated emphatically; but sympathy with lowly forms of life was nurtured as a by-product of the drifting, pervasive Oriental doctrines that elsewhere had been embodied in pantheist or dualist creeds. To Francis's mystical mind these intimations of affinity with Creation in all its manifestations were congenial, and they became sacramentalized as integral elements in his outlook. Support for this view is provided by a remarkable passage in the *Opuscula* attributed to Francis:

> Holy Charity overcomes all the temptations of the devil and the flesh, and all the fears of the flesh. Holy Obedience overcomes all carnal desires, and keeps the body under discipline, ready to obey its brother in the spirit; it renders a man submissive to all things in this world, not only to men but even to wild beasts, so that they may do their will with him in whatsoever way God may permit.[5]

Man should subordinate himself to the animals in so far as he believes they are the instruments of God's will. Here, again, is the vision of the Earthly Paradise in which man and beast are in harmony. This is at the opposite pole from the mentality that boasts

[4] J. B. Pratt, *The Pilgrimage of Buddhism* (New York, 1928), p. 93.
[5] *Opuscula S. Patris Francisci*, ed. L. Lemmens, *Bibliotheca Francisca Ascetica* I (Quaracchi, 1904), 21; L. Sherley-Price, *S. Francis of Assisi, His Life and Writings* (London, 1959), p. 166.

of man's conquest of nature and arrogantly regards the human species as entitled to exploit the material environment in defiance of its status as God's Creation and regardless of his own true nature as a spiritual being.

The saint's reverence for Creation was carried to an extreme in his attitude to fire. When his face was about to be cauterized with a hot iron in an effort to remedy his eye ailment, he said: "My Brother Fire, noble and useful among all other creatures, be kindly to me in this hour, because formerly I have loved thee for the love of Him who created thee." Even when his clothes caught fire, he was reluctant to have them extinguished, and he objected to glowing wood being carelessly thrown out; it should be set on the ground "on account of the reverence for Him of Whom it is the creature" (*Spec. Perf.* 115, 116). If we are to assess the saint's attitude toward nature, we must take no less account of this intensity of response than of the tales of his dealings with birds and beasts in which it is depicted in picturesque and imaginative detail.

For Christian parallels to this intense nature mysticism, we have to go to the Christian mystics of the East. According to one of these saints, the sincere follower of Christ experiences "a kindling of the heart for all creation—for mankind, the birds, the animals, the demons, the whole creation. And whenever he thinks of them or contemplates them, tears pour from his eyes, because of the strong sympathy which possesses his heart." [6] As it is difficult to point to Christian nature mystics in the West with this kind of outlook prior to Francis, apart from, to a lesser degree, the Irish, it has been too readily assumed that his nature mysticism was derived from heretical, pantheist sources. Historians frequently refer to the importation of Eastern ideas to Europe as a consequence of trade relations and the Crusades. We are well informed concerning the heresies they generated, but insufficient attention has been paid to the influence in Europe of the Eastern Christian mystical outlook. [7]

[6] Isaac the Syrian, 48, Sermon. Eng. trans. A. J. Wensinck, *Mystic Treatises by Isaac of Nineveh* (Amsterdam, 1923).

[7] This tradition may be traced back to the *Book of Revelation*. The persistence of Christian nature mysticism in the East is sufficiently indicated by a

Bees and Flies

Insects evoked the Little Poor Man's practical sympathy. "He ordered honey and the best wine to be provided for bees that they might not perish from want in the cold of winter. He called by the name of brother all animals, though in all their kinds the gentle were his favourites" (2 *Cel.* 165; cf. 1 *Cel.* 80). Nowadays it is routine practice for beekeepers to feed ill-provided stocks in winter by means of an appliance containing syrup or honey introduced at the top of the hive; but before modern hives were available, honey was obtained in the autumn by smoking out the colonies from the skeps. This was an unpleasant, wasteful, and dysgenic procedure as the most efficient strains tended to be eliminated. Using a bee excluder and a centrifugal extractor, the beekeeper now obtains the honey without damaging the frames and combs or causing casualties among the bees.

The saint's kind-heartedness was well intentioned, though it is very doubtful whether wine, except perhaps in minute traces, is good for bees. They tend to become stupefied when they suck over ripe fruit in autumn. In Italy there was a tradition more than twelve centuries old of giving it to the wintering stocks. Virgil's instructions to the beekeeper were to gather clumps of *Aster amellus*, a plant wth a daisy-like, bluish flower: "This plant's roots you must boil in fragrant wine, and set for food at their doors in full baskets." [8] The modern beekeeper would dismiss this as an absurd device to maintain bees in winter. In Italy, except high in the mountains, it is easier to keep bees through the winter than in northern Europe. Nowadays an apiarist considers it something of a reproach to himself if his bees die of hunger in the winter. In preserving his stocks he is, of course, mainly motivated by self-interest; but many beekeepers, like

---

quotation from Dostoievsky. In *The Brothers Karamazov* Zosima remarks: "Love all God's creation, the whole universe, and each grain of sand. Love every leaflet, every ray of God's light; love the beasts, love the plants, love every creature. When you love every creature you will understand the mystery of God in created things."

[8] *Georgics* iv. 271–280.

1. The Sermon to the Birds. Window in the choir of Kloster Königsfelden, Switzerland. Photographer: M. Stittler. Courtesy of Kanton Aargau Denkmalpflege.

2a. The Sermon to the Birds. Matthew Paris. Courtesy of the Master and Fellows, Corpus Christi College, Cambridge.

2b. The Sermon to the Birds. Eton College. Courtesy of the Provost and Fellows.

2c. The Sermon to the Birds. Luttrell Psalter. Courtesy of the British Museum.

3. The Sermon to the Birds. Giotto. Courtesy of the Louvre, Paris.

4. St. Francis gives his cloak to a poor knight. Giotto.
Upper Basilica of San Francesco, Assisi. Courtesy of Fratelli Alinari.

5. St. Clare reading. Courtesy of Bibliothèque Nationale, Paris.

6. St. Francis receiving the stigmata. Beaufort Psalter.
Courtesy of British Museum.

7. St. Francis and incidents of his life. Bonaventura Berlinghieri.
San Francesco, Pescia. Courtesy of Fratelli Alinari.

8. St. Francis and scenes from his life. Unknown master of the Sienese school. Courtesy of Fratelli Alinari.

9.   St. Francis converts the Wolf of Gubbio. Sassetta.
Courtesy of the National Gallery, London.

10a. A nun playing a psaltery and a Franciscan friar playing a mandolin.

10b. A nun, a Franciscan, a nun, and a Dominican join in a stately dance.

Music and dance among Franciscans. Queen Mary's Psalter.
B. M. Royal 2 B. VII. ff. 176 and 177. Courtesy of British Museum.

11. Christ enthroned. Centrepiece in gilded copper of the altar in the church of Città di Castello, Italy. Photographer: Leonard von Matt.

12. St. Francis in ecstasy. Giovanni Bellini.
Courtesy of Frick Collection, New York.

13. St. Francis presents roses at the altar. Tiberio d'Assisi.
Santa Maria degli Angeli, Assisi. Courtesy of Fratelli Alinari.

14. Landscape with St. Francis. The Stigmatization. Jan Breughel II.
Courtesy of Herner Wengraf Ltd.

15. St. Francis and the Christmas Crib. Gozzoli.
Church of San Francesco, Montefalco.
Courtesy of Fratelli Alinari.

16. The Sermon to the Birds. Wall painting.
Wiston Church, Suffolk. Tim Armstrong,
after a drawing by E. W. Tristram.

17. The Sermon to the Birds. Wall painti
All Saints Church, Little Kimble,
Buckinghamshire. Tim Armstrong, after
sketches by E. A. Armstrong and photogr
by Patrick Armstrong and Ruth Meyler.

18. St. Francis institutes the Christmas Crib at Greccio. Giotto.
Upper Basilica of San Francesco, Assisi. Courtesy of Fratelli Alinari.

19. The Stigmatization of St. Francis. Master of St. Severin.
Courtesy of Wallraf-Richartz-Museum, Cologne.

Saint Francis, have an affection for their bees, and the ancient tradition of "telling the bees" matters of family concern has not yet died out.[9]
The tradition of beekeeping at monasteries goes back to the Desert Fathers. In Ireland it was recorded that Saint Madomnoc introduced beekeeping. The inscription for the festival of the saint on 13 February in the *Félire* or *Calendar of Oengus* records:

> In a little boat from the east,
> over the pure-coloured sea, my
> Domnóc brought—vigorous cry!—
> the gifted race of Ireland's bees.

It was said: "Madomnoc brought bees, the full of his bell." He came from the heart of Ireland to study under Saint David at Menevia in Wales and was given charge of the abbey's wealth, its bees. When he left for Ireland, they would not leave him but followed his ship far out to sea. Saint David open-heartedly acknowledged their love for their bee-master and blessed them, reconciling himself to a future in which bees would no more thrive in Menevia. The story was interpreted later as meaning that the real bees from Menevia were the saints who brought sweet treasures of Christian charity and knowledge to perfume Ireland's woods with the Gospel spirit of tenderness and grace.[10] The custom of keeping bees at monasteries continued and is still maintained, for example, at Buckfast Abbey.

[9] In East Anglia when there was a death in the family, the hives were tapped gently and the bees informed. A piece of crêpe was pinned to the skeps. These practices are reputed to be derived from ancient beliefs that the bees were messengers of the gods, carriers of souls to the hereafter. Cf. G. E. Evans, "Folk Life Studies in East Anglia," in *Studies in Folk Life*, ed. G. Jenkins (London, 1969), pp. 35–46.

[10] *Félire Oéngusso Céli Dé. The Martyrology of Oengus the Culdee*, ed. W. Stokes, Henry Bradshaw Soc., XXIX (London, 1905), 60, 113; *Works of Giraldus Cambrensis*, ed. J. S. Brewer (London, 1861–1891), III, 396–397; L. T. de Barneval, *Legendary History of Ireland*, trans. J. G. Shea (Boston, 1857), p. 97; Sister Donatus, *Beasts and Birds in the Lives of the Early Irish Saints* (Philadelphia, 1934), pp. 98–107. Albeus also brought bees across the sea, calming them by making the sign of the Cross over them. Cf. Plummer, *op. cit.* I (1910), 54.

From ancient times moralists quoted the activities of honey bees as a reproof to the indolent. Francis greatly admired them: "Their nimble activity and their wondrous science could move him to glorifying the wonders of the Lord so enthusiastically that he would often speak of nothing else for a whole day, praising the bees and the other creatures. . . ." These insects, then, as earlier, were regarded as paragons of industry and foresight. In the Septuagint there is an addition to Proverbs vi. 6-8: "Go to the bee, and learn how diligent she is, and what a noble work she produces; whose labour kings and private men use for their health. She is desired by all, and, though weak in strength, yet since she values wisdom she prevails." About 1260 Thomas Cantimpratanus wrote *Bonum Universale de Apibus* in which he exemplified many moral principles from the virtues of bees.

Celano (2 *Cel.* 169) relates a little tale about bees which breathes the poetic fragrance of Franciscan romanticism. The saint once spent forty days of prayer and contemplation in a mountain cell so remote that for a long time afterward it remained unvisited. At length some folk who reverenced him made a pilgrimage to it. They found there an earthen vessel from which he had been accustomed to drink, and within it bees building their cells—surely signifying, says Celano, the sweetness of contemplation the saint had there enjoyed (cf. Ezekiel iii. 3; Psalm xix. 10). He, or his informants, were apparently unaware that honey-bees would not hive in a receptacle so small as a beaker or drinking bowl. Either the vessel was a large pitcher or the bees were of some wild species. But criticism from the point of view of the apiarist is only relevant in so far as it reveals, not the biographer's deficiencies as a naturalist, but his attitude and sources. We may detect in this pleasing anecdote not only the delight in symbolism which underlies so many stories in the Legend but also, perhaps, the echo of ancient tales such as that of Saint Madomnoc who transported honey-bees in his bell, and the Irish priest who, having lost the Host, was aided by pious, obliging bees who carried it to safety and built a dome of wax over it.[11] In this story we have yet another

[11] *Liber Flavus Fergussiorum*, trans. E. J. Gwynn, *Eriu* II, 82: Giraldus Cambrensis, II, 42, 122.
Those interested in associative imagery may notice that Bonaventura (ix. 6),

glimpse of the Earthly Paradise in which God and all His creatures are in harmony.

Francis conjoined the well-worn theme of the lazy drone with an uncomplimentary reference to flies. A certain friar was notorious as being "a friend of the belly" and happy to enjoy what others obtained by their begging. Obviously some of the early disciples were not perfect. He reproved him thus: "Go thy way, brother fly, for thou wouldst eat the sweat of thy brethren and be lazy in God's work. Thou art like brother drone who though he does not undergo the toil of the bees is the first to eat of the honey" (2 *Cel.* 75; *Spec. Perf.* 24; *Leg. Ant.* 62). Unpleasant as the idea of flies sucking perspiration may be, it is an apt description of the social parasite. Playfully, and perhaps facetiously, Francis called these insects "brother," but we may believe the term was used sincerely, for he accepted erring friars as brothers and considered all or practically all animals as within the divine community. He called an idle or stingy fellow "brother fly" and also referred to coins as "flies" (2 *Cel.* 75, 77; *Bon.* v. 6, vii. 3, 10). One of the greatest of his followers, Saint Bernardino, expressed his contempt for money in similar fashion. According to the panegyric by Bernardino da Feltre, Duke Filippo Maria tried to bribe him; but when courtiers arrived bearing a bowl of five hundred golden ducats, he laughed at the sycophants and said: "I value them no more than so many flies." Francis reproved some soldiers for confiding in "fly-gods and pence" (*Spec. Perf.* 22, 24). The insects might be viewed with tolerance, but their connotation in reference to man was mean behaviour. As close-fisted people could be dubbed "flies," so tale-bearers were as biting flies or fleas—to be avoided (2 *Cel.* 182). According to an ancient saying, flies and devils come and go in the same way—*muscas tamquam daemonies venientes*—and should be repelled. A thirteenth-century illustration in the De Quincey *Apocalypse* shows a woman shielding herself from an arrow discharged by a horned, clawed devil while

---

relating a rather trivial anecdote telling how Francis, during Lent, made a little vase and then burnt it—an odd thing to do—introduces the words "flies," "sweetness," and "honey-sweet." It seems that Bonaventura assimilated Celano's tale about the bees and, borrowing its imagery, produced an odd little story of his own.

overhead an angel swats a swarm of flies representing devilish temptations. For centuries diseases were associated with demons, but the connexion between them and their insect carriers and vectors was unperceived. The name of the god of Ekron, Baal-zebub or Baal-zebul (2 Kings i. 2) was mistakenly interpreted as "Lord of the flies." In the New Testament (Matt. x. 25) he is alluded to as master or prince of the demons.

To be patient with flies in the insanitary medieval towns and villages where they were pernicious pests called for considerable charity. Those who have seen these insects in a dense black moving mat completely covering the meat on butchers' stalls and clustering around people's eyes in North Africa can form some idea of what dwellers in thirteenth-century towns in southern Europe had to endure. Probably the eye disease from which Francis suffered was trachoma which can be transmitted by flies and has long been endemic in the Near East and the countries bordering on the southern shores of the Mediterranean. He may have caught the infection in Egypt. Only recently has a vaccine been introduced to counter it. An Irish story-teller was able to describe Saint Colman's fly as a friendly, obedient helper, marking his place when he had to leave off reading, because in Ireland with its sparse and scattered population and "soft" climate, flies were not as great a menace as in countries further south.[12]

The Scorpion

Although the scorpion is not an insect but an arachnid, related to the spiders, it is sometimes assumed to be an insect. It was, and is still, greatly feared in many areas. In the visionary journey reported in the *Fioretti* (26), based on Tundale's Vision, of which more will be said later (p. 181), the bridge traversed by the friar spanned a gorge "filled with serpents and dragons and scorpions"—a description based on Deuteronomy viii. 15. Wicked men were called scorpions (Ezekiel ii. 6), and "serpents and scorpions" (Luke x. 19) symbolized the powers of evil. Scorpions became synonymous with suffering and the

[12] N. Colgan, *Vitae Sanctorum Hiberniae*, I (Louvain, 1645, and Dublin, 1948), 244a.

terror it can inspire. Rehoboam had said: "My father chastised you with whips, but I will chastise you with scorpions" (1 Kings xii. 11; 2 Chron. x. 14), probably referring to scourges armed with iron spikes or spines. The followers of Antichrist were compared to scorpions (Rev. ix. 3). During the Middle Ages the fear that scorpions inspired owed a good deal to tradition, especially where folk had no acquaintance with them. In England so little was known of the scorpion that in the *Ancren Riwle* it was mentioned as "a kind of serpent that has a face like that of a woman and puts on a pleasant countenance"—a description reminiscent of the painting by Hugo van der Goes of the *Temptation of Eve* in which the human-headed serpent is shown with four legs like a lizard. The date of this work in Middle English is uncertain, but probably the writer was translating the remarks of Vincent of Beauvais: *Scorpio blandum et quasi virgineum dicitur habere vultum.*[13] In an illustration in a British Museum manuscript (Harley 4751) dating from the late twelfth century the scorpion is depicted with a human head, oval body, and four legs with three-toed feet. The creature is many times larger than the hand impaled on its spear-like sting. Evidently the artist had no idea what a scorpion looked like. Until after Shakespeare's time, it commonly symbolized the dangerous, poisonous, and sinister. "Seek not a scorpion's nest," says King Henry (2 *Henry VI*. III. ii. 86); and *Macbeth* (III. ii. 36) confesses, "O, full of scorpions is my mind, dear wife." In the *Bestiaries* and even in biblical concordances up to the nineteenth century, it was defined in horrific terms as a reptile whose young kill their mother. The less that was known of it, the more representative of the frightful it became. The virulence of the venom of Egyptian and Near Eastern scorpions has been much exaggerated though occasionally a man may die if stung so that his respiration is affected.[14] Species found in the Sahara and Mexico are more dangerous. The Venetians were renowned for the preparation of "treacle," a medicinal compound regarded during the Middle Ages as an effective antidote against

[13] Vinc. Bell., *Spec. Doctr.*, XVI. iii; *Spec. Mor.* II. xxvii. Cf. P. A. Robin, *Animal Lore in English Literature* (London, 1932), pp. 114–116.

[14] H. B. Tristram, *The Natural History of the Bible* (London, 1877), p. 303.

snake venom and other poisons. Among the notable *Sayings of Father Giles* (1) quoted in the *Fioretti*, we find: "Vices and sins are poison and deadly venom; but virtue and good works are healing treacle." Chaucer wrote: "Christ which that is to every harm treacle." "Treacle" came through French from *theriacum*, Greek for "of a wild beast," and was used to mean an antidote against venomous creatures.

The Ant and the Cicada

The ant, so active in gathering stores, was regarded as a model of industry by the Hebrews: "Go to the ant, you sluggard" (Proverbs vi. 6; xxx. 25); and one of the desert monks, Malchus, thought it a profitable exercise to spend a whole day watching ants and moralizing from their behaviour.[15] The only legend in which Francis is said to have concerned himself with ants is still told at Citerna on the borders of Tuscany. Folk there say that he banished these insects from where he intended to preach because their bites might have distracted the members of his congregation.[16] This may be assumed to be merely a version of the Expulsion motif concocted by villagers intent on not being outdone by other countryfolk who also claimed a connexion between their village and the saint.

In the *Sayings of Friar Giles* (7) we read:

> Friar Giles said that the ant was not so pleasing to St. Francis as other living things because of the diligence she hath in gathering together and storing up in the time of a summer, a treasure of grain for the winter; but he was wont to say that the birds pleased him much more, because they laid not up one day for the next. But yet the ant teacheth us that we ought not to be slothful in the summer of this present life, so that we be not found empty and barren in the winter of the last day and judgement [Cf. *Friar Giles* 9].

This last comment carries a reminiscence of Aesop's fable, "The Ant and the Cicada." Acting on the Gospel injunction (Matt. vi. 34)

[15] E. W. Budge, *Paradise: Stories of the Holy Fathers* (London, 1934), pp. 304–305.

[16] H. E. Goad in *St. Francis of Assisi, 1226–1926: Essays in Commemoration* (London, 1926), p. 160.

Francis even forbade the cook to put the dried beans for next day's meal in warm water the previous night (*Spec. Perf.* 19), but the deposition made by the friar who helped in the saint's kitchen (p. 132) suggests that any such instructions were not always to be taken seriously.

The story, related by Celano (2 *Cel.* 171), of the Poverello's duet with the cicada combines the Aesopean notion that this sun-loving insect sings joyously with the Franciscan belief that singing creatures praise God. He tells us that one of these insects used to perch on a fig tree, "singing sweetly," near his cell at the Portiuncula, and he would sometimes hold out his hand in a kindly way and invite her to him, saying, "My sister cicada, come to me." "She immediately came up on his hand, as though endowed with reason. Then he said to her: 'Sing, my sister cicada and praise the Lord thy Creator with a joyful song.' And without delay she began obediently to sing, and ceased not until the man of God mingled his own praise with her songs and bade her fly back to her accustomed place, where she remained for eight days in succession, as if bound." It is a pleasant picture, the little man with the mellow voice (1 *Cel.* 83) and the small insect singing a duet.[17] Celano states further that when Francis came to his cell he used to touch her with his hands and bid her sing. She was always eager to do his bidding. At length he said to his companions: "Let us give sister cicada leave to depart, for she has now gladdened us enough with her praise; that our flesh may not have occasion for vainglory by such things." Forthwith she went away and was never seen again. All this caused the brethren to marvel greatly. Bonaventura (viii. 9) paraphrases Celano. He has the insect chirp and sing but avoids "singing sweetly," perhaps thinking it inappropriate in reference to a cicada. In his usual style he emphasizes even more than Celano the insect's obedience and Francis's

[17] The story is probably a variation of the Nightingale Duet theme, but it is not far from actuality. Insects of this group have been known to duet with the tapping of a typewriter and synchronize with buzzings made with the mouth. Cf. R. D. Alexander, "Sound Communication in Orthoptera and Cicadidae," in W. E. Lanyon and W. N. Tavolga, *Animal Sounds and Communication* (Washington, 1960), pp. 45, 84–85. A grasshopper will leap on to a radio and stridulate if the pulse of the music attracts it.

authority, for he states that she did not return because she dared not disobey the saint's command—the kind of false track into which his stress on the miraculous was apt to lead him. He lays less stress on Francis's friendly attitude to the insect, but emphasizes that he had learned to marvel at the glorious handiwork of the Creator manifested in little things. In a legend told of John of Capistrano, we seem to have a version of this theme of the cicada which sings and departs when commanded to do so combined with the Stilling the Swallows motif, for he ordered the cicadas to be silent as they disturbed his preaching.[18]

The Saint and Cicada Duet combines elements we have already found in connexion with bird legends: the singing, exuberant, co-operative creature, the duet in praise of God, the dismissal with blessing mentioned or implied, and the non-return, allying the anecdote with the Expulsion motif to emphasize the saint's supernatural power. All these elements occur in various combinations in legends prior to the time of Saint Francis, and literary accounts of the Bird and Saint Duet or Bird Colloquy appear much earlier than any such story involving an insect, so we may assume that the cicada legend is derivative in spite of arguments which might be presented that, being more realistic, it is an independent episode. True, a cicada is more likely to alight on a man's hand than a nightingale and we know that Francis frequented the Portiuncula whereas definite evidence is not available of his having stayed at the Carceri, the setting of the nightingale duet. But argument along these lines serves no purpose and would obscure the main point to which this whole discussion has led, namely, that all these nature stories must be examined and assessed primarily as legends. Only then are we entitled to form an opinion as to their factual basis. This approach has been overlooked or avoided by practically all writers on Saint Francis, and until it is accepted we cannot know the truth about him. What is true of the nature legends is valid also of much else in the *Lives* as earlier incidental comments will have made apparent. Human

[18] *Acta Sanctorum*, Oct. X. 451, col. 2. Cf. C. G. Loomis, *White Magic: An Introduction to the Folklore of Christian Legend* (Cambridge, Mass., 1948), pp. 66, 180.

nature is such that it craves picturesque and personal anecdotes to illustrate the lives of great men and momentous turning points of history. Moreover, stories of this kind, such as Alfred and the Cakes and King Canute and the Waves, although mythical, have had historical and moral value, emphasizing to simple folk great events and bringing vividly before their minds important personages. Whatever its foundation in fact—and there is no reason to doubt that the Duet stories picture the happy relationship between the saint and living creatures—Saint Francis and the Cicada is poetry. To become pedantically concerned in regard to its factual precision is akin to arguing that Romeo and Juliet could not really have confused the songs of skylark and nightingale. These Duet stories show us a blossoming of sympathy with and tenderness toward nature such as had not hitherto appeared in continental Europe. Their attachment to an outstanding saint and nature mystic is confirmation that his love for all Creation was such that he is rightly honoured as one who gave new inspiration and direction to Western thought.

❀ VI ❀

Fish, "Reptiles," and Dragon

So different is the way of life of fish from that of human beings that there are fewer traces in literature or folk-lore of the sympathy or compassion that higher forms of life elicit being extended to them. In general an anthropocentric point of view has prevailed, and the degree of fellow-feeling or empathy for an animal has depended on the extent to which it happens to exhibit characteristics capable of being interpreted as having affinities with or resemblances to those of man. The recognition and acceptance of these similarities is often below the level of conscious realization. It would be possible to draw up a list on this basis grading the features that render animals unattractive or attractive to man. At one end of the scale would be such characteristics as divergence in number of limbs, amorphousness, or its contrary hard integuments, sliminess, and fetid odour; at the other, soft, warm covering, such as fur or feathers, bipedal gait, resemblance to man facially or in general form, similarity in voice or other forms of behaviour. Some creatures, especially apes, arouse ambivalent responses as their resemblances to mankind are so great as to suggest grotesque caricatures of ourselves. The animals we find most attractive are those with a social sense, especially the dog, which behaves in a confiding way, due partly to its social instincts but also to breeding and training, and birds whose voices, coloration, and activities seem gay. A few are able to imitate human speech. Some creatures very different from ourselves have characteristics that tend to offset obvious external differences. Thus, as we have already noted, honey-bees, with their ability to live socially and build geometrically, to store food and to communicate with one another, are found interesting apart from their products being valued. Fish, living in another element from man, employing very different means of locomotion, and being usually silent, have seldom aroused empathy.[1] Moreover, as many species are edible and comparatively easy to catch by one or other of the devices man has contrived, fish have been regarded from the earliest times as primarily important as food, and it is difficult to sympathize with anything that is a regular article of diet. Even those keeping religious fasts have regarded them as permitted fare. Thus evidence of compassion for fish is scarce. Where it occurs it betokens a notable degree of humane feeling.

Fish

Naturally some of the Franciscan references to fish are inspired by Gospel texts. According to Celano (1 *Cel.* 27, 28) the Little Poor Man foretold the success of his movement, envisaging a concourse speaking many tongues converging on Umbria. He prophesied: "At last it shall happen even as if a man cast his net into the sea or into some lake, and should enclose a plenteous multitude of fish, and, when he has put them all into his boat, should, disliking to carry them all because of their multitude, choose out the larger and those that best pleased him to put into his vessels and throw the rest away." This parable has some similarity to the Miraculous Draught of Fishes (Luke v. 4–9) which may have inspired it and we may suspect was designed by Celano to reflect a situation later than that in which it is said to have been uttered, when it had become apparent that the Order contained some unworthy members.[2] The same writer

---

[1] A number of fish species utter sounds, but only investigating scientists are likely to hear them. Cf. W. E. Lanyon and W. N. Tavolga, *Animal Sounds and Communication* (Washington, 1960), pp. 93–138.

[2] In the apocryphal *Gospel of Thomas* the parable of the Great Fish resembles the Franciscan simile: "Man is like a wise fisherman, who cast his net into the sea and drew it out of the sea when it was full of little fishes. Among them the wise fisherman found a large fish. He cast all the little fishes into the sea. He selected the large fish without difficulty. He who has ears to hear, let him hear." Cf. R. M. Grant and D. N. Freedman, *The Secret Sayings of Jesus* (London, 1963), pp. 120–121. Neither Francis nor Celano could have known this parable which cannot be an authentic saying of Jesus but has affinities with the Pearl of Great Price. Cf. E. A. Armstrong, *The Gospel Parables* (London, 1967), pp. 44–46, 154–157, 205. The similarity between the parable of the Great Fish

quotes another vision of the natural world. In it Franciscan success was adumbrated (1 *Cel.* 33). The saint saw a beautiful, lofty tree and felt himself growing until he was able to touch the topmost boughs. This was a foreshadowing of the Pope's acquiescence to his petition that the friars be licensed to preach. The vision is also a reminder of the Little Poor Man's high spirituality. There are earlier and later variants of the theme.[3]

Bonaventura (xi. 14), in a passage that adroitly and elegantly associates Francis with the greatest prophets and saints, as well as with the Gospel parables, refers to God's mysteries being revealed unto babes and the simple. He mentions David as "the most lofty of the prophets," Peter as the "Prince of the Apostles," and Francis as "the little poor one of Christ." All these, though simple, "were made famous by the teaching of the Holy Spirit; the first a shepherd to feed the flock of the Synagogue that was brought forth out of Egypt, the second a fisher, to fill the great net of the Church with a multitude of believers; the last a merchantman, to buy the pearl of Gospel life, when that he had sold and disposed of all things for the sake of Christ." Bonaventura (iv. 7) had earlier referred to poverty as "this rare pearl" (cf. *3 Soc.* 8).

Francis is one of the very few saints of whom it is recorded that he manifested humane feeling for fish. He took pleasure in returning one to the water. When a fisherman on the lake of Rieti caught a

---

as told by Thomas and as told by Celano is due to their both being based on Gospel narratives and imagery.

[3] This version may be regarded as a modification of the motif of the Tree that Bows which appears to be a variant of the story of Joseph's Brethren (Gen. xxxvii. 7) in which their sheaves bowed to his. A tree bowed to permit St. Guido, Abbot of Pomposa, to gather dates from it (*Acta SS. Mart.* III. 915) and when Saint Rose of Lima went forth in the morning, the trees bowed to her. Cf. L. Hansen, *Rosa Peruana: Vita Mirabilis et Mors pretiosa S. Rosae a Sancta Maria* (Ulyssipone Occidentall, 1725); R. de Bussière, *Le Perou et Ste. Rose de Lima* (Paris, 1863), p. 256. Trees bowed as the funeral cortège of Saint Firman passed by. Cf. W. Caxton, *The Golden Legend*, ed. F. S. Ellis (London, 1900), II, 217. It may be more than coincidence that the Bishop of Assisi mentioned in this chapter by Celano as honouring Francis and the brethren was also called Guido. We may assume the anecdote of Francis's vision to be one of Celano's inventions as, apart from other considerations, the likelihood of the humblest of saints dreaming thus and relating the dream afterward is slender.

large tench and brought it to him as he sat in a boat, he called it "brother," leaned over the side and slipped it back into the lake (1 *Cel.* 61; *Bon.* viii. 8).

As usual the biographers felt bound to give the incident a miraculous tinge in order to add radiance to the saint's halo, but from our point of view their statements that the fish lingered around the boat and only swam away after Francis had said a prayer (Celano) or blessed it (Bonaventura) distract attention from the novel situation of a man, of his Christian charity, calling a fish "brother" and treating it kindly. Bonaventura, however, speaks of the tench playing around the boat "as though drawn by the love" of the man of God, while Celano makes the point that the saint was in all things obedient to God and therefore "the creatures obeyed him." [4] He thus harks back to the time before the Fall when there was harmony among God, man, and beast. His statement carries the nuance that if man were to give full allegiance to God, harmony would again reign throughout nature; the Earthly Paradise would become a reality.

Typically, Thomas of Celano runs on to mention, almost in an aside, Francis's turning water into wine for his own benefit when he was ill, proceeding as hagiographers were apt to do from what might be interpreted as highly remarkable to the miraculous. He concludes: "And truly he is a Saint whom the creatures thus obey and at whose nod the very elements are transmuted for other uses." Similarly, he records (2 *Cel.* 46) another miracle—again following earlier biblical precedent—the bringing forth of water from a rock to assuage the thirst of the peasant who lent the saint an ass (*Fioretti. 1st consid. of the stigmata; Bon.* vii. 12).[5] Thus as Celano had said in his *First Life* (1 *Cel.* 90), "Through him the ancient miracles were renewed, while in the wilderness of this world there was planted by a new method but after ancient custom a fruitful vine bearing sweet flowers, fragrant with holy virtues and stretching out everywhere the tendrils

---

[4] It was said of Saint Brigid that the fishes honoured her more than any other saint. Cf. Lady Gregory, *A Book of Saints and Wonders* (London, 1920), p. 9.

[5] According to a local legend he commanded the torrent at the Carceri to be silent because the noise interfered with his prayers. Cf. M. Rowdon, *The Companion Guide to Umbria* (London, 1969), p. 171.

of a hallowed Religion." The transformation of water into wine ranks as hardly more than the introduction of a conventional prodigy. The miracle had been attributed to so many saints, including Saint Columcille, that it became a way of emphasizing how closely a man, famous for his sanctity, followed in the footsteps of Christ. Apparently Celano inserted the miracle in this context because he deemed it appropriate to emphasize that if a saint could have control of a creature belonging to another element he could be thought of as having power over the element itself. Here we have another example of the incremental exaggeration and ordering of prodigies from the less to the more extraordinary of which we have already had a number of instances. Bonaventura (v. 12) goes even further in endowing Francis with control over nature: "Consider how wondrous was the purity of this man, how great his merits, that at his beck the fire should temper its heat, water should change its flavour, angelic music should afford him solace, and light from heaven leading; thus it was evident that the whole frame of the world was obedient unto the consecrated senses of the holy man." [6] High praise, indeed, but the humble saint has become a wizard.

[6] Because we find it difficult to understand the peculiarities of medieval thought, we may be inclined to dismiss such comments as instances of "doublethink." But this would be too facile. The writers with whom we are concerned believed that what was edifying had therefore a truth of its own. According to our standards they were credulous and distorted facts but they were under pressure owing to the differing interpretations of Francis's ideals and the obligation to work for harmony in the Order. They may, perhaps, have had in mind that the more educated members of the church would be able to interpret with discretion accounts of miracles required as authentication of sanctity for which there was a popular demand. In the Middle Ages church doctrine and policy were sometimes adapted to conform with the demands of the laity. Such popular clamour was responsible for the institution of the festival of Corpus Christi. Pressure groups then, as now, could determine policy and sometimes over-ride reason.

As a further instance of incremental sequential exaggeration, we may note that after Bonaventura mentions the Stilling of the Swallows (xii. 5) he goes on to relate that Francis's boat went where he wished it to go, first taking him out into the lake and then "of its own guidance" putting in to land. Thus after a miracle concerning the animate he follows with another involving the inanimate. This miracle of the self-guiding and self-propelling boat conforms to an ancient Celtic miracle motif. When Saint Brendan's crew saw an island in the distance, they began to row with might and main toward it; but the

Saint Anthony of Padua's Sermon to the Fish (*Fioretti* 40) is obviously modelled on the Sermon to the Birds as quoted in the *Fioretti* (16) or a version of it and carries the theme further. The theme of a saint holding forth at Rimini to gaping fish ranged in orderly ranks according to size might seem far-fetched, if not positively ludicrous, to most folk today, but we would be much mistaken if we were to take it at its face value. The two Sermons illustrate once more the gradation from the more or less plausible to the fantastic, demonstrating the inapplicability of our usual criteria to medieval tales. The Sermon to the Flowers (1 *Cel.* 81) was a call to them to praise God; the Sermon to the Birds has a certain amount of not very serious allegorical significance (although a pointed moral was soon attached to it), whereas the Sermon to the Fish is patently

---

Abbot called out: "Do not be so foolish. You will tire yourselves out. Is not the Lord our Captain and Helmsman? Then leave it to Him to direct us where He wills." Cf. C. Selmer, ed., *Navigatio Sancti Brendani Abbatis* XVI. (*Univ. of Notre Dame Publ. Med. Studies*, 1957), p. 39. The story of Saint Brendan's voyage was so widely known that Bonaventura must have been acquainted with it.

This kind of belief had a practical application in Ireland as justice was sometimes meted out by setting an alleged delinquent afloat in a coracle on the principle that thus his fate was placed in the hands of God. According to Muirchu's *Life of St. Patrick*, the chieftain Maccuil, converted by Saint Patrick, was set adrift in an oarless boat and committed to God's providence. He drifted to the Isle of Man, where he became a bishop. Some support for the story is available from Manx traditions. Cf. H. J. Lawlor, *The Monastery of St. Mochaoi of Nendrum* (Belfast, 1925), pp. 35–36. Perhaps it was recalled that the infant Moses had been placed in a rush basket daubed with clay and tar by the Nile (Exodus ii. 1–10). The *Anglo-Saxon Chronicle* records that in the year 891 "three Scots [Irish] came to king Alfred in a boat without any oars from Ireland, whence they had stolen away, because they desired for the love of God to be in a state of pilgrimage, they recked not where. The boat in which they came was made of two hides and a half; and they took with them provisions sufficient for seven days; and then about the seventh day they came on shore in Cornwall, and soon after went to king Alfred." (A "state of pilgrimage" signifies a penitential exercise). The staff that Saint Cainnic left behind on Iona overtook him on his way back to Ireland, and the two cedar doors given to Saint Giles for his monastery in Provençe preceded him of their own accord. (Cf. J. Ryan, *Irish Monasticism* (London, 1931), p. 324.) The theme of a person, sometimes a child, being cast adrift and attaining eminence in another land is found in Greek, Russian, and Welsh mythology.

almost entirely allegorical. There are indications that this is so in the allusions to the fish being spared during the Deluge and the preservation of Jonah through the good offices of the great fish. The book of Jonah is itself an allegory, teaching that in spite of man's errors and sins Gods pardons those who repent; He even has regard for cattle (Jonah iv. 11)—one of the earliest expressions in literature of God's compassion for animals. The fish that listened so attentively to the saint provided an idcalized picture of what the people of Rimini, stiff-necked as they were, might become; and so the parable ends with all of them, including even the heretics, repenting, as the citizens of Nineveh had done. Hugely impressed by this amazing spectacle they ran to Saint Anthony and prostrated themselves in devotion at his feet. Again we are reminded of the ideal world in which all nature, including man, is obedient to God's will and participates in His purpose. The humour and kindliness of this rebuke were designed to win the hearts of the citizens of Rimini. Here and elsewhere throughout the Franciscan Legend animals set an example to men. In the secular literature of the Middle Ages, they often figured as representative of human vices and follies, but this is less evident where the spirit of Saint Francis prevailed.

The Sermon to the Fish, as quoted in the *Fioretti*, indeed shows the influence of the Sermon to the Birds, but scrutiny of an earlier version, preserved in the "Florentine Legend," reveals the framework on which it was built: When Saint Anthony was preaching beside a river to heretics and was derided by them, he turned to the river and proclaimed: "O ye little fishes I have a message for you from Christ." And the fishes came at his will and remained with their heads out of the water until he had finished speaking to them and had given them his blessing. Then they swam away.[7] Granted the assumption that the shoal came and went obediently at the saint's will, there is

[7] L. de Kerval, *S. Antonii de Padua Vitae Duae* (Paris, 1904), pp. 47–52. Cf. E. Gilliat-Smith, *St. Anthony of Padua* (London, 1926). A late legend that Saint Francis preached to the fish in the Tiber from a boulder near Pantenello, which is still pointed out, is evidently an offshoot of the Saint Anthony legend. Cf. H. E. Goad, *St. Francis of Assisi, 1226–1926. Essays in Commemoration* (London, 1926), p. 70; J. Maritain, *Terres Franciscaines* (Paris). It was also said that Saint Anthony's nephew was restored to life after being found drowned in a fisherman's net.

nothing miraculous or even unusual in this account apart from the abnormality of fish holding their heads out of the water—a detail inserted here to make it evident that they listened attentively. From early times men were said to commune with birds and beasts and to apostrophize nature and the elements. In this story we have an example of the type of hagiography in which the natural is exaggerated or extrapolated to become supernatural, as in a story about Saint Cainnic which might, perhaps, have influenced the author of the Florentine Legend. The Irish saint went to the near-by river to beg some fish, but the surly fishermen would not give him any, so he lent his staff to a companion who thrust it into the water, whereupon a huge fish came and was drawn ashore.[8] When he replaced his staff, another fish offered itself; but the saint, who had remained at home and was enlightened by the Holy Spirit, called out to his disciple, "O Scellanus, what has already been caught is sufficient for us," and the fish was allowed to go free into the sea. Thus the saint acted on the principle of respecting and not exploiting nature, a relationship that is essentially Christian but has been extensively disregarded.[9] This is one of the rare Christian legends prior to Saint Francis in which compassion is shown for a fish. It is noteworthy that

[8] C. Plummer, Vitae Sanctae Hiberniae I (Oxford, 1910), 157. In Irish hagiography the saint's bachall or staff serves various miraculous purposes, such as drawing water from the rock. When Francis did so he did not use a staff because, according to Celano (1 Cel. 22), "Francis hearing that Christ's disciples ought not to possess gold, silver, or money, not to carry on their way scrip, wallet, bread or staff, not to have shoes, or two tunics, but to preach the Kingdom of God, and repentance, straightway cried, exulting in the spirit of God: 'This is what I wish, this is what I am seeking, this I long with all my inmost heart to do.'" He was acting according to Matt. x. 10 and Luke ix. 3 rather than Mark vi. 8 which permits the use of a staff. As Celano (2 Cel. 7) had mentioned that during his unregenerate youth Francis carried a staff as master of the revels, relinquishment of it could be interpreted as symbolical of his renunciation of loose living. His statement did not prevent the tradition being established that a tree grew from his staff.

[9] The principle of not depleting the stock of any animal unnecessarily was observed by shamanistic hunting peoples such as Siberian tribes and North American Indians. Their motives were not merely utilitarian for they were based on magico-religious beliefs and respect for the animals. Cf. C. A. Burland, North American Indian Mythology (London, 1965), p. 34; E. Lot-Falck, Les Rites de Chasse chez les Peuples Sibériens (Paris, 1953), p. 163; L. von Schrenck, Reisen und Forschungen in Amur-Lande III (Kaiserlich Akad., 1881), 550–589.

in the Irish story the fish is caught in the river and released into the sea—suggesting that it was a salmon rather than a pike, a fish that will lunge at an oar in the water—while Saint Anthony preached from the bank between the river and the sea, addressing the fish in both. Visitors to Rimini are still shown the exact spot from which the saint preached.

Analysis of the genesis of the Sermon to the Fish reveals principles which may be applied to most of the other legends we have been considering. We can usually point to a factual basis, sometimes implying minimal observation—in this instance, that fish shoal and may come close inshore. Second, we have the proximate influence of the Florentine Legend. So far as other animal legends are concerned, the proximate legend, if it existed, may or may not have been preserved in writing. Third, there is the more distant reminiscence of the Sermon to the Birds tradition. Fourth, as a background to such legends, there is the medieval outlook with its acceptance of the supernatural and miraculous together with the belief that holiness endows a saint with power from on high through which he can influence Creation and manifest his sanctity to men. In any legend it may be difficult to distinguish the relative importance of such intermingled contributions, but each and all of them have to be taken into consideration. We must always remember that the distinctions we make between accurate reporting, parable, and legend had little significance for medieval hagiographers.

Two legends about Saint Anthony tell of miraculous transformations of food. According to one of these, he was preserved from breaking his fast by the capon served to him turning into a fish. The other concerns an amphibian. He was invited to a meal, but his malicious host tricked him, taking advantage of the saint's humility and Saint Francis's endorsement of the Gospel injunction to eat whatever was served (Luke x. 7). A toad was placed before him. But the man's wickedness was foiled. The toad, transformed into a fat capon, was relished by the saint.[10] Readers of Celano's *Second Life*

---

[10] Gilliat-Smith, *op. cit.* (1926), p. 64. This motif, which we may call the Miraculous Substitution, appears in a number of versions. Caesarius Heisterbacensis (*Dial. Mir.* IV. lxxxvi) relates that monks dining late while Shrove Tuesday passed into Ash Wednesday procured a cock to cook, but when one

will recognize something familiar in this tale. It is evidently an adaptation of his story (2 *Cel.* 78) of what happened when Francis was being entertained at Alexandria in Lombardy—as usual, Celano locates miracles precisely. "His host asked him to observe the Holy Gospel by eating all that was set before him." He prepared and cooked a capon seven years old. While the meal was being eaten, an evilly disposed person came to the door pretending to be a beggar. Francis gave him a portion of the bird on a slice of bread; but next day, while the saint was preaching, the man appeared waving the piece of fowl and shouting, "See what kind of person this Francis is whom you honour as a saint. He gave me this while he was feasting last night." But the piece of capon was seen to be a fish. Thus was the rascal put to shame. When he confessed and sought forgiveness, the fish once more became a piece of capon.

We can be sure that neither Saint Francis nor Saint Anthony was involved in such events, not merely because we are unable to believe in such miracles but because the biographers of both saints can be shown to have appropriated the story from an earlier source. Voragine, in his *Golden Legend*, relates that, when Saint Thomas Becket arrived in Rome on St. Mark's Day, his servant could not obtain any fish. So Thomas instructed him to procure whatever was available. Meanwhile the Pope, hearing of Becket's arrival, sent a cardinal to greet him. His astonishment was great when he found him eating capon. The Pope, unable to believe the cardinal's report, sent another. He, too, found Thomas eating capon. In order to validate

---

of them tried to extract the entrails he pulled out a toad. When Saint Gunther was pressed by Saint Stephen, King of Hungary, to eat peacock, he prayed to be delivered from sin and the bird flew away. Similarly, when Saint Nicholas of Tolentino was invited to dine on partridge, it took flight. Cf. Père Ch. Cahier, *Caracteristiques des Saints dans l'Art Populaire* (Paris, 1867), I, 330; II, 586.

Bandits of the period sometimes tortured their victims by forcing toads into their mouths. These creatures, when seized, exude two separate poisons whose actions resemble the effects of digitalis. In medieval art toads were associated with snakes as symbolic of evil, impurity, and temptation. Snakes and toads are represented in the carving at Strasbourg entitled *The Seducer of Unfaithful Virgins* climbing up a handsome youth's back while he holds forth an apple. Cf. V. H. Debidour, *La Bestiaire Sculpté en France* (Paris, 1961), pp. 316–317. Toads were associated with witchcraft (Cf. *Macbeth* IV. i. 6; *Tempest* I. ii. 340); E. A. Armstrong, *Ency. of Man, Myth, and Magic* (London, 1972), pp. 2855–2856.

his word to the Pope, he stole one of the capon's legs and carried it off in his kerchief; but when he disclosed what was inside, instead of the leg there was a carp. The Pope was so impressed by the miracle when Becket explained what had happened that he ordained that at Canterbury when St. Mark's Day fell on a fast day flesh could be eaten. Voragine's *Golden Legend* was compiled in the second half of the thirteenth century from earlier sources; but even if he borrowed this motif from Celano, its appearance in Caesarius Heisterbacensis's *Dialogues* is evidence of its being current before Celano wrote.

Celano's appropriation of this motif to adorn his *Vita Secunda* illuminates his character and methods. Saint Francis was not a stickler for vegetarianism, and, as we have seen, kept Christmas as a feast even when it fell on a Friday (p. 137). There is no mention of his refusing the cooked pork brought to the friars (p. 120), and he gave his cook gentle hints not to take some of his remarks about fasting too seriously. He picked grapes from a vineyard and drank wine, though in reporting such indulgence the biographers are careful to mention extenuating circumstances (*Spec. Perf.* 28). In his view dietary rules should be interpreted with charity and commonsense. He said: "As we are bound to beware of superfluity of eating which harms body and soul, so also must we beware of too great abstinence, nay, even more, since the Lord will have mercy and not sacrifice" (*Spec. Perf.* 27). But Celano, who sympathized with the stricter brethren, had to sail between the Scylla of representing his hero as lax in these matters and the Charybdis of depicting him as conforming to every tittle, and more, of the law. As the text quoted by Francis was from a passage that constituted the mainspring of his ideas and mode of life, his biographers could not ignore it. Celano compromised by making the capon no chicken but seven years old—and seven could be interpreted as meaning still older—a very ancient bird. If Francis contemplated eating a fowl, it was because it was very tough! Celano was not inclined to make unnecessary concessions to the liberalizing faction even when he thus became involved in wriggling out of inconsistencies. Bonaventura (v. 1), anxious to do what he could to heal the differences between the opposing factions and to smooth his narrative, characteristically slides over the difficulties by omitting the story, merely stating: "Howbeit, when he went forth abroad, he adapted himself—as the Gospel biddeth—unto them that entertained him in the quality of their meats, yet only so as that, on his return unto his own abode, he strictly observed the sparing frugality of abstinence."

We cannot interpret these and other narratives in which Francis's asceticism is mentioned without taking into account the controversies that divided the Franciscans even in the saint's lifetime. The extreme bitterness that developed between the "Spirituals" or rigorists and their opponents is indicated by the burning at the stake at Marseilles of four Spirituals in 1318. Celano (1 *Cel.* 52) records that Francis, having eaten a morsel of chicken while ill, caused himself to be dragged with a rope round his neck like an animal or a robber as a penance through the streets of Assisi crying out: "Come, look at the glutton who has been battening on poultry when you did not know it." As we have noted (p. 130) the *Mirror of Perfection* (61) goes further and states that he was hauled naked through Assisi while proclaiming that he had eaten flesh and partaken of broth.

We must treat such tales with discretion and even with suspicion, first, because of discrepancies in the records; second, because the biographers' accounts are known to be tendentious; and, third, because of the inconsistencies they involve. The evidence that Francis was not a fanatical stickler for dietary observance is strong, as also is the evidence for his modesty. Hagiographers were caught between the dilemma of not allowing their hero to be outdone in asceticism by any other saint and, on the other hand, depicting him as possessing in supreme degree the finer Christian virtues—which was certainly true of Saint Francis. So they allowed imagination and exaggeration to carry them away. If we were to credit the more extreme statements of the biographers, we would be forced to accept much of Voltaire's sneer as valid—that Francis was "a mad fanatic, who went about naked, who spoke to beasts, who catechized a wolf, who made himself a woman of snow." [11] He was not the first rationalist, nor the last, to misunderstand the nature and aims of hagiography.

11 *Oeuvres Complètes de Voltaire*, ed. L. Moland (Paris, 1877–1885), XII, 338.

"Reptiles"

Although one might have expected the rôle of the snake as depicted in Genesis, augmenting whatever natural repugnance man may feel for reptiles, to have excluded these creatures from Christian sympathy, it is a testimony to the power of Christ in generating love for the despised and repellant that, from time to time throughout the centuries, there have been Christians charitable enough to express compassion for reptiles—a term that in the past was applied to creatures ranging from scorpions to crocodiles. Fantastic as is the story of the blind dragon that crawled to the foot of Saint Symeon Stylites' pillar to be cured, it would not have gained currency if the notion had been unacceptable that even a monstrous reptilian creature deserved pity. The sixth-century hermit, Isaac the Syrian, quoted earlier (p. 147), declared that the truly charitable Christian "cannot bear to see, or to learn from others of any suffering being inflicted upon a creature. . . . He will pray even for the reptiles, moved by the infinite pity which reigns in the hearts of those who are becoming united to God." [12] This Christian charity for creatures commonly regarded as sinister or repulsive is all the more noteworthy as even Linnaeus wrote in very unfavourable terms of what he called the Amphibia, including in that group more animals than are now so classified: "These foul and loathsome animals are distinguished by a heart with a single ventricle and a single auricle, doubtful lungs and a double penis. Most amphibia are abhorrent because of their cold body, pale colour, cartilaginous skeleton, filthy skin, fierce aspect, calculating eye, offensive smell, harsh voice, squalid habitation, and terrible venom and so their Creator has not exerted His powers (to make) many of them." [13] Other writers of the eighteenth century also disliked these creatures. Still there are many, influenced by innate antipathies, ancient tradition, or community prejudice, who feel

[12] V. Lossky, *The Theology of the Eastern Church* (London, 1957), p. 111.
[13] Cf. M. Smith, *The British Amphibians and Reptiles* (London, 1951), pp. 7–8. Presumably the serpent is sometimes represented with legs during the Temptation because later it received the condemnation: "On your belly you shall crawl" (Gen. iii. 14).

revulsion on seeing, and still more, on handling, amphibia and reptiles.

Celano states that Francis was much distressed if he saw any poor man harshly spoken to, or, if he heard any one utter a curse against any creature, and continues: "He overflowed with the spirit of charity, pitying not only men who were suffering need, but even the dumb brutes, reptiles, birds, and other creatures without sensation." He also wrote (1 *Cel.* 59) "He diligently exhorted all winged creatures, all beasts, all reptiles and even creatures insensible, to praise and love the Creator, since daily, on calling on the Saviour's name, he had knowledge of their obedience by his own experience." [14] Thus Celano indicates what he understood only incompletely: the saint's rapport with animals. Francis no more allowed himself to show repugnance because of the strange appearance and seemingly uncouth ways of some creatures, nor, indeed, to feel it, than he permitted the hideous deformities of lepers to alienate his sympathy. He would have endorsed the opinion of Sir Thomas Browne in *Religio Medici* (1642), so different from that of Linnaeus a century later: "I hold there is a general beauty in the works of God, and therefore no deformity in any kind or species of creature whatsoever." Saint Lukas fed snakes, but perhaps Francis might have had qualms concerning them.

He was said to have silenced noisy frogs as he quieted the swallows. This achievement has been attributed to ten saints.[15] Thus

---

[14] In the fifteenth century altar-piece by Botticini depicting Saint Francis with the Virgin and Child, together with Benedict, Sylvester, and the Abbot Anthony, the symbolic light- and salvation-seeking lizard is shown with a snake at Sylvester's feet, and a tortoise, representing chastity, is near Saint Francis's feet. Saint Anthony's pig is beside him. These were introduced because of their symbolism and decorative effect. Francis's known love of nature may, perhaps, have had some minor influence in motivating the painter to depict a wealth of animal and plant life. Cf. H. Friedmann, "The Iconography of an Altarpiece by Botticini," *Bull. Metrop. Mus. Art* (Summer 1969), pp. 1–16.

[15] Cf. Bernard de Besse, *Liber de Caudibus B. Francisci* VI, ed. P. Hilarin (Rome, 1897), p. 41. Saint Anthony imposed silence on the frogs that disturbed the devotions of the Friars Minor at Montpellier. Cf. L. de Kerval, *St. Anthony of Padua* (London, 1926), p. 263: Cahier, *op. cit.,* I, 274–276; C. G. Loomis, *White Magic: An Introduction to the Folklore of Christian Legend* (Cambridge,

among saints' legends mentioned, we have the silencing of Birds,
Insecta, and Amphibia; also, perhaps, a Mammal, the ass, if we suppose it to have been braying (p. 124). This version of the Power
over Beasts motif, of which the Expulsion motif is a category,
cannot have originated in Ireland because the frog was unknown
there until toward the end of the seventeenth century when a Fellow
of Trinity College, Dublin, placed spawn in a ditch in the University
grounds. Centuries earlier Giraldus Cambrensis remarked that in
France and Italy frogs were noisy and garrulous, in Britain they were
silent and in Ireland non-existent.[16] Yet earlier, Saint Donatus,
writing in 824, considered the absence of frogs one of the commendable features of Ireland. As Bishop of Fiesole he had evidently
found their loquacity disturbing, though it is just possible that he
was prejudiced against them and their croaking because he remembered that in the Apocalypse (xvi. 13–14) spirits of devils were
reputed to issue from the mouths of false prophets in the likeness
of frogs.[17]

Mass., 1948), pp. 64, 179. Cahier does not give his source for Francis's silencing
of the frogs, but the motif, like the finding of a lost object in the belly of a fish,
is pre-Christian. Suetonius recorded that Augustus silenced the frogs croaking
near his grandfather's house and added that ever since they had remained silent.
St. Benno ordered frogs to be quiet; but on reflecting that their songs might be
more acceptable to God than his praying, he bid them praise God in their own
peculiar fashion. Cf. H. Waddell, *Beasts and Saints* (London, 1934), pp. 71–
72. Saint Bernardino did not think it undignified to imitate the sounds made
by frogs and other animals in order to hold the attention of congregations to
which he was preaching. Cf. I. Origo, *The World of San Bernardino* (London,
1963), p. 24.

[16] *Topographia Hiberniae*, trans. T. Wright (London, 1863), p. 64.

[17] His eulogy of Ireland is among the most moving of the many expressions
by Irish exiles of love and nostalgia for their homeland: "Far in the west they
tell of a matchless land which goes in ancient books by the name of Scotia;
rich in resources this land, having silver, precious stones, vestures and gold, well
suited to earthborn creatures as regards its climate, its sun and its arable soil;
that Scotia of lovely fields that flow with milk and honey, hath skill in hus-
bandry, and raiments, and arms, and arts, and fruits. There are no fierce bears
there, nor ever has the land of Scotia brought forth savage breeds of lions. No
poisons hurt, no serpent creeps through the grass, nor does the babbling frog
croak and complain by the lake. In this land the Irish race are worthy to dwell, a
renowned race of men in war, in peace, in fidelity." Cf. D. Hyde, *Literary
History of Ireland* (London, 1967), p. 164.

Naturally the composer of the legend of Saint Anthony of Padua's Sermon to the Fish, seeking to mollify and convert rather than to ridicule the citizens of Rimini, represented them as fish rather than frogs which, with their wide mouths and grotesque resemblance to human beings when swimming and mating, have never been popular. Dante (*Inf.* xxii. 27–29) compared sinners in hell to these batrachians:

> As in a trench, frogs at the water side
> Sit squatting with their noses raised on high,
> The while their feet, and all their bulk they hide—
> Thus upon either hand the sinners stood.

But Francis extended his spirit of charity to creatures commonly treated as not merely unattractive but even disgusting.

The Satanic Serpent

From early times snakes have been regarded not only as dangerous, as, indeed, many are, but as representing or embodying evil powers. The Temptation of Eve (Gen. iii. 1–13) brought the concept into Christian thought (2 Cor. xi. 3) and established the serpent as a symbol or embodiment of Satan. Such symbolism constantly recurred in the art and literature of the Middle Ages and, as we might expect, appears in the Franciscan Legend. Celano (2 *Cel.* 64; cf. 1 *Cel.* 3; 2 *Cel.* 115) makes an odd reference to the devil as associated with opulence and the temptations it brings: "None the less does the Old Serpent fly from a naked man, either because he despises the company of the poor, or because he fears the height of poverty." There was a popular belief that a viper is afraid to look at a naked man whereas when it sees him clothed it darts at him.[18] Perhaps Celano was merely illustrating vividly the lesson that poverty insulates a man from some temptations, but nakedness did not protect Adam and Eve from the wiles of the Serpent. The biographer, or Francis, was evidently influenced by the conventional notion of serpents as creatures of the dust. The saint is quoted as saying that the devil carries dust to cast into the conscience to defile it: "When spiritual joy fills the heart, in vain does the Serpent shed his deadly poison.

18 K. Bartsch, *Chrestomathie Provençale*, p. 334.

Devils cannot hurt Christ's servant when they see him filled with holy mirth" (2 *Cel.* 125). Celano was prone to portray Francis as the severe ascetic, but a remark such as this gives us another, and a truer, aspect of the saint's character.

Bonaventura (viii. 4) quoted an ancient saying when he referred to Francis's shrinking from slander "as from a serpent's tooth." The expression lived on to reappear in Shakespeare's *King Lear* (I. iv. 310). The anguished king laments:

> How sharper than a serpent's tooth it is
> To have a thankless child!

Perhaps the proverb came the more readily to Bonaventura's mind as shortly before (viii. 1) he had mentioned the Fall, thereby bringing to the surface of his mind the image of the snake.

In a passage that may, indeed, express Francis's attitude to scholarship but appears to be given prominence to alleviate the bitterness between those in the Order who emphasized the importance of learning and the Spirituals who stressed the preeminence of piety, poverty, and good works, Bonaventura (xi. 1) pointed out that, although the saint

> had no instruction or learning in the sacred writings—yet illumined by the beams of eternal light he searched the deep things of the Scriptures with marvellous intellectual discernment. For his genius, pure from all stain, penetrated into the hidden places of the mysteries, and where the learning of a theologian tarrieth without, the feelings of the lover led him in . . . . I am fain (saith he), that my Brethren should be learners of the Gospel, and thus make progress in the knowledge of the truth, that they should grow in the purity of guilelessness, so that they sever not the harmlessness of the dove from the wisdom of the serpent, which twain the greatest Teacher hath joined together with His blessed mouth.

To clinch his argument Bonaventura reports that the saint expounded divine mysteries so luminously to a Sienese doctor of theology that he exclaimed: "Verily, the theology of this Holy Father, borne aloft by purity and meditation as though by wings, is as a flying eagle, while our learning creepeth on its belly on the earth" (xi. 27; cf. *Spec. Perf.* 53). As it is so likely that Bonaventura's associations ran on from the Fall to the scriptural antithesis between serpent and dove (Matt. x. 16) and then to serpent and eagle, we may perhaps assume that he put these words into the scholar's mouth—and may even have invented him and his comment. The antithesis between eagle and serpent, representing the contrasting and sometimes conflicting powers of heaven and earth, is among man's earliest cosmic symbolical representations. A Babylonian seal of the third millennium B.C. depicts an eagle holding a snake in the talons of each foot.[19] Shelley realized the cosmic importance of the symbol when he wrote in *The Revolt of Islam*, "When the Snake and Eagle meet—the world's foundations tremble."

Brief reference to the eagle as it appears in the Franciscan Legend is included here rather than in chapter iii because of its association with the serpent and its being more mythological and symbolical than real in medieval thought. Saint Francis and his biographers regarded the eagle's concern for her eaglets as an image of God's loving and protective care. Biblical texts represented the eagle as bearing her young on her wings and fluttering over them (Exod. xix. 4; Deut. xxxii. 11). According to Celano (2 *Cel.* 173): "Whenever the hardness of his own life was blamed he answered that he had been given to the Order for a pattern, so that like an eagle he might incite his young ones to fly." Eagles will, indeed, shelter their young with their wings from sun or rain but do not bear them up in flight to save them from falling, and the impulse of eaglets to fly matures rather than is incited. As the eagle, the emblem of Saint John, noted for its ability to soar to great heights, symbolizes aspiration, so hindrances to its power of flight represent impediments to moral and spiritual achievements such as preoccupation with worldly affairs (*Fioretti. Sayings of Friar Giles*, 7).[20]

19 O. Weber, *Altorientalische Siegelbilder* II (Leipzig, 1920); Armstrong, *The Folklore of Birds* (New York, 1970), pp. 125–140. Various species of eagle prey on snakes.

20 In the course of time the eagle legends became elaborated and the belief that the bird could gaze on the sun was combined with the biblical statements concerning her care for the young. In Berthelet's edition of *Bartholomeus de Proprietatibus Rerum* XII. i (London, 1535) we read: "Among all fowls, in the

Celano (2 *Cel.* 63) tells a peculiar tale about a serpent which Bonaventura (xi. 5) repeats with some minor modifications. Saint Francis was travelling with a companion through Apulia to Bari when he received a revelation of the snares laid by the devil to entrap the greedy. They came on a large purse (*fionda*) bulging with coins, and his companion urged him to pick up the money and use it to relieve the needy. Francis refused, maintaining that this was a trap laid by Satan: "My son," said he, "it is not lawful to take away the property of others; and to give away what belongs to others involves punishment for sin, not honour for merit." (Was Celano feeling compunction for having represented Francis as doing this very thing [1 *Cel.* 1] or is this another instance of inconsistency?) They proceeded on their way, but the friar became increasingly uneasy and chided Francis for his lack of compassion toward the poor. At last the saint agreed, not to comply with his request, "but to show to the fool a Divine mystery." He turned back and called a lad who was sitting on the wall by the roadside to note what happened. First, he forbade him or the friar to approach and then withdrew a stone's throw to pray. He instructed the brother, who was now filled with foreboding, to take up the purse. Timid and shuddering he stretched

---

Eagle the spirit of sight is most temperate and most sharp in act and deed of seeing and beholding the sun in the roundness of his circle. . . . Also there is one manner Eagle that is full sharp of sight, and she taketh her own birds in her claws and maketh them to look even on the sun . . . and if any eye of any of her birds watereth in looking on the sun, she slayeth him, as though he went out of kind; or also draggeth him out of the nest, and despiseth him, and setteth not by him." Cf. Shakespeare, *Love's Labour's Lost* IV. iii. 334. This is another example of the accretion of motifs which explains many of the more fantastic medieval beliefs. Comments in older editions of the standard biblical concordance (Cruden) retain some of these ancient ideas.

In the Florentine Codex, sometimes appended to the *Fioretti,* Saint Francis is said to have appeared to Brother Leo with wings and golden claws like an eagle. In reply to Leo's inquiry Francis says that the wings represent the aid to be given to the brethren in their tribulations and the talons the power against demons and those who stray from his Rule. Salimbene, in the *Liber de Praelato,* remarked of the dictatorial Elias that the provincial ministers held him in such awe that they trembled before him as a lark trembles before the pursuing hawk.

forth his hand to seize it. Lo! a huge serpent sprang out. Francis commented: "To God's servants, brother, money is nothing else but a devil and a venomous snake." Bonaventura (vii. 5) edited the story. He disapproved of the possible interpretation that it was through the saint's prayer that the purse contained the snake and omitted the passage that might suggest this. He states that the youth was called to be a witness of God's power and adds that the purse and snake suddenly vanished.

There is plenty of circumstantial detail in the story. The location is mentioned, and we are given the vernacular term for the purse: *fonda* or *fionda* ("a sling"). The original setting however, was nowhere near Bari but far to the east. Buddha, walking with a companion, came on a heap of gold and precious stones. He cried out, "Behold—a venomous serpent!" Celano may have introduced the details to cover up the traces of his having borrowed the story, or he may have added embellishments to an already elaborated tale. It might be objected that the similarity between the two tales is a matter of coincidence, but this is demonstrably not so because the story is known to have been one of the sources of the Italian *Novellino*.[21]

21 A. d'Ancona, *Studi di critica e storia letteraria* (Florence, 1890), p. 337; S. Julien, *Les Avadânas* I (Paris, 1859), 60–63. This Indian story was found by the translator in a Chinese encyclopaedia. In Hindu mythology serpents are reputed to guard treasures, and in the *Arabian Nights* we are told of serpents guarding the Valley of Diamonds. Eastern influence may be traced in the story told by Matthew Paris of a Venetian miser, Vitalis, who fell into a pit containing a lion and a snake. When a woodcutter rescued them, the lion gave him a goat, the snake a jewel, but only under duress did the miser reward his rescuer. The diffusion of serpent stories is further illustrated by the occurrence in early Irish literature of legends connecting snakes with treasures despite the absence of these reptiles from Ireland (cf. T. P. Cross, *Motif-Index of Early Irish Literature*, Folk-lore series no. 7 [Bloomington, Ind., 1936], pp. 58, 62). A remark made by Columban when forced to leave Germany seems to be derived from the same kind of source which later influenced Celano: "We have found a shell of gold but it was full of serpents." The belief, recorded in the *Bestiaries* and mentioned by Shakespeare (*As You Like It* II. i. 13), that the toad's head contains a jewel is apparently a development of the snake-treasure motif.

The legend told on the north-east coast of England where Irish missionaries were active, that Saint Hild turned the snakes into stone, appears to be a modifi-

In view of the history of the tale of Barlaam and Josaphat, which became one of the most popular medieval romances in spite of being a Christianized version of the Life of the Buddha, we need not be surprised to find Francis's biographers retailing unwittingly a version of a Buddhist story.[22] Much Eastern lore, illustrative fables, and moral exempla spread through Europe with developments of this romance. They were included in the great source book, the *Gesta Romanorum*. Some of Boccaccio's stories were based on Eastern tales.

The story may have made some impression in Assisi as the chapel of the Portiuncula was said to have been first named Santa Maria di Josaphat by the hermits of Palestine who, so the story went, built it in the fourth century.[23] This tradition is apocryphal, but in view of other evidence of Eastern influence it has interest as another indication that the Desert Fathers were not forgotten in Assisi.

Celano's borrowing and elaboration of this Eastern tale—probably in ignorance of its provenance—throws light on his mentality and methods. When it seemed to him appropriate, he introduced material from elsewhere, disguising it somewhat and giving it a Franciscan setting and flavour. Bonaventura apparently associated the snake story with the Gospel parable of the Hidden Treasure (Matt. xiii. 44) for he mentions it earlier in the same chapter as if preparing

cation of the saying that Saint Patrick rid Ireland of snakes suggested by the finding of ammonites in that area. On the Whitby coat of arms and the badge of St. Hild's College in Durham an ammonite is depicted.

As there is still apt to be scepticism concerning the transmission of folktales and folklore the reader might be interested in the following instances: In his essay "Cinderella in China" by R. D. Jameson in *Three Lectures on Chinese Folklore* (Peiping: San Yu Press, 1932), the travels of versions of this story in the Far East as well as the West are traced. The Lady Godiva legend of Coventry appears to have originated from a tale brought back by returning crusaders (cf. H. R. E. Davidson *in* J. C. Lancaster, *Godiva of Coventry* [Coventry, 1967]). The references made by the Franciscan friar Odoric to the generation of geese from shellfish in his report of his journey from India to China seem to have been based on what his Irish companion Friar James told him during their journeys together in the Far East (cf. M. Komroff, *Contemporaries of Marco Polo* [New York, 1928], p. 243; Armstrong, *op. cit.* [1970], pp. 232, 236).

22 J. Jacobs, *Barlaam and Josaphat* (London, 1896).
23 O. Englebert, *Saint Francis of Assisi* (London, 1950), p. 72.

the ground for what we may call the Parable of the Snake. (His mind also carried reminiscences of the Pearl of Great Price, which occurs in the same context [Matt. xiii. 46], and the saying, Pearls before Swine [iv. 7].)

The Dragon

Apart from two references to the dragon, mythological creatures hardly appear in the Franciscan Legend. As contrasted with much medieval literature and homiletic material, the great preponderance of references to real animals indicates the new sympathetic interest in nature which Francis introduced. Most of the curious and fabulous lore contained in the *Physiologus* and elaborated in the *Bestiaries*, which survived to decorate Shakespeare's plays, is disregarded. There are a few casual allusions, more in the nature of clichés than mythology. Celano's "lion unchained" (2 *Cel.* 194) as a symbol of freedom and power is a counterpart to the eagle with weighted wings (*Fioretti: Friar Giles*, 7). As we have noted, the scorpion is alluded to in a formal way as a terrifying creature, but the dragon is the only truly mythological animal to figure on the Franciscan scene.

This monster is one of the most ancient, widespread, and long-lived mythological beasts, originating in the Mesopotamian cultures and mentioned in the Old and New Testament.[24] We hear of dragons in the tales of the Desert Fathers and European legends and romances. They live on in Eastern and Western symbolism. At festivals in Chinese villages and towns, their gambols still provoke merriment.

The dragon is mentioned by Bonaventura (iii. 5) when he embellishes Celano's description of Brother Sylvester's vision of a golden cross issuing from Francis's mouth. Sylvester had looked askance at the way of life of the saint and his Brethren before this experience— perhaps the biographer's way of showing sympathy with the Spirituals and gently rebuking the laxer Brethren—until "in a dream he beheld the whole city of Assisi beset by a great dragon, whose bulk seemed to threaten the whole countryside with destruction. Then he saw a Cross of gold proceeding out of the mouth of Francis, the top

[24] G. Elliot Smith, *The History of the Dragon* (Manchester, 1919).

whereof touched heaven, and its arms outstretched at the side
seemed to reach unto the ends of the world, and at its glittering
aspect that foul and loathly dragon was utterly put to flight." [25]
Asceticism was thus vindicated and the victories of the Franciscans
recognized and prophesied. Such monsters, however, had appeared
before. In the *Gesta Romanorum* [26] we are told of a city beset by
dreadful venomous beasts, the worst of which was a dragon. It
exacted from the citizens an animal every day. Should they default,
it threatened to devour men instead.

Various horrifying creatures appear together in the strange and
interesting tale in the *Fioretti* already mentioned in connexion with
the scorpion, describing the weird visionary experience of another
friar. Led by an angel he travels over mountains scarred with jagged
rocks and crags amid which he stumbles and falls. It seems as if all
his bones are broken, but the angel restores him and they reach a
plain covered with sharp stones and thorny briars where he has to
run with bare feet. At length he comes to a fiery furnace with devils,
armed with iron forks, thrusting sinners into it. He enters the furnace
and meets a couple condemned because during the famine Francis
had foretold they gave false measures of corn and wheat. The angel
again heals him, and they come to a frail bridge without rails beneath which lurk dragons, serpents, and scorpions. With great
trepidation he tries to cross, fearful lest he fall into the jaws of the
monsters. After two abortive attempts, he grows wings and arrives
at the door of a great palace to be greeted by Saint Francis and
Friars Bernard and Giles. Saint Francis recognizes, welcomes and
commends him, saying: "Let him enter for he is one of my friars."
Then he sees the saint adorned with fairest stars—and finally, with
laggard steps, he seeks the world again.

The significance of this visionary pilgrimage representing the
tribulations the faithful friar must endure lies in its being based on
Irish traditions. It thus reinforces the evidence of Irish influence

[25] That Bonaventura should not scruple to add a lurid fiction of his own to
the story as it came to him provides insight into the liberties he took with his
sources.

[26] Ed. W. Dick (Erlangen, 1890), *c.* 217 (230); N. Tamassia, *Saint Francis
of Assisi and his Legend* (London, 1910), p. 233.

on the Franciscan movement which has been accumulating throughout this work.

The origin, development, and diffusion of this tradition have been set forth by C. S. Boswell.[27] He traces its history to the Vision of Adamnan, the *Fis Adamnáin*, which embodies Eastern and classical elements and dates from about the tenth century, possibly the ninth, and notes its influence on literature up to and including the *Divina Commedia*. The tale relates the visionary journey made by Adamnan accompanied by a guardian angel. The episode that concerns us describes the pilgrim's crossing of a fire-filled glen, spanned by a bridge, beneath which lurk eight serpents with eyes like coals of fire. The chaste, the penitent, the diligent, and the martyrs find the crossing easy because for them the bridge is wide. Those who had resisted God's will but became obedient find the bridge narrow at first, but afterward broad. For recalcitrant sinners it is so narrow that they fall into the glen.[28]

The most influential work inspired by the *Fis* was the Vision of Tundale, composed at Ratisbon by Marcus, an Irish monk, about the year 1149. It achieved popularity at once and was translated into most European languages. Tundale also goes on a visionary journey during which, like Adamnan, he endures vicissitudes amid strange and terrifying scenery. He, too, comes to a glen, bridged by a narrow plank, beneath which he sees an "uncouth, intolerable monster" with eyes like hills of flame, into whose yawning jaws demons drive sinners. He is forced into the belly of the monster where, with other souls, he is bitten by lions, vipers, and hounds. Eventually he finds himself outside the beast and after surviving other perils issues from this Hell. Passing through a forest and a goodly plain bright with flowers and fragrant with herbs, and in its midst the

---

27 C. S. Boswell, *An Irish Precursor of Dante* (London, 1908).

28 The concept of the Bridge of Judgement appears to have originated in the East. In the *Gathas* of Zoroaster (ca. 570 B.C.) the Bridge of the Separator (*Cinvato paratu*) refers apparently to a bridge guarded by a stern deity which the dead had to attempt to cross. According to Moslem belief, the bridge *al-Sirat* could readily be traversed by believers but others fell into the fires of hell. Gregory the Great (*Dial.* IV. 36) mentions a bridge beneath which flows the infernal river.

Well of Life, he enters Paradise. Around a majestic blossoming tree, crowded with birds making every kind of music, the redeemed sit on thrones with golden crowns on their heads praising the King.

Those familiar with early Irish literature and with the *Divina Commedia* will have noticed reminiscences of the one and adumbrations of the other. The plain through which the Irish pilgrim passes on escaping from Hell has a considerable resemblance to the Italian poet's Earthly Paradise; but discussions of Irish influence on Dante may be found in Boswell and other works. That the passage in the *Fioretti* is based on Tundale's Vision can hardly be doubted. Nearly a century ago it was pointed out that a similar passage occurs in the writings of Joachim of Fiore, whose influence on the Franciscans was very great.[29]

In endeavouring to trace the transmission of ideas, imagery, and motifs from age to age and country to country, certainty is necessarily elusive, not only because of the difficulty in establishing unquestionable sequences of linkages between writers or tellers of tales so long ago but because it can always be argued that communities similar in a great many respects are likely to generate spontaneously similar ideas, legends, motifs, and symbols. But such communities seldom or never evolve without antecedent traditions in common which contribute to the formation of cultures favourable to the acceptance, modification, and transmission of such data. We have a rough analogy in the spread of the Black Death or forms of influenza virus which, originating in the Far East, eventually penetrated to Europe, finding in the human organism a congenial milieu. The influenza virus may become modified and adapted in the course of time or in certain areas, as a legend may, and attain new vigour and more widespread dispersal in new surroundings.

The characteristics of the Celtic Church (influenced as it was by Eastern Christendom) and Franciscanism merged so smoothly that, as we have already noted, it has been possible to deny that Hibernian traditions influenced the later movement (p. 40); but Francis, in going back to the Gospels, was, as has been suggested, reviving and reproducing much that was of the essence of Celtic Christianity with

[29] A. d'Ancona, *I Precursori di Dante* (Florence, 1874).

its simplicity, evangelistic fervour, community spirit, comparatively loose organization, love of nature, and devotion to adventurous missionary enterprise.[30]

The Irish penetration of the Continent contributed to and prepared an ambience favourable to the emergence and success of Franciscanism. Even if St. Francis was himself unaware of these influences, he could not and did not escape them. So far as the early days of the movement are concerned, as revealed, for example, in the *Fioretti*, the evidence that lies a little below the surface is all the more cogent because it indicates that the Franciscans themselves were largely unaware of the location in the West of the spring from which flowed one of the most important streams that refreshed and inspired them.

[30] There are such similarities between Adamnan's *Life of St. Columcille* and the *Fioretti* that so cautious a scholar as C. S. Boswell (*op. cit.* [London, 1908], p. 11) commented on "a certain kinship between them." This Adamnan was not the Adamnan of the *Fis Adamnáin*.

❧ VII ❧

The Furred Beasts of Saint Francis

The Mouse

The Franciscan records give so much prominence to the mutual regard in which Francis and the animals held one another, that it is somewhat surprising to find an account of any creature tormenting him. When the swallows of Alviano were unduly garrulous, he had only to reprove them and they became silent; but although during his stay at St. Damian's two years before his death a plague of mice irritated him greatly, he accepted the nuisance patiently. He was suffering so much with his eye affliction that for more than two months he was practically blind. By day and night the mice ran over him, and even when he sat at table to have a meal they managed to climb up and worry him (*Spec. Perf.* 100). At the time he was living in a reed hut, so they had no difficulty in entering. This was during the summer of 1225, possibly one of those years which tend to occur in fairly regular cycles when a peak population of these rodents had been reached. The most familiar of such infestations are the lemming "population explosions" which occur from time to time, but on a minor scale rapid increases in numbers occur in many related species. Occasionally one sees a hillside alive with voles leaping here and there, giving an odd impression of brown herbage intermittently coming to life. Field mice may produce litters even in an occupied tent.

Such a plague of mice could be extremely annoying to a blind man, for mice lose their timidity fairly rapidly if they feel free to run about with impunity. Francis prayed that he might be given grace to endure this and his other trials patiently. He is said to have regarded the irritations caused by the mice as "a diabolical temptation," but there is no mention of his waging a campaign against them or even making attempts to exclude the annoying little beasts. Nor is there any reference to his wielding miraculous powers to tame or exorcise them. Saint Cainnic drove the mice from his Irish island,[1] but Saint Francis accepted the rodents' activities in his hut as a trial of his patience. Indeed, he rejoiced in his infirmities and tribulations, composing "a new Praise of the Creatures of the Lord," breaking into song and reminding his friends that when about to preach they should announce themselves as "minstrels of the Lord."

The point of view is that animals can be exasperating and even may be regarded as instruments of the devil without themselves deserving exorcism or extermination—an advance in compassion from the sentiments and actions of some earlier saints as represented by their biographers. In Francis's attitude to the animate creation there was an acceptance of mutual friendliness which was based on humility and even attained the point of acknowledging subordination to the animals (p. 146). But the main purpose of the story is to illustrate his patience and cheerfulness in adversity. His attitude was very different from that of the desert hermits who, as a penance, exposed themselves naked to the bites of insects.

The Fox

The fox, so prominent in Irish saints' legends and secular tales in many parts of the world, is mentioned in only two contexts in the Franciscan Legend. The absence of more references to this animal may be accidental, but if any explanation were needed it could be found in the reputation of Reynard in the Beast Epic and Fable, as well as in other Continental legends, as a crafty, deceitful creature. (In the Far East it is regarded as tricky, sinister, and uncanny.) In contrast, the legends of the Irish saints depict the fox as, at times, naughty, but on the whole friendly and capable of reform. Living as a monk he might revert to evil ways but he could be brought back to the straight and narrow path, as in the legend of Saint Ciaran, Brother Fox, and Brother Badger. Naturally, as the continental fox

---

[1] C. Plummer, *Vitae Sanctae Hiberniae* I (Oxford, 1910), 161. Saint Colman had as companions a mouse, cock, and fly, Saint Moling a fox, and Saint Ciaran a fox and badger. Cf. H. Waddell, *Beasts and Saints* (London, 1934), pp. 101–109, 145–147.

had a bad reputation, Reynard did not appeal to moralistic hagiographers elsewhere as an animal whose symbolism would enrich their tales and edify readers. Moreover, from the time of Gregory the Great, heretics had been called "foxes." [2]

Saint Francis, who went directly to the Gospels to learn God's design for his life, seized on the text: "Foxes have their holes and the birds their roosts but the Son of Man has nowhere to lay his head" (Matt. viii. 20; Luke ix. 58); (2 *Cel.* 56; *Bon.* vii. 2; *Spec. Perf.* 9).[3] It is scarcely possible to lay too much stress on these words as the *leitmotiv* of Francis's life. They express the two most characteristic aspects of his aspirations: to follow as literally as possible in Christ's footsteps, and in so doing to accept a life of vagabondage, renouncing home and property. We must remember, however, that this text does not represent the positive, creative, redemptive aspects of the missions of Jesus and Francis. "Christ for the joy that was set before Him endured the cross" (Heb. xii. 2), and joyfully the Poverello followed. Celano remarks (2 *Cel.* 210): "Amid countless labours and grievous sicknesses, Francis, God's herald, trod in the footprints of Christ." The Umbrian saint envisaged Jesus as constantly on the move

---

[2] Frederick II, in his fury against the mendicant Orders, declared that they should be burnt tied in couples "like foxes." Cf. A. Boulanger, *Histoire Génerale de l'Église* II (Paris, 1935) v. 12.

In the Bible the fox, sometimes confused in translation with the jackal, is associated with destructiveness and craftiness. In the Song of Songs (ii. 15) we hear of "the little foxes that spoil the vines," and Samson tied firebrands to the tails of jackals rather than foxes to destroy the crops of the Philistines (Judges xv. 4). Herod is called "that fox [jackal]" (Luke xiii. 32). In the Middle Ages *vulpeculae* was a term of opprobrium. Gregory the Great and later writers called heretics *vulpes* (N. Tamassia, *Saint Francis of Assisi and his Legend* (London, 1910), p. 40). The wariness of foxes led to highly ingenious stratagems being attributed to them. They were said to urinate on their tails and strike them on the faces of pursuing dogs, to frighten wolves from their dens by laying sea-onion at the entrance holes, and to attain long life by eating the resin of pine trees. Incremental exaggeration thus turned the fox into the most cunning of animals, and it acquired associations with the powers of evil to whom "devilish ingenuity" has long been attributed.

[3] The only other reference to the fox occurs in the advice given to Francis to wear a fox skin under his tunic to ease a stomach ailment (2 *Cel.* 130; *Leg. Ant.* 40). He agreed on condition that a patch of the fur should be sewn outside so that he could not be accused of deceit.

along the hill-paths of Galilee and felt himself to be most truly His disciple as he trudged the dusty tracks, preached in the villages, prayed in the woods, and spent nights in caves, hovels, or bowers of reed or branches. Umbria was his Galilee.

In the early days a Franciscan settlement was simply called a place, *luogo*. As divergence on such matters as loyalty to the life of poverty and the importance to be attached to scholarship led to the divisions that arose in the Order between the Spirituals and those of liberal views, we must take account of the saint's declared ideals (*Spec. Perf.* 10):

> He was in no wise willing that friars should possess any places by right of ownership, in the houses or gardens or other things which they used, but should sojourn therein as travellers and pilgrims; and therefore he wished that friars should not be gathered together in great numbers in their dwellings, because it seemed to him difficult to observe poverty in a great multitude. And his intention from the beginning of his conversion even unto the end was that poverty should be altogether observed in all things. . . . Let them make poor little houses of wattle and daub, and some little cells in which from time to time the friars may pray and work, for greater seemliness and to avoid sloth. Let them also build small churches.

They were to live "ever as guests and strangers and pilgrims" (*Spec. Perf.* 11). In the *Fioretti* (18) we are told: "For shelter they made them little wicker cots of willow and rush matting." Celano (2 *Cel.* 190) summed up the Franciscan outlook thus: "Simplicity followed the Saint in life and went before him into Life." As already mentioned (p. 37), the régime of Francis and his companions was in many respects a recapitulation of the life of the Irish missionaries in Northumbria.

It might be thought that men who wandered the roads of medieval Europe, traversing at times tracts of mountain, marsh, and forest, would find many wild creatures forcing themselves on their attention as bears, wolves, squirrels, and birds attracted the notice of Saint Columban and Saint Gall, but the travels and search for solitudes of these two Irishmen six centuries earlier took them off the beaten track and into the forests while the friars kept mainly to the principal routes through countrysides more populated than in the days of Columban and less congenial habitats for predatory mammals or deer.[4] The Life of Columban and, indeed, the Legends of many other Irish Saints, bring us into closer contact with real animals deep in the woods than the Lives of St. Francis. The Irish hagiographers were more interested in animals than all except a few Franciscans. The prominence of animals in Hibernian hagiography may have been partly due to their importance in pagan Celtic religion. In the Franciscan nature stories, as the reader will now be aware, there is archness and artificiality. Moreover, while the animal anecdotes in the biographies of the two great Irish missionaries to the Continent continued an established Hibernian tradition which persisted for centuries, the Franciscan interest in animals was not the upsurge of any local tradition and, as we have seen, before long it almost withered away.[5] This is explicable only on the assumption that the friars' sympathy with nature was aroused by Francis's own intense nature mysticism, nurtured in a milieu where the troubled waters of social and ecclesiastical life were being gradually assuaged by an increasing awareness of Creation's loveliness. The tradition was only tenuously maintained by followers such as Saint Bernardino and Saint Douceline. But it is at least as true of nature mysticism as of other types of mysticism that the wind bloweth where it listeth. Seldom has a great mystic been able to bestow his mantle on a successor.

When we compare the wild mammals of the countryside in the Franciscan stories with those in the Irish legends, the second-hand character of the former becomes evident; the animals have little reality, and their appearances are perfunctory. They peep from the leaves of books, not from among the trees. The few still to be men-

---

[4] The Life of Saint Sturm, written about A.D. 820, contains passages giving vivid impressions of the wildness of the German countryside at that time. He is described as alone in the forest near Mainz among "gloomy woods, seeing nought but beasts (whereof there was an innumerable multitude in the forest) and birds and vast trees and wild and solitary glades." Cf. G. G. Coulton, *Life in the Middle Ages*, IV (Cambridge, 1930), 45.

[5] It has already been pointed out that later stories, such as the stilling of the unruly ass and the account of the nightingale duet, appear to be elaborations or variations of earlier Franciscan themes derived from elsewhere.

tioned are the deer, hare, rabbit, and wolf; but the allusions to these, with the exception of the wolf, are rather trivial and conventional— and the wolf, as we shall see, travelled to Gubbio from afar. In the Irish stories practically all the main familiar indigenous mammals appear—the deer, fox, wolf, otter, seal, badger, and mouse. The squirrel, recorded as perching on Queen Medb's shoulder, came at Saint Columban's call from the tree-tops to do likewise and run in and out of his cowl.[6] The hare takes a minor place but this can be explained. The rabbit was not introduced to Ireland until the thirteenth century or later. Granted that it is unfair to compare a series of stories, the products of a number of centuries, with those gathered together within about one century, yet the Franciscan mammals do not seem really to belong to the Umbrian countryside. We may assume that most dwellers in medieval walled towns in Italy knew little of wild nature—the educated and wealthy, probably much less than those who worked in the fields, forests, and vineyards. Their interests were elsewhere. Not until Dante, the summator of the past and herald of the future, whose exile brought him into contact with the countryside, do we find a great man of letters who looked at nature, including its minor organisms and phenomena, with interest, insight, and admiration. The naturalist reading the *Divina Commedia* experiences as he comes upon vivid, terse references to nature, similar pangs of delight to those gained roaming a hillside, finding here a blossoming plant new to him or there a bird he has never seen before.[7] Francis, indeed, attentively observed the crested lark, but we are able to view most of the creatures he loved only through the uncomprehending eyes of his biographers whose alienation from the wild life of the countryside is apparent.[8]

[6] This mammal was exterminated from Ireland, perhaps four centuries or more ago, but was reintroduced in the nineteenth century.

[7] L. O. Kuhn's *The Treatment of Nature in Dante's 'Divina Commedia'* (London and New York, 1897).

[8] St. Bonaventura's attitude toward nature appears in his statement: "The creatures of this sensible world signify the invisible things of God; in part because God is the source, exemplar, and end of every creature; in part through their proper likeness; in part from their prophetic prefiguring." Cf. J. A. W. Bennett and G. V. Smithers, *Early Middle English Verse* (Oxford, 1968), p. 165.

The treatment of nature, and particularly of landscape, in Italian painting from the time of Giotto onward manifests an interest in scenery which became possible only when man felt fairly secure against the perils, often imaginary, of the woods, waters, and mountains. In the relatively densely populated areas of Italy, the environment had been subdued. The menacing spirits Saint Columban and Saint Gall heard wailing around were in retreat, though the strange Etruscan gods may not have been entirely forgotten. The ferocity of the only animal that was still a menace to man's herds, the wolf— for the bear had taken refuge in mountain fastnesses—had been exaggerated by town dwellers who had comparatively little acquaintance with it. Sometimes those most familiar with some menace, whether the sea, a volcano, or an animal, are less fearful of it than people whose knowledge is by hearsay.

The Hare

Apart from the narrative of the Wolf of Gubbio, the most vivid story of Francis's compassion for a wild mammal is the description of his fondling a leveret. When he was staying at Greccio, a leveret that had been caught in a snare was brought to him:

> When the blessed man saw it he was moved with compassion and said "Brother Leveret, come to me. Why didst thou let thyself be deceived?" And forthwith the leveret, on being released by the brother who was holding him, fled to the holy man, and without being driven by any one, lay down in his bosom as being the safest place. When he had rested there a little while the holy father, caressing him with maternal affection, let him go, so that he might return freely to the woodland. At last, after the leveret had been put down on the ground many times, and had every time returned to the holy man's bosom, he bade his brethren carry it into a wood which was hard by [1 Cel. 60].

Bonaventura (viii. 8), unable to refrain from adding a decorative touch, says the leveret "at the call of the kindly Father leapt with flying feet into his bosom," which implies that it was already a fairly large and active animal. There is no mention of any rebuke being administered to the man who snared the hare. The blame for being caught was gently laid on the poor animal.

It seems unkind to submit this pretty tale to critical scrutiny, but we must do so if we are to gain further insight into the mentality of the biographers and assess their veracity and the value of the natural history they retailed. Probably in that age it was not realized that, as the countryman in Britain believes, it is inadvisable to handle a leveret lest the dam, on returning and perceiving that it has been touched, refuse to suckle it. But, as the little creature had already been handled, Francis could not make matters worse by fondling it. However, it is incredible that a recently snared leveret would leap repeatedly into a man's bosom to be cuddled as the fleeing responses of the hare can only be overcome gradually and with difficulty. When hares are kept in captivity, the cages have to be so arranged that a keeper never enters an occupied enclosure. If he did so the animal would probably break its skull or neck attempting to escape.[9]

A leveret reared from an early age and treated gently may be tamed to behave somewhat as Francis's hare is said to have done. The poet Cowper, a fragile soul himself, described his three pet hares in one of his letters to the *Gentleman's Magazine* (June 1784, p. 412):

Puss grew presently familiar, would leap into my lap, raise himself upon his hinder feet, and bite the hair from my temples. . . . Finding him extremely tractable, I made it my custom to carry him always after breakfast to the garden, where he hid himself generally under the leaves of a cucumber-vine, sleeping or chewing the cud till evening. . . . Puss was tamed by gentle usage; Tiney was not to be tamed at all; and Bess had a courage and confidence that made him tame from the beginning.

Apart from other considerations, the notion of a wood being the safest place for a leveret betrays ignorance of the way of life of an animal that, beyond all other European mammals, is a creature of the open. A leveret's form is never in a wood, where the animal would be very vulnerable because woodland is the habitat of nearly all tem-

[9] H. Hediger, *Wild Animals in Captivity* (London, 1950), pp. 138–142.

perate zone carnivores and the hare is adapted to outdistance pur-
suers in open country. Hares may enter woodland to feed but are not
at home there. The hagiographers were interested in the animal only
as the means whereby the compassion and marvellous power at the
command of the saint could be demonstrated.

The element of truth in the story is that Francis was the sort of
person to whom people would naturally bring a distressed animal.
Piety interpreted and exaggerated this into something akin to spell-
binding. "It is certainly wonderful," says Celano, "how even the irrational creatures recognized his tender affection towards them and
perceived beforehand the sweetness of his love" (1 Cel. 59). We may
discount this as natural history, but what Celano is telling us of the
saint's character is all the more valuable because of the oblique way
he does so. A leveret, with its soft fur and limpid eyes is a most
engaging creature. Even a full-grown hare, timid and defenceless,
arouses sympathy. There has come down to us a remarkable Middle
English poem in which a hare mourns her unhappy fate—to be
hunted, killed, and skinned. In many verses we are told how "she
mad herc monc."

THE HUNTED HARE

But all this most I goo,
    By no banke I may a-byde;
lord god, that me is woo!
    Many a hape hath me bytyde.

.   .   .   .

As sone as I can ren to the laye,
    A-non ye grey-hondys wyl me have!
My bowels heth I-throwe a-waye,
    And I am bore home on a stavfe.

Als sone as I come home,
    I ame I-honge vpon a pyne.
With leke-waltes I am cette a-none,
    And whelpes play with my skyne! [10]

[10] R. H. Robbins, *Secular Lyrics of the XIVth. and XVth. Centuries* (Oxford, 1952), pp. 107–110; ren-run; pyne-pin; leke-waltes vegetables; cette-eaten.

Something of the same empathy with a hare is expressed in a Gaelic song sung on the island of Benbecula in the Outer Hebrides. The animal mourns its sad plight after being caught and complains of its skull smashed, its coat removed:

THE HARE

Whoever reads my testimonial
I was unquestionably virtuous
Without gloom or servility
    In my nature.

. . . .

'Tis a sad tale to tell
That I am to-night laid low
And that my brain-pan
    Is being mangled.

After they had removed my coat
Right down to my paws
And roasted my carcase
    On embers.

Not thus was I at
The Martinmas season
Frisking and sporting
    Mid the rough hills

. . . .

Without thought at that time
That the villain would come
With his gin to ensnare me
    In the gloaming.

I was at home on the heaths
Where my father and ancestors
Were sportive, merry
    And spirited; [11]

There is no definite evidence that the earlier poem influenced the later; but it is noteworthy that in both the poet identifies himself

[11] A. Carmichael, *Carmina Gadelica* V (Edinburgh and London, 1954), 395–397.

with the persecuted hare, both express compassion for the animal, and both describe its roving ways, the hazards it encounters, its ignominious, brutal treatment, and its being flayed.

As Celano's hare lacks reality, it is worth inquiring whether he, or less probably Saint Francis, could have been influenced by earlier precedents. The motif of the Rescued Hare first appears in Christian hagiography in Sulpicius Severus's *Dialogues*. The story of the saint commanding the hounds chasing a hare to stand immobile was well known throughout the Middle Ages. A statue of Saint Martin dominating the hounds occupies a conspicuous position on Chartres cathedral. Saint Marcoul protected a hare pursued by the king's courtiers which took refuge in his robes and cured one of the hunts-men who hurt himself while dismounting from his horse to kill it. The account of the hare that sought and found sanctuary under Saint Anselm's horse—a somewhat improbable action, though less so than seeking shelter in a person's clothes or bosom—continues the motif.[12] Anselm (1033–1109), like Saint Francis, was a native of Italy, born in Aosta in Piedmont. He lived a gay life in his youth, enjoyed mystical experiences, fell out with his father, left home, became a monk, travelled, reached high eminence, and acquired a great repu-tation for sanctity. His views were strongly influenced by the teaching of the Irishman, John the Scot (Eriugena). Aosta maintained close connexions with Ireland, and lively devotion was offered to the Irish saints Brigid and Ursus.[13]

The similarities between the experiences of the two saints may be coincidental, though Francis's biographers, who were well acquainted with traditional hagiography, may be assumed to have known of details in the Life of Saint Anselm. At all events the facts mentioned

---

[12] W. Caxton, *The Golden Legend*, ed. F. S. Ellis (London, 1900), VI, 148; V. H. Debidour, *La Bestiaire Sculpté en France* (Paris, 1961), pp. 276, 388; M. A. le Grand, *Les Vies des Saints de la Bretagne Armorique* (Quimper, 1901), p. 730; Sulpicius Severus, *Dial.* II. ix.

[13] The market of wooden implements still held on the eve of Saint Ursus is said to be a continuation of the saint's custom of distributing wooden sabots to the poor. Cf. A. N. Tommasini, *Irish Saints in Italy* (London, 1937), pp. 125, 246, 265–279.

suggest that Irish influences may have operated indirectly where they have not been suspected.[14]

Pagan traditions in Celtic areas differed from the Christian theme of compassion for the animal. Julius Caesar wrote that the natives of Britain would not eat hare.[15] They evidently considered it a magical taboo animal. This is borne out by the statement of Dio Cassius that Boudicca, "queen" of the Iceni, released a hare from within her garments at the beginning of a campaign—which strongly suggests that there was among the Celts, as elsewhere, a connexion among the hare, goddesses, and the moon.[16] So strongly held were convictions concerning the magical nature of the hare that they persist to this day in East Anglia, the land of the Iceni, the Isle of Man, and some regions of Ireland.[17]

Thus lingering heathen associations may have prevented the hare from appearing in the Legends of the early Irish animal-loving saints. They may also be responsible for the association of the hare with female saints in the later hagiography of Celtic areas. Saint Motacilla, the Welsh princess, was patroness of the hunted hare. In Ireland,

[14] There were contacts between Saint Anselm and the Irish. He wrote to the Irish bishops as a metropolitan to his suffragans. Eadmer, his confidant, states that in 1115 the Bishop of Limerick assisted the Archbishop of Canterbury at the consecration in the Church of the Blessed Peter at Westminster of one of the queen's chaplains to the See of St. David's. Cf. Tommasini, *op. cit.*, pp. 138–139.
[15] *De bell. Gall.* V. 12. J. W. Layard, *The Lady of the Hare* (London, 1944).
[16] Dio Cassius, LXII. 2.
[17] E. Porter states in *Cambridgeshire Customs and Folklore* (London, 1969), p. 55: "A Thorney man said in 1956 that his grandmother, who died in 1897 at the age of 90, would never eat jugged hare because 'she might be eating a witch.'" My wife tells me that when staying on a farm at Thorney (near Peterborough) during the 1920s she noticed that the maids would not eat hare when it was served for the rest of the family. No doubt this aversion was due to a lingering association with witchcraft. At the end of the nineteenth century it was stated in *The Zoologist* (1892), p. 63 that in the Isle of Man "the natives would not think of eating a hare."
Across Asia into Mongolia and China, occult and sometimes sinister powers are attributed to the hare, perhaps because of its lively mating activities on moonlight nights which may have caused it to be associated with the moon as a goddess and hence with witchcraft. Cf. G. Willoughby-Meade, *Chinese Ghouls and Goblins* (London, 1928), pp. 107, 168, 314.

where according to Giraldus Cambrensis, the hare was common, as it is today, Saint Mona is said to have checked the hounds chasing a hare; hence Irish children call hares "Saint Mona's lambs," and when they see a hare being hunted murmur a prayer: "God and St. Mona succour thee." [18] Thus the hare by long tradition is associated with female personages. When we trace the story to a period after Saint Francis, we find that it has returned to the earlier form in which a saintly woman is involved. The Blessed Oringa, lost at night in the woods, made friends with a little hare which rested in her lap when she sat down. Probably the influence of Celano's tale is apparent in the setting of the incident incongruously in the woods and the mention of the leveret nestling in Oringa's lap.[19] She was born in 1237, and her Life is known from a manuscript preserved in the convent of Saint Clare (Clara) at Florence. Thus there can be no doubt that this legend is a continuation of the Franciscan tradition. Perhaps the association of the hare with Saint Francis came naturally to biographers, obsessed with prejudices against women (p. 233), for in him they found represented the virtues that men have always valued in the female sex. Their emphasis on his "maternal" relationship with the hare may indicate their subconscious transference of their suppressed admiration of femininity to him.

The Rabbit

To the story of the hare, Celano (1 Cel. 60) appends the comment: "Something of the same kind happened with a rabbit (which is a very wild creature) when he was in the island in the lake of Perugia." This was Isola Maggiore in Lake Trasimene where Hannibal routed

---

[18] Giraldus Cambrensis, *Topographia Hiberniae*, trans. T. Wright (London, 1863), p. 43; Sister Donatus, *Beasts and Birds in the Lives of Early Irish Saints* (Philadelphia, 1934), p. 127. Saint Godric banished a hare from his garden where he was growing vegetables for the poor, but he fastened a bundle of greens to it so that it would not be without provisions! He sheltered hares, fleeing from huntsmen, in his hut, freed snared animals, warmed frozen ones and "in his wise solicitude watched over the very reptiles and creatures of the earth." Cf. Geoffrey of Durham, *Acta Sanctorum*, May 21; Reginald of Durham, *Libellus de Vita et Miraculis S. Godrici*, Surtees Society, XX (1845), 148.

[19] S. Baring-Gould, *The Lives of the Saints* I (Edinburgh, 1914), 147.

the Roman forces in 217 B.C.—the island where Francis kept a lone Lenten retreat (*Fioretti* 7) in the manner of the Desert Fathers and Celtic saints. If, as Bonaventura records (viii. 8), the animal was brought to the saint while he was on this uninhabited island, the incident must presumably have occurred on some unrecorded visit; but it is very much more likely that Bonaventura took it upon himself to manufacture details, assuming they would make his narrative more effective. Both writers, as we have seen, tend to buttress the account of one prodigy with another. The intention in this instance appears to have been to indicate that all sorts of animals responded to the saint's tender sympathy. Apparently Celano was writing for townees when he thought it necessary to explain that the rabbit is very timid, but the wilder the animal the more the saint's power would be exalted. However, it may not have been common in Umbria at this period.

Celano, using a technique with which we are now familiar, gives us a series of increasingly remarkable prodigies—the Sermon to and Stilling of the Swallows, the Persistent Pheasant, the Taming of the Hare, the Rabbit Rendered Docile, the Charming of the Tench, and the Turning of Water into Wine, concluding: "And truly he is a Saint whom the creatures thus obey and at whose nod the very elements are transmuted for other uses." The final words are significant. The Little Poor Man of Assisi becomes transformed into a magician before our eyes, and Celano has allowed himself to regard and extol power over the elements as the supreme manifestation of sanctity. Bonaventura (xii. 4–6), as we have seen (p. 162), followed the same procedure, recounting the exploit of the Parmesan scholar who reduced a swallow to silence by invoking the saint's name and then mentioning the boat that found its own way to Francis's desired destination. His concluding words go further than Celano's and are positively minatory: "Who then could be of so obstinate and wicked mind as to despise the teaching of Francis, by whose wondrous might it came to pass that not only creatures lacking reason were amenable unto correction but that even lifeless objects, as though they had life, ministered unto him while preaching?" Thus does contemplation of the exercise of power seduce even good men's minds. The performance of prodigies is enthroned above holiness and covert threats substituted for the benign suasion of goodness.

There is more than natural history interest in all this. These anecdotes and incidental remarks reveal an aspect of medieval ecclesiasticism which enables us to understand some of the vicissitudes which befell the Franciscan Order after, and even before, the saint's death. We already perceive the blurring of the distinction between, on the one hand, the pure beauty of holiness and its power to refine those who become acquainted with it, and, on the other, crude thaumaturgy and sensationalism. We shudder to notice the fist of authoritarianism behind the sanctimonious phraseology.

Those who have seen the devastation and misery left by political despotism and national aggrandizement are affronted by this exaltation of power on the part of the biographers of the gentlest of saints, but in our time we arrogantly and inconsiderately assert our power over nature. In his relationships to God, nature, and his fellows, man's judgement falters. The Middle Ages knew no better than to seek to magnify holiness by means of power; we exalt power and despise sanctity.

The Deer

Bonaventura's concept of Francis's relationship to animals as involving the ability to dominate them appears in an illustration in one of his sermons.[20] Saint Francis, he said, had power not only over men but over the fishes of the sea, the birds of the air, and the beasts of the field. On one occasion when he was going through a wood, the deer fled from him and his companion, but he said to one of them, "Why do you run away? Stand still!" At the word of the saint the animal stood where it was, and he went up and laid his hands on it. Then he said, "Now go, and praise God", and it bounded away. So, too, with birds, continued Bonaventura; they sang or kept quiet at his bidding (p. 72). The picture is of a wonder-worker, not of an animal lover. The point of view agrees with that of the chronicler of Saint Cainnic to the extent that he represented him as dismissing the

[20] Bonaventura, *Opera Omnia* (Quaracchi ed.) IX, 587; cited in J. R. H. Moorman, *A New Fioretti* (London, 1946), p. 66.

noisy birds, but it differs from it and the themes of many Irish legends in that the emphasis is mainly on Francis's miraculous power over wild animals rather than day to day friendliness with them.

> Cainnich of the mortifications loved
> To be in a bleak woody desert
> Where there was none to attend on him
> But only the wild deer.[21]

The Wolf of Gubbio

Among all the birds and beasts of Franciscan story, the Wolf of Gubbio stands supreme in dramatic appeal, and, it must be added, in the challenge presented to interpreters of the Franciscan Legend. In confrontation with this beast, the attitude of scholars to the historical records of the saint's life and their assessment of the accuracy of his biographers become apparent. A critic's success or failure in this encounter can be sufficient to show whether romanticism, sentimentality, or credulity has clouded his judgement, or, on the other hand, poverty of imagination or lack of sympathy with the saint has led him astray.

Toward the end of the nineteenth century, Sabatier commented on the Wolf as the third state of the story of the robbers of Monte Casale linked with a legend of La Verna; but he produced no evidence for the existence of this legend.[22] Most writers since attribute greater or lesser reality to the Wolf. Nearly thirty years after Sabatier's book appeared, Father Cuthbert remarked that "in his marvellous way he tamed the beast." [23] Writing in this decade M. de la Bedoyère comments: "It is hard not to believe that this story was founded on fact since it squares so well with Francis' undoubted power of taming animals." [24] The present Bishop of Ripon, the Rt. Rev. J. R. H. Moorman, remarks:

[21] P. F. Moran, *Essays on the Origin, Doctrines and Discipline of the Early Irish Church* (Dublin and London, 1864), p. 145.

[22] Paul Sabatier, *The Life of St. Francis of Assisi* (London, 1920), pp. 133, 418.

[23] *Life of St. Francis of Assisi* (London, 1921), p. 195.

[24] M. de la Bedoyère, *Francis: A Biography of the Saint of Assisi* (London, 1962), p. 162.

Wild animals seem to have had no fear of him and when, after fondling them, he wanted to get rid of them, he often found difficulty in persuading them to go away. The flock of swallows which interrupted his preaching at Alviano was silenced by a word from the saint, and a hawk at La Verna became his knocker-up and woke him for Mattins each morning. Wolves and other wild beasts gave him no fear and became perfectly docile in his company, while the fierce wolf of Gubbio became so tame that it lived to be quite a popular figure in the town and died universally mourned.

Elsewhere he asks, "What could be more convincing than . . . the story of the Wolf of Gubbio?" [25] Even more recently E. M. Almedingen says of the story: "Its core does not seem to belong to legendary lore." [26] Englebert expresses as his opinion: "It may be that one is dealing here with a famished animal or as ferocious a Signore or brigand." [27] Joergensen's interpretation followed Sabatier's to some extent. He regarded the story as the legendary transformation of a pact established through the good offices of the saint between the small republic of Gubbio and one of the fierce gentleman-brigands who at that time occupied fortified castles in the Italian mountains. He finds a parallel in the confrontation between Saint Anthony of Padua and the tyrant Ezzelino, but fails to explain why such a pact should be recorded only in this cryptic form.[28] Writing as an authority on mysticism rather than a biographer of Saint Francis, Evelyn Underhill generalized from his rôle of "ambassador from the terrified folk of Gubbio to his formidable brother the Wolf." She commented: "The result of the interview, reduced to ordinary language, could be paralleled in the experience of many persons who have possessed this strange and incommunicable power over animal life." [29]

[25] Moorman, *Saint Francis of Assisi* (London, 1963), p. 76; cf. Moorman, *A New Fioretti* (London, 1946), pp. 66–67.

[26] Almedingen, *Francis of Assisi* (London, 1967), p. 88.

[27] Englebert, *Saint Francis of Assisi* (London, 1950), p. 169.

[28] J. Joergensen, *Saint François d'Assise*, trans. T. de Wyzewa (Paris, 1922), p. 147.

[29] Underhill, *Mysticism* (London, 1960), p. 260. This point of view is by no means a thing of the past as the following quotation shows: "The wonderful fascination that emanated from his whole person acted even on irrational creatures. The conversion of the wolf of Gubbio and the sermon to

There are precedents, though insufficiently convincing, for regarding the Wolf of Gubbio as a human marauder. Francis treated brigands as kindly as he did the Wolf. (*Spec. Perf.* 66; *Actus* 29; *Fioretti* 26). From early times the wolf had been proverbial for its ferocity, and traditionally savage men were compared to wolves. "Benjamin shall ravin as a wolf" (Gen. xlix. 27). Christ spoke of false prophets as ravening wolves (Matt. vii. 15) and told His disciples that He sent them forth as sheep in the midst of wolves (Matt. x. 16), a text that, according to Bonaventura (ix. 8), Francis quoted to a companion. "He saw very many raging like wolves against the little flock" (2 *Cel.* 23). Celano remarks that Francis's father "rushed on him like a wolf on a sheep" (1 *Cel.* 12), and Bonaventura (ix. 8) records that the Saracens seized him and his companion "like wolves making haste to fall upon sheep."

If the recalcitrant citizens of Rimini could be reproved in a parable about fish, could not a despot or bandit be represented in similarly veiled language? Medieval outlaws were treated as wolves. "Let him bear the wolf's head" was the traditional sentence on a man being outlawed. Like the wolf, he was to be killed on sight. In Italy such a malefactor was a *capo lupino*, and in France he was excommunicated as a *loup-garou*. At Bergamo the magistrate responsible for the formal procedure of outlawing a malefactor had as his emblem a wolf's head. The critic Tamassia, himself a professor of the history of law, taking account of such facts and the details of the animal's behaviour provided by the *Fioretti*, came to the conclusion that in the Wolf of Gubbio we have such an outlaw "reconciled to his city with the exact forms and ceremonies prescribed by law and practically observed at that epoch." [30] But he acknowledges that the notion of an animal observing human etiquette comes from the Desert Fathers, a tale in the *Historia Lausiaca*.

---

the birds . . . are the best known of many episodes in which all creation was subject to his mysterious charm." Cf. J. Leclercq, F. Vandenbroucke and L. Bouger, *The Spirituality of the Middle Ages*, trans. Benedictines of Holme Eden Abbey (London, 1968), p. 291.

[30] Tamassia, *op. cit.*, pp. 229–231; cf. J. Grimm, *Deutsch Rechtsalterthümer* II (Berlin, 1899), 334.

In spite of the support such a view has received from some scholars, it cannot be accepted as having more than an element of truth. It is incredible that, if Francis had brought about reconciliation between the people of Gubbio and some brigand or tyrant, the fact should only have been recorded in so oblique a manner. The biographers were candid enough in speaking of the saint's encounters with robbers and would have had no inhibitions about referring to such an achievement (1 *Cel.* 16; *Bon.* ii. 5; *Fioretti* 26).[31] It is, therefore, no more probable that the biographers had any wicked individual in mind than that the shepherd of the Gospel parable was a particular Galilean. The story of the Wolf is a parable relying on traditional associations and natural emotional responsiveness to conventional imagery, an offshoot of that ideal and myth which has been embodied in different guises throughout history, depicting man, no longer at strife with nor subject to nature, establishing harmony with it, an ideal that in this its religious form differs profoundly from the magical concept in which man as sorcerer or magician, or in league with unnatural powers, subordinates nature and its processes to his will and wishes. The magician is the instrument of crude power, the saint the vehicle of moral and spiritual power, whose influence resides in his approximation to the state of the Blessed who are able to say "In His will is our peace" (*Paradiso,* iii. 85). The parable of the Wolf portrays the consummation of man's dreams: reconciliation by virtue of holy power between nature and himself. Elsewhere we are told how Francis, by making himself a channel of Divine, loving power, reconciled families and cities;[32] here we are given a further and deeper insight into the concept of the Earthly Paradise, the ideal realm in which man's animal nature no longer is

[31] Sabatier, *op. cit.,* p. 133.

[32] There is no more authentic and vivid portrait of Saint Francis than that preserved to us in the description by Thomas of Spalato, then a theological student, of the saint as he saw him preaching in the piazza at Bologna in 1222: "The whole matter of his discourse was directed to the quenching of hatred and the establishment of peace. His dress was mean, his person insignificant, his face without beauty. But with so much power did God inspire his words that many noble families, sundered by ancient feuds were reconciled for ever" (*Historia Salonitanarum, Monumenta Germaniae Historica, Scriptores,* XXIX, p. 980). Cf. T. Okey, *The Little Flowers of St. Francis* (London, 1944), p. xi.

felt to be at war with his spiritual aspirations. Francis himself is shown as a man of compassion and peace, idealized man wholly possessed by God.

Not only were evil individuals in the Middle Ages regarded as wolfish, but wolves were sometimes treated as if they were wicked men. In spite of being denied souls, they were sometimes tried, condemned, and executed according to legal procedure. They were hanged as malefactors. Gratiano's vituperation against Shylock combines reminiscences of this procedure with belief in possession by an animal. He cries,

> thy currish spirit
> Govern'd à wolf, who, hang'd for human slaughter,
> Even from the gallows did his fell soul fleet,
> Infused itself in thee; for thy desires
> Are wolfish, bloody, starved and ravenous.
> *Merchant of Venice* IV.i.133

As a number of allusions in the Franciscan Legend show, the medieval mind was confused concerning where to draw the line between regarding animals as in an altogether lower category than man and attributing human faculties and sensibilities to them. Thus, in one of the anecdotes told by Caesarius Heisterbacensis to which reference has already been made (p. 73), a bird seized by a hawk calls on Saint Thomas of Canterbury and is miraculously released—a combination of mechanistic ideas concerning prayer and anthropomorphic ideas about birds with which our minds find it difficult to come to terms.[33] Orthodoxy forbade ascribing souls to the beasts, yet human qualities, including sinfulness, were attributed to them. In one of the earliest versions of the story of the Jackdaw of Rheims, sentence of excommunication is pronounced on the unknown thief of the ring. From that time the jackdaw was observed to pine and look sickly, but when

---

[33] Cf. chap. iii n. 47. Souls could appear as birds, but birds had no souls. Animals could be punished for impiety, like the fly that fell dead after hovering over a chalice, but oxen that revealed where a stolen pyx was concealed and mice that gnawed wafers reverently avoided the sacred monogram. Cf. Caesarius Heisterbacensis, *Dial. Mir.* IX. vii, x, xi. A dog mischievously baptized by students went mad. *Ibid.*, X. xlv.

the ring was discovered in the bird's nest it began to recover and was soon quite well "by a plain miracle of God" as the narrator is careful to add. There is ample evidence that animals were indeed excommunicated.[34]

Having noted the lack of evidence that the monster of Gubbio was a man in wolf's clothing, we must now consider the evidence for the animal's reality. Undoubtedly during the thirteenth century starving wolves became bold and entered villages. Not long after Francis came to Gubbio these beasts were roaming the countryside. Salimbene remarked that in the year after the religious revival of 1233, called the Great Halleluia: "There was so great snow and frost throughout the month of January that the vines and all fruit-trees were frost-bitten. And beasts of the forest were frozen to death, and wolves came into the cities by night: and by day many were taken and hanged in the public streets. And trees were split from top to bottom by the force of the frost, and many lost their sap altogether and were dried up." He also mentions that one winter when staying at Hyères in Southern France he heard multitudes of wolves howling at night. To a fearful man a pack could sound like a host.

The conflict between the Pope and the Emperor resulted in such destruction, chaos, and loss of life that wolves became a serious

[34] Migne, *Patrologia Latinae* CLXXXV, col. 1144.

Saint Thomas Aquinas, who was a Dominican, taught that animals could be instruments of the powers of hell, possessed by the devil. Legal action taken against such animals was directed against Satan. As Canon Law was God's law and all creatures were subject to God, they could be excommunicated. The ambivalent medieval attitude to animals arose from the belief that they could be used by, or be manifestations of, supremely good or utterly evil powers. This preconception stood in the way of any objective assessment of the behaviour of animals. For a recent popular discussion of how theological ideas determined the legal treatment of animals, cf. G. Carson, "Bugs and beasts before the law," *Nat. Hist.*, LXXVII, 4(1968), 6–19; Tamassia, *op. cit.*, p. 229 gives references to authorities on the penal treatment of animals. In the *Alcoran des Cordeliers* (ed. 1734), p. 215, Saint Francis is represented as parleying with the Devil in the form of the Wolf!

The excommunication of animals continued into the sixteenth century and possibly later. Purchas, in *His Pilgrimes* ([4th ed.; London], II, 1047) gives a detailed account of the procedure by which Francis Alvarez excommunicated locusts in Ethiopia during the infestation of 1560. Soon there followed a storm and such a deluge of rain that not one was found alive.

menace. Bandits swarmed in the countryside, driving away cattle, carrying off men in order to extort ransoms, torturing those who could not find the money. Salimbene says the robbers were more cruel than devils, and the land was made desert. "The wolves found no beasts in the villages to devour according to their wont; neither sheep nor lambs, for the villages were burned with fire. Wherefore the wolves gathered in mighty multitudes round the city moats, howling dismally for exceeding anguish of hunger; and they crept into the cities by night and devoured men and women and children who slept under the porticoes or in waggons. Nay, at times they would even break through the house-walls and strangle children in their cradles." [35]

In conditions such as Salimbene describes, and when the forests in the Apennines extended over wider areas than at present, wolves were much more numerous and bolder; but even nowadays whenever there is a hard winter, wolves are reported as appearing in the villages of northern and central Italy. In December 1968 and again in February 1969 the English press carried such reports. Salimbene exaggerates when, for example, he writes of "mighty multitudes" of wolves, but we may accept his statement that they occasionally attacked small children and villagers incapacitated through illness and starvation. A determined, hungry wolf could force its way through a dilapidated wattle and daub wall. In normal conditions wolves might prey on sheep but would very seldom, if ever, be able to attack and kill an able-bodied man. In default of further evidence, all such accounts should be treated as legendary.[36]

[35] C. G. Coulton, *From St. Francis to Dante* (London, 1906), pp. 33, 56, 172. Celano (2 *Cel.* 53) refers to a famine that occurred after Francis's death such that "nutshells and the bark of trees were made into bread."

[36] The story of wolves pursuing travellers in a sledge has long been current in many versions, the most lurid of which describes the occupants being thrown to the wolves one after another, or a baby being sacrificed to them in order to delay their onslaught. As a boy I listened to a German visitor describing his terror when his sledge was thus chased by a pack in Russia. None of these stories has been shown to be authentic. In *Travels with a Donkey*, Robert Louis Stevenson mentions "wild Gévaudan, mountainous, uncultivated and but recently disforested from terror of the wolves." Lois Crisler (in *Arctic Wild* [London, 1959], pp. 264–267), who lived among wolves and investigated such tales, was

A number of writers mention the finding of the remains of a wolf at the base of a wall of the church of San Francesco della Pace in Gubbio, but the evidence produced does not stand scrutiny. A canon of the church claimed to have been shown the skull by the workman who uncovered it and told an English visitor that it had passed into the possession of a man living not far away, but nobody took the trouble to verify the tale, retrieve the relic, or ascertain whether it was a wolf's rather than a dog's skull. The story is unreliable and of a genre commonly found at places closely associated with saints. In later accounts the find became magnified into the skeleton of the animal. The bones may be recovered from the legends more readily than from the ground. At the church itself there is a crude carving representing the Wolf signifying its submission to Saint Francis and a stone on which he is said to have preached. The scene is also depicted in a painting by Sassetta in which the beast is shown placing its paw in the saint's hand (pl. 9).[37]

Thus there is no evidence of the reality of the Wolf as an actual animal any more than of him as a ferocious man though the legend has the frail basis in fact that wolves may at times have come to the gates of Gubbio and alarmed its inhabitants. However, we have no reason to query the substantial truth of another story concerning Francis and wolves. It is related that after he had received the stigmata, being in a frail condition, he rode a donkey; and as he was passing close to San Verecundo, a farm labourer hailed him and advised him to go no further as there were fierce wolves further on

---

able to find only a single instance of wolves chasing a man. One of the two beasts had a broken jaw and was behaving abnormally. They were too wary to close in on him. A wolf that attacked two Canadian Pacific railwaymen was found to be suffering from rabies.

[37] P. Cavanna, *Umbria Franciscana*, pp. 374–378; L. McCracken, *Gubbio Past and Present* (London, 1905), p. 283; H. E. Goad, *Franciscan Italy* (London, 1926), p. 70; M. Rowdon, *The Companion Guide to Umbria* (London, 1969), p. 209.

Gubbio is the ancient Iguvium, and archaeologists have found evidence of the sacrifice of a dog to Jupiter there as well as in Rome on the Capitol. Cf. P. Grimal, *In Search of Ancient Italy* (London, 1964). In Celtic tradition and custom the rôles of the wolf and dog were very similar. Cf. A. Ross, *Pagan Celtic Britain* (London, 1968), pp. 341–342.

which would bite him and eat his donkey. Blessed Francis replied: "I have done no harm to Brother Wolf that he should want to kill and eat our donkey. Good night my son, and fear God." [38] And so he went safely on his way. We may note that it was not suggested that the pack, however fierce, would kill the saint. Some such incident may have contributed to the inclusion of the story of Brother Wolf in the Legend.

In view of various comments made earlier, it is hardly necessary to emphasize the unsoundness, whether as psychology or natural history, of the views implying that Francis wielded unique power over animals or was among an élite specially endowed with the capacity to subdue fierce animals. Such ideas, characteristic alike of Orphism, Buddhism, and Christianity, express a poetic ideal and are valuable as such.[39] But it must be reiterated that there are no grounds for believing that sanctity, or indeed any virtuous qualities other than interest, tenderness, gentleness, understanding, patience, sympathy, and experience enable people to become on good terms with animals. Some truly gentle folk readily establish friendly relations with animals; others, able to ingratiate themselves with domestic pets, such as dogs or cats, do not appreciate that this may be due in part to so prosaic a characteristic as their scent. Disregard for human beings as potentially dangerous on the part of wild animals, due to unfamiliarity on the one hand, or the familiarity that breeds unconcern or confidence on the other, should not be assumed to be evidence of the animal's regard or affection, nor should cupboard love be mistaken for devotion.[40] In short, the Wolf of Gubbio, interesting

[38] M. Faloci-Pulignani, Legenda de passione Sancti verecundi, *Miscellanea Francescana* X (1906), 6–7.

[39] The Buddha is said to have radiated such gentleness that a wild elephant released maliciously against him paused with trunk uplifted and did not harm him. Cf. A. Schweitzer, *Indian Thought and its Development* (London, 1936), p. 106.

[40] When a wild monkey crept up behind me in North Africa, it was not treating me as another Saint Francis but trying to steal the sandwiches in my pocket. A deer nuzzling me at Nara in Japan was expecting to be fed, and an agouti in the Panamanian forest which fed from my hand was motivated merely by hunger. The lions in African National Parks which permit car-loads of tourists to approach within a few yards treat both cars and people as of no

animal as he is, should not be regarded as an outstanding illustration of the power of holiness to soothe the savage breast.

Before coming to closer quarters with the beast, we may recall the treatment of a few comparable stories by the early biographers as, in quest of the truth in these matters, the behaviour of hagiographers is no less worthy of notice than the behaviour of the animals in their legends. Attention has already been drawn to the cumulative exaggeration and use of reinforcing incident and near-parallels which mark their work (pp. 112, 162). Thus in the Sermon to the Birds the adornments of the story, more than its theme, place it beyond the bounds of credibility, whereas the Sermon to the Fish is in itself plainly incredible. Both are, to some extent, allegorical, the latter much more so than the former; but they must be understood in relation to one another. Bonaventura, after mentioning the Confiding Hare (viii. 8), refers to Obedient Wolves (viii. 11). He captures his reader's sympathy with his story of an inoffensive creature's affection for Saint Francis and then proceeds to rely on the same reader's acquiescence when he alludes to the saint's authority over an exaggeratedly fierce and harmful beast. Here Bonaventura is, as usual, following Celano who, in his *Vita Secunda* (35, 36) tells how the people of Greccio were plagued with wolves and hailstorms from which Francis delivered them.[41] When the citizens fell back into their wicked ways, they were afflicted by fire, sword, and pestilence in addition to more wolves and hail. A cautionary tale, indeed, as Celano does not fail to point out in uncharitable terms: "Verily it is just that those who turn their backs on benefits should come to destruction." His reference to wolves may have served to bring them

---

significance. A leopard took no notice when I photographed it at a distance of twelve feet. A ringed plover remained brooding with my hand beneath her.

[41] Bonaventura (viii. 11) also follows Celano (2 *Cel.* 35) in relating that when the citizens of Greccio repented, the hailstorms veered aside to neighbouring lands—though how this climatic anomaly was regarded by the owners of neighbouring vineyards is not mentioned. The concept of the elements sparing the just and rewarding the righteous is at least as early as the myth of the Deluge recorded in Genesis. It frequently occurs in legends of the saints. While all around is drenched the saints, their clothes, or dwellings remain dry. In Celtic hagiography a book or other precious perishable object is retrieved undamaged from the water.

into the forefront of the biographers' minds and so to the gates of Gubbio.[42]

The Wolf is not the only abnormally fierce native wild animal in the pages of the Fioretti (*1st consid. of stigmata*). When Orlando of Chiusi di Casentino made arrangements for the visit of two of the brethren to La Verna, "he sent with them full fifty men-at-arms to be their defence against wild beasts." It is as if lions and tigers lurked in every Umbrian thicket. We need no further evidence of the story-tellers' delight in hyperbole nor of the source of the Wolf's ferocity.

Apart from these considerations it is sufficiently evident that we are in the realm of fable when we read: "All the citizens went in fear of their lives. . . . And when they went abroad they armed themselves as they were going to battle; and at last it came to pass that for fear of this wolf no man durst leave the city walls" (*Fioretti* 21). If the beast had been a dragon, it could scarcely have created a greater reign of terror; and indeed there is an affinity between the Wolf of the *Fioretti* and Bonaventura's terror-inspiring "foul and loathly dragon" (iii. 5) which "seemed to threaten the whole countryside with destruction."

Outside the gates of Gubbio we see the Wolf bounding forward with jaws agape, but the saint makes the sign of the Cross and commands him, as saints had done since the days of the Desert Hermits, in the Name of Christ to hurt no man. When the Wolf lies down at his feet, "gentle as a lamb," he treats him with restraint and courtesy, urging the acceptance of a peace pact. The assurance is given him that, if he will refrain from his depredations, "neither man nor dog shall pursue thee more." Francis thus boldly makes a pledge, not only on behalf of the citizens of Gubbio, but of all the city's dogs, disregarding the abject terror which the wolf had aroused in them. The monster bows his head in token that he accepts the terms offered and follows the saint into the city where the assembled citizens pledge themselves to feed him all his days. He then publicly renews

[42] Tamassia (*op. cit.*, p. 225) points out in connexion with this passage that the biographer N. Papini scribbled a marginal note on a manuscript of the *Fioretti* at Assisi: *Chi lo dice il primo?* ("Who says it first?").

the promise already given to Saint Francis: "The wolf knelt down and bowed his head and with gentle movements of tail and body and ears, showed by all possible tokens his will to observe every pact of peace." He gives further assurance of his good faith by placing a paw in the saint's hand. Thereupon all the citizens cry aloud to heaven, praising and blessing God.

If this story were merely the contemporary fabrication of rustic admirers of the saint or of his learned biographers, we might treat it as an *ad hoc* manufactured fable and pass on, but the Wolf of Gubbio is descended from a long line of beasts. He emerges, not from the Apennine hills, but from his ancient lair deep within the monastic library and behaves as animal denizens of the Earthly Paradise, living reconciled with mankind, had done for many centuries. Indeed, his behaviour is so similar to that of the hyena befriended by Saint Macarius (or wolf, in some versions) [43] that we may be confident that the Franciscan story is a late version of the tale told in the desert and brought to Europe. Probably the inspiration was direct, for the Lives of the Desert Fathers were favourite reading in thirteenth-fourteenth-century Italy, and the writings of Sulpicius Severus, to whom a traveller from Egypt, Postumianus, told a number of desert stories on arriving in Gaul, were known to the biographers of Saint Francis.[44]

[43] E. A. W. Budge, *Lives of the Ethiopian Saints* III (London, 1928), p. 857; *Stories of the Holy Fathers* (Oxford, 1934), p. 164; *Hist. Laus*, 19, 20.

[44] Tamassia, *op. cit.*, pp. 61, 71, 212; H. Waddell, *Beasts and Saints* (London, 1934), pp. xiv, 6-7, 13-15. The Coptic version is closest to the Franciscan. Cf. E. Amélineau, *Monastères de la Basse Egypt*, pp. 233 ff. Sulpicius Severus (*Dial*. I. xiv) has his own story of a wolf that fed from an anchorite's hand. Tamassia may be thought to lay rather too much stress on the influence of the *Lives of the Fathers* on the Franciscan Legend, but the first followers of Saint Francis may have copied some of the practices of the Eastern monks and hermits. Saint Clare, like Paul the Hermit, kept count of her prayers with pebbles, and the friars wove rush baskets and bartered them for food (*Fioretti. Giles*, 3) as the Desert Fathers had done. But some of the customs the Franciscans had in common with the Desert Fathers were probably mediated through the Irish who had early been influenced by Eastern practices and had brought some of them to the Continent already in the sixth century. The Desert Fathers, when observing the tradition of Christ's fast in the wilderness, went apart into the desert; but during later times fasts of forty days

In the version of the story which he related to Sulpicius Severus, the penitent wolf bowed her head and fixed her eyes in shame on the ground, seeking pardon. The Wolf of Gubbio, like Macarius's hyena, gave his pledge twice. He knelt down, bowing his head, as she bowed her's, making movements of assent. As the people of Gubbio praised God for their deliverance, so Macarius "gave glory to God"; and as they fed their wolf, so he fed his hyena.

Thus the lineage of the Penitent Wolf can be traced from the fourth century to the thirteenth, from the Egyptian desert to the forests of Ireland and continental Europe—and to the gates of Gubbio. The motif, reaching Celtic countries, became popular apparently because of prior pagan sentiments of respect or awe. The Cornish saint Meriadoc tamed a wolf, an immense, fierce beast which "had slain many men and women in the country." Like the wolf that came to Francis "gentle as a lamb," the monster, on being touched by Meriadoc, became tame and followed him like a lamb.[45] Making use of the power inherent in Saint Modwenna's staff, a shepherd compelled a wolf to come to the saint, like a dog, shamefaced, as if conscious of its guilt. When Saint Fechin ordered a wolf that had killed a calf to approach, the beast signified obedience with movements of its tail and ears. It then obligingly tied itself up.[46] We have indications of these Celtic traditions taking root in Italy in connexion with Saint Donatus, the Irishman who became Bishop of Fiesole in the ninth century. A wolf stole a baby, but when the bishop made intercession for it, the animal brought the child safely back.[47] A picture over the altar in the cathedral of Fiesole represents the saint

---

were kept on mountain tops, due, no doubt, not only to these being lonely regions but also to memories of the Mount of Transfiguration. Thus, according to tradition, Saint Patrick spent forty days on the summit of Croagh Patrick, still a place of pilgrimage and vigil, Saint Francis spent forty days on Mount La Verna, and Friar Giles kept Lent on a high mountain. But evidence of Eastern traditions, transmitted through Irish channels, has already been quoted (p. 132).

45 The episode is mentioned in a play dated 1504 but the Latin Life of St. Meriadoc, now lost, cannot have been written later than 1199. Cf. G. H. Doble, *The Saints of Cornwall*, pt. i (Truro, 1960), p. 126.

46 Donatus, *op. cit.*, p. 131.

47 *Acta Sanctorum*, Oct. IX, for 22 Oct.; pp. 648 ff.

with an Irish wolf-hound (or wolf) at his feet. In the Life of Saint Clare as told in *The Golden Legend* compiled by Voragine about 1275, there are two stories that seem to be versions of the Saint Donatus legend. In one a mother prays to Saint Clare with the result that the wolf that has run off with her baby returns it; in the other, a woman carried off by a wolf prays to Saint Clare and is released.[48] Consistently saints' wolves, including the Wolf of Gubbio, conform to ancient tradition and manifest their penitence with appropriate polite and humble gestures. Apart from other evidence, this is sufficient to indicate that in the Franciscan Legend we are dealing with a beast from the books, not from the woods.[49]

[48] Caxton, *op. cit.*, pp. 197–198.

[49] These stories suggest that the wolf was regarded ambivalently in Celtic countries and not, as in Germanic areas, considered a daemonic being of the wilderness. Cf. J. de Vries, *Altgermanische Religionsgeschichte* II (Berlin, 1937), 305, 369–370. In mountainous continental areas, winter snows have always tended to drive wolves into the valleys in search of prey. In Ireland's milder climate such intrusions must have been less frequent and the animals would have been less feared. Their howling, however, is mentioned in Early Irish poetry, and during the dreadful massacres and famine at the time of the Flight of the Earls they attacked people dying of wounds and hunger.

There are Irish stories of wolves set to guard flocks, even "standing in" for a cow's calf so that the lactating animal would continue to yield milk. In a Life of Saint Cainnich we hear of a bitch wolf that came, morning and evening *cum humilitate et penitentia* to provide milk for a motherless calf. Saint Kentigern yoked a wolf to his plough to take the place of one of his two stags which it had killed. Cf. A. P. Forbes, *Lives of St. Ninian and St. Kentigern.* (Edinburgh, 1874), pp. 61–67. We have already noted that Columban set a predatory bear to work (p. 37). Saint Munn had the help of two wolves in guarding his sheep and wolves acted as swineherds for Saint Brigid. When Saint Patrick was a small boy, he was reproved for allowing a wolf to steal a lamb; but next morning, in response to his prayer, the wolf returned the lamb. Saints even fed wolves from their flocks and Saint Molua provided a feast for wolves. Giraldus Cambrensis tells a story of a wolf which besought a priest to give the viaticum to his mate.

Caesarius of Heisterbacensis (*Dial. Mir.* X. lxvi) tells a story of the Androcles and the Lion type. A wolf dragged a girl into the forest to extract a bone from another wolf's jaw and then led her safely back. Saint Gudwalus helped a wolf in a similar way. Wolves sometimes aided saints. One guided Treverius when he had lost his way in the forest just as a hyena or wolf guided Saint Anthony to the hermitage of Paul in the desert. A wolf protected Saint Alban's corpse from other animals, and another that guarded Saint Edmund's head between its forepaws is portrayed on a choir-stall of Walpole St. Peter,

Other animals from the time of the Desert Fathers onward had shown their penitence by conforming to human etiquette or ritual, but the Wolf of Gubbio was particularly punctilious. On three occasions he bowed his head in token of giving his pledge to Saint Francis, and on the third occasion he knelt as he did so—as the saint's lamb was wont to kneel at Mass at the Portiuncula (*Bon.* viii. 7). Another incident of this kind is particularly worthy of note. Gregory the Great tells a story describing how King Totila found Cerbonius, bishop of Populonia, giving shelter to some imperial soldiers. He was condemned to be devoured by a huge bear. Crowds such as attended the Roman circus gathered and the bishop was led forth. The bear was released and advanced toward the prelate, but suddenly abandoning his ferocity, bowed his neck, lowered his head in humble submission, and began to lick the bishop's feet. The crowd which had expected to witness the man's death loudly expressed their admiration and veneration.[50] This, of course, follows the ancient motif of the animal—in some cases previously befriended—which refuses to attack the innocent man as in Androcles and the Lion, but the point of greatest interest is that elsewhere in the same book a monk on good terms with a bear calls him Brother. Florentius, in dire need of a guardian for his flocks, prayed for Divine aid. A bear appeared, and "bowing his head to the ground and showing nothing hostile in his behaviour, clearly gave it to be understood that he had come to serve the man of God." Florentius acquired great affection

---

Norfolk. The wolf guarding Saint Edmund's body is also represented on the central boss of the roof vaulting in the chapel dedicated to him in Tewkes- ˈ bury Abbey. This legend may be connected with the story of the hound that led people to his murdered master. It came into English literature by way of Scandinavian saga. (Cf. Cross, Plummer, Donatus, and Loomis, *opera cit.*)

To a minor extent the ambivalent attitude to wolves is represented in the Franciscan Legend. Friar Giles said that "the true religious are like unto wolves for they seldom issue forth in public places save for hard necessity, and continently do strive to return to their hiding-place without much converse or dwelling with men" (*Fioretti. Friar Giles,* 11). His remark gives a clear impression of the normal behaviour of wolves in Italy at that period. If wolves had been a serious, persistent menace he would scarcely have ventured to make such a comparison.

[50] *Dial.* III. 15; Tamassia, *op. cit.,* pp. 100, 234–235.

for the obliging beast and "of his simplicity often called him 'Brother.' " The story of this pet, as of so many, has a sad ending, for jealous monks belonging to another monastery slaughtered the kindly creature.

It is unlikely that Francis was familiar with these anecdotes, though his biographers may have known them; but they influenced later literature, and together with the anthropomorphic concepts of other animal stories, religious and secular, created a situation in which eventually Francis could speak perfectly naturally of all created things as Brother and Sister and not be regarded as eccentric, esoteric, or heretical. In the Beast Epic and Fables, animals behaved as human beings; and in Irish legends various creatures, large and small, associated with a saint, constituted a pious community of monks. It is significant that in the *Fioretti* a distinction is made between *frate*, meaning "friar" or "brother" in the religious sense, and *fratello*, "brother" in the sense of family relationship; Frate Lupo is therefore "Friar Wolf" and addressed as if he were a member of the community, like the erring fox in Saint Ciaran's woodland community.[51] He is treated almost as a "brother in Christ." Bonaventura's remark (viii. 6) penetrated to the fundamentals of Francis's attitude to nature: "When he bethought him of the first beginning of all things he was filled with a yet more overflowing charity, and would call the dumb animals, however small, by the names of *brother* and *sister*, forasmuch as he recognized in them the same origin as himself." This is a significant statement for it implies the recognition of an affinity between man and animal which, until Darwin, was often denied. Bonaventura was re-stating what he had found in Celano (1 *Cel.* 80–81), that Francis had regard for worms, preached to the flowers and fields, and "called all creatures by the name of brother." He spoke of his ailing frame as "Brother Body." "*Coepit hilariter loqui ad corpus: 'Gaude frate corpus.'* "

There is nothing surprising in the bear being the first animal in Christian legend to be called Brother. Probably as far back as the Old Stone Age men regarded it as having human affinities.[52] Ainu

---

[51] Okey, *op. cit.*, p. 1.

[52] Armstrong, *op. cit.* (New York, 1970), p. 9, fig. 8. This Old Stone Age engraving of the animal on its hind legs and an ivory carving representing a bear in

women suckled bear cubs as if they were children, not desisting when a missionary was preaching to them;[53] and before sacrificing a bear, the Gilyaks paraded him through the village and feasted him on fish and brandy. In our own society the appeal of the Teddy Bear is an indication of a subconscious recognition of the animal's "human" characteristics. As has been mentioned amenable bears appear early in Christian legend (p. 37). They obeyed the commands of Saint Columban and, like the obliging wolves of Irish stories, a bear atoned for its misdeeds by taking the place of a domestic animal. Bear folklore illustrates the tenacity of tradition. Writers from Aristotle to Chester in *Love's Martyr* state that it eats ants to cure itself of sickness.

The scrutiny of Friar Wolf's credentials has taken us far afield, but it is fundamental to this discussion to show that any restricted explanation in terms either of history or natural history of this and other animal stories in the Franciscan Legend cannot but be inadequate. The stories are more interesting than those who make such attempts appreciate. They give us illuminating glimpses into the workings of the medieval mind, and reveal how important it is to understand something of the mentality of the hagiographers if we are to get to know the saints of whom they wrote. They were writing in terms of edification, poetry, and even romance, as well as of history; and those for whom they wrote expected to be told of the church's heroes in such terms. Moreover, as we have seen, such writing must be viewed in depth, for the authors lived immersed in tradition with very many of their illustrative ideas drawn from the well of the past. They did not always know from what ancient sources they received inspiration, nor were they or their readers concerned to explore subliminal motives as we in our critical and self-conscious age must do, for we, too, are children of our time.

Thus, like some other Franciscan stories, the Legend of the Wolf

---

a similar attitude being reproved by Saint Gall indicate how impressed were men of very different cultures by this two-legged posture. Cf. M. Joynt, *The Life of St. Gall* (London, 1927), Frontispiece.

[53] J. Batchelor, *The Ainu and their Folklore* (London, 1901), 484; L. von Schrenck, *Reisen und Forschungen in Amur-Lande* (St. Petersburgh, 1891), pp. 550–589.

of Gubbio is composed of interwoven strands from many sources, and to try to explain it in a matter of fact way is mistaken. It is a romantic parable in which ideas from the past are given a new moralistic setting.[54] The Wolf represents the forces of brutality, lust, greed, and power-seeking which have always horrified, daunted, and sometimes dismayed the Christian. Saint George, armed and astride his charger, symbolizes one way of overcoming them; Saint Francis, in his tattered habit subduing the beast by the influence of courage, sanctity, persuasiveness, and confidence in the power of goodness, stands for another, and, where it is feasible, better way, based on the happily inextinguishable belief that every Christian can play a part in realizing man's age-old dream: "The wolf and the lamb shall feed together. . . . They shall not hurt nor destroy in all my holy mountain, saith the Lord" (Isaiah, lxv. 25).

The animal stories in the Legend can be understood along these lines as teaching patience, tolerance, sympathy, and outgoingness. In telling them, the biographers were writing better than they knew, although they were manifestly portraying the saint as the personification of holy love, able to elicit affection and establish concord among all the creatures of God. Animal instincts are shown overcome by virtue, not only as a power exercised by man in the person of Francis, dominating and subduing them, but as a divine, benignant influence, pacifying, appeasing, redeeming, and converting. In the milieu of Franciscan brotherhood from which the *Fioretti* emanated, an atmosphere permeated with the Christian charity of the thirteenth chapter of Saint Paul's First Letter to the Corinthians, the gentle idealism and heartfelt longings of the friars crystallized into this dramatic

[54] The Wolf of Gubbio was to achieve fame in the New World much later. Toribio de Benavente (Motolinia), in his *Historia de los Indios de Nueva Espana* (ed. F. B. Steck, Acad. Amer. Franc. Hist. [Washington, D.C., 1951]) relates that the Aztecs performed a play in which Saint Francis preached to the birds. A "beast" representing the Wolf—probably a man in disguise as no wolves occur in Mexico—then rushed out from the hill, but the saint made the sign of the Cross and reproved him. He then led him to the town where the chiefs had assembled. Here the beast signified his willingness to obey Francis. As an addition to the legend, an Indian feigned drunkenness and fiends seized him. No doubt this performance was introduced and encouraged by the Franciscans as a substitute for what they considered less edifying myths and customs.

form through the spirit of Saint Francis fervent in their hearts. By natural growth as well as artifice, the parable became touched with some of the dramatic, timeless beauty of ancient mythology. Writers who dwell on the reality of the beast at the gates of Gubbio have been beguiled into giving picturesque details a historicity which they were never intended to possess; but the story has its own truth as a glimpse of the Earthly Paradise.

❈ VIII ❈
The Canticle of Brother Sun

Despite the well-intentioned but misguided efforts of Celano and Bonaventura, writing with an eye to satisfying authority and popular demand, we are able to discern the lineaments of Saint Francis through the rosy mists of hagiographical adulation. Although our primary purpose has been neither to subject the Lives to critical scrutiny nor to attempt another biography of the saint, we have seen that when exploring one facet of his personality—his attitude toward nature—we have had to take into consideration the bias and propagandist aims of the biographers. Thus, by discounting a good deal of adventitious matter and evaluating anew what remains, we have been able to come closer to the Little Poor Man. On the one hand he has been presented as a figure of superhuman, indeed even, at times, supernatural sanctity, wielding magical power, and on the other as an ascetic subjecting himself and his companions to disciplines so harsh as to savour of mental disorder. These exaggerations tend to cancel out one another. Studying the Lives with discernment, and not infrequently finding it necessary to read between the lines, Francis comes before us as a warm and lovable personality. In fairness to the early biographers, we must recognize that, apart from the pressures to which they were subjected, it was no easy task to depict him faithfully. His outlook included piety and gaiety, contrition and exuberance, adventurousness and severe· self-discipline, ecstatic love of nature and absolute devotion to God. High-ranking clergy and scholars who had never kissed lepers nor felt tender concern for worms could not readily understand him.

Enough remains in the records to show that he retained much of the joviality, delight in beautiful things, and pleasure in music of his unregenerate days, as we might expect, for conversion does not revolutionize a personality but gives it new orientation and ardour. Celano remarked (1 *Cel.* 51): "He had by grace become simple though he was not so by nature." This is no more than a half truth, though a valuable one. As a youth he indulged in the distractions of other young men, but he was, and remained, whatever the diverse aspects of his personality, essentially a simple soul. Single-minded devotion to Christ gave unity to his life. Clothing himself like Sister Lark he set aside the parti-coloured garments that had astonished and amused the citizens of Assisi and made his own the gay flowers of field and forest; instead of ribald *canzoni* he sang the glory of God and taught his companions to sing Christ into men's hearts. God's troubadour, the birds were his choristers, and for him Lady Poverty was more deserving of homage than any knight's *belle dame*. Inspired by the Gospel injunctions, enthralled by tales and songs of high romance, his heart kindled by the crusading ardour of the age, he set forth in utmost humility to live as nearly as he could the life of Christ and to bring the world to His allegiance. All this, although already stressed in these pages and by many earlier writers, needs repetition here lest it should seem that in scrutinizing the natural history in the Legend we have lost sight of the saint. He was not a naturalist but a man whose loving sympathy for all aspects of Creation invigorated his insight, pioneering the way for poets, artists, and scientists. In his Discourse on Perfect Joy he emphasized that bliss does not lie in understanding "the qualities of the birds, and of fishes, and of animals, and of men, and of trees, and stones, and roots and waters" but in knowing how to "suffer patiently with joy and gladness" (*Fioretti* 8). A saint, indeed, but as such the inheritor of a tradition of enjoyment of Creation as God's handiwork stretching back to Old Testament times and shining forth in the Gospels and Christ's exhortation, "Consider the lilies . . ." (Matt. vi. 28; Luke xii. 27). More than a millennium of Christian concern for the creatures of field and forest crystallized in his Legend and reached its consummation in the épopée of stories told about him and in his own Canticle of Brother Sun, commonly called the Canticle of the Sun.

Biographers and critics, well aware that he who would become acquainted with Saint Francis needs to use his imagination, have allowed it to lure them into pitfalls. Paul Sabatier, to whom admirers of the saint owe so much, initiated the genre of romantic biography which influenced many later writers. His treatment of the circumstances in which the Canticle was composed illustrates alike his vivid portrayal of events and persons and a more generous use of the imagination than the records justify. He describes Francis, ill and nearly blind, taking refuge at St. Damian's and welcomed by Saint Clare:

And first she kept him near her, and, herself taking part in the labour, she made him a large cell of reeds in the monastery garden, that he might be entirely at liberty as to his movements.

How could he refuse a hospitality so thoroughly Franciscan? It was indeed only too much so: legions of rats and mice infested this retired spot; at night they ran over Francis's bed with an infernal uproar, so that he could find no repose from his sufferings.[1] But he soon forgot all that when near his sister-friend. Once again she gave back to him faith and courage. "A single sunbeam," he used to say, "is enough to drive away many shadows!"

Little by little the man of the former days began to show himself, and at times the Sisters would hear, mingling with the murmur of the olive trees and pines, the echo of unfamiliar songs, which seemed to come from the cell of reeds.

One day he had seated himself at the monastery table after a long conversation with Clare. The meal had hardly begun when suddenly

[1] J. R. H. Moorman, *Saint Francis of Assisi* (London, 1963), p. 101, also mentions "swarms of rats," but neither in the *Fioretti* (19) nor the *Mirror of Perfection* (100) is there any reference to rats. The black rat *Rattus rattus*, carried probably in ships returning from the Crusades or in Italian trading vessels, may have reached some localities in Europe during the twelfth or early thirteenth century from its home in Central Asia, but the outbreak of the Black Death (bubonic plague) is attributed to the rats from the Crimea bearing the fleas that are the vectors of the disease to Constantinople, the Near East, Sicily, and Provençe in 1347. During 1348 the Black Death ravaged Italy, Spain, northern France, and southern England. It is very unlikely that the rodents had established themselves in Umbria at the time of Saint Francis's death. The brown species *Rattus norvegicus* arrived in Europe as an immigrant from a region, probably around the Caspian, early in the eighteenth century. Cf. G. E. H. Barrett-Hamilton and M. A. C. Hinton, *A History of British Mammals* III (London, 1916), 579–582; P. Ziegler, *The Black Death* (Penguin Books, 1970), pp. 27–29, 43, 106–107, 131–132, 157.

he seemed to be rapt away in ecstasy. *Laudato sia lo Signore!* he cried on coming to himself. He had just composed the Canticle of the Sun.[2]

Let us be content with accepting that the Canticle was composed or, much more probably, completed when Francis, suffering from an eye affliction, was staying in a hut close to St. Damian's with a few of the friars around him (*Fioretti* 19).[3] The Song itself, rather than the circumstances of its composition, will occupy our attention. After Francis prayed that he might endure his infirmities patiently, cheerfulness returned and he reflected that man is amazingly privileged: he is like a slave to whom an emperor has given a kingdom. Inspired by this thought, which involves the acceptance of God, the world, and human life as good and is the foundation of thankfulness, he sang the Song of the Sun, and then taught it to his companions so that when they halted to preach on their journeyings they might proclaim themselves as God's minstrels and sing together with spiritual jubilation (*Spec. Perf.* 100, 119, 120; 2 *Cel.* 213; *Leg. Ant.* 43). Similarly Saint Aldhelm had sung by the roadsides to attract a crowd to hear the Gospel (p. 22).

The ideas that found expression in the Canticle of the Sun had long been maturing in the saint's mind. Celano (1 *Cel.* 116) remarks that "many a time as he was walking on his way meditating and singing of Jesus, did he forget whither he was going, and invite all the elements to praise Jesus." It is recorded that in 1213, years before his illness at St. Damian's, he caused a tiny chapel to be erected between San Gemini and Porcaria and arranged for the following sentences to be inscribed on the antipendium above the altar: "All who fear the Lord, praise Him! Praise the Lord, heaven

---

[2] Paul Sabatier, *The Life of St. Francis of Assisi* (London, 1920), p. 304.

[3] According to Celano (2 *Cel.* 217) the saint was on his deathbed when "he invited all creatures to praise God; and in certain words which he had composed before exhorted them to the love of God." In one chapter of the *Mirror of Perfection* (100) the Canticle is said to have been composed two years before his death and in another (118) "a little before his death." For discussions of the *Canticum Solis*, cf. *Misc. Fr.* III (1888), 2–7; VI, 43–50; *Franz. Stud.* II (1915), 241–265; *Archiv. Fr. Hist.* XIII (1920), 269–273.

and earth! Praise Him, all rivers! All creatures, praise the Lord! All birds of heaven, praise the Lord." [4] It is a pity that his example in this respect has not been more widely followed and that, instead of the lonely prominence often given to the Crucifix in churches, the symbols of Creation should not also appear in glowing glass or sparkling mosaic proclaiming to the worshipper the wonders of Creation as well as the grace of Redemption. We have already contemplated the possibility that Francis may have visited the churches of Ravenna and been inspired to more ecstatic delight in nature, viewed as the handiwork of God, by what he saw there (p. 107). In San Apollinare in Classe (A.D. 549) built in the lovely forest destroyed in World War II where Dante located the Earthly Paradise, the gay apsidal frieze still illustrates the beauties of the countryside —the saint with his flock among meadows gay with birds and flowers —and not far away is the Mausoleum of Galla Placidia with its dome a night sky radiant with golden stars. Here Francis would find portrayed in splendour the relationship between God and His Creation which he constantly extolled: "Praise the Lord, heaven and earth!" But he need not have gone so far to receive such visual inspiration. He is said to have stayed a month at Città di Castello on the way from La Verna to St. Damian's where he composed or completed the Canticle (1 Cel. 70). In the central section of the ancient altar-piece in the church there he would see a majestic figure of God the Father surrounded by sun, moon, and stars (pl. 11). [5]

This exultant cry in which man, offering adoration, assumes that all Creation joins joyously with him in appreciation and thanksgiving had been characteristic of the church's worship from its beginnings and still remains so, though in our time secularized man, master of nature as he assumes himself to be, seldom dwells on the

---

[4] The texts are from the Psalms and the book of Daniel. Cf. Wadding, op. cit., ann. 1213, n. 17; H. Thode, Franz von Assisi und die Anfänge der Kunst der Renaissance in Italien (Berlin, 1885) p. 107, Johannes Joergensen, St. Francis of Assisi, trans. T. O'C. Sloane (London, 1912), p. 310.

[5] L. von Matt and W. Hauser, St. Francis of Assisi (London, 1956), p. 78; pls. 146, 147, 153. Eleventh-century mosaics in St. Mark's, Venice, portray the creation of the heavenly bodies. Adam and Eve are depicted "naked and unashamed."

thought of his voice joining in the chorus of delight and wonder rising from the earth, sea, stars, and sky. Space occupies his thought more than eternity, and for many the subtlety of the computer is more relevant than numinous insight. Contemplation as practised in the past has become the Cinderella of the religious life. To such Lorenzo's reflections, inspired by Platonic and neo-Platonic Christian traditions, may seem but frothy words:

> Look, how the floor of heaven
> Is thick inlaid with patines of bright gold:
> There's not the smallest orb which thou behold'st
> But in his motion like an angel sings,
> Still quiring to the young-eyed cherubins,—
> Such harmony is in immortal souls;
> But whilst this muddy vesture of decay
> Doth grossly close it in, we cannot hear it.
> (*Merchant of Venice*, V. i. 58–65)

But the church still proclaims triumphantly in the Te Deum, as it has done since the time of Saint Augustine or earlier:

> We praise thee, O God, we acknowledge thee to be the Lord.
> All the earth doth worship thee: the Father everlasting.
> To thee all Angels cry aloud; the Heavens and all the Powers therein.
>
> Heaven and earth are full of the Majesty: of thy glory.[6]

One of the hymns of Synesius of Cyrene (ca. 373–ca. 414), probably inspired by Psalm cxlviii, is more specific in mentioning the Creatures of God:

> To thee all things offer endless praise:
> Day and night, lightnings, snows

[6] The authorship of the Te Deum was ascribed to Saint Ambrose or to him and Saint Augustine, but it is composite, derived in part from such Eastern sources as the Eucharistic Hymn of the Liturgy of Jerusalem and the Morning Hymn of the Eastern Church. Verses 7–9 appear to be taken from a passage of Saint Cyprian's writings. Ultimately it owes inspiration to the Psalms. The writer of Ecclesiasticus (xlii. 17) refers to the angels telling forth the marvels of Creation. Plato had written of the Music of the Spheres, each sphere making its own music. Christian thought adopted the theme of the separate elements of Creation singing the praise of the Creator.

The heavens and the aether, roots and growing things,
Beasts and birds and shoals of swimming fish.[7]

Most detailed and best known of the Christian hymns in which man
feels himself to be joining with all Creation in worship is the Benedicite, sung in both East and West in the Office of Lauds. As the
Song of the Three Children, it is an apocryphal addition to the
book of Daniel and constitutes a link between Jewish and Christian
worship. This Song was included in the Irish *Liber Hymnorum* compiled at the end of the eleventh century and later set in the prayer
books of the Churches of Ireland and England to be sung at Mattins
during Lent, but now, regrettably, less often heard since the introduction of new Orders of Service in England. The Works of Creation are marshalled in all their magnificent array and called on, each
and all, to add their voices to the cosmic chorus:

> O all ye works of the Lord, bless ye the Lord: praise him and mag-
> nify him for ever.
> O ye Angels of the Lord, bless ye the Lord: . . .
> O ye Heavens, bless ye the Lord. . . .
> O ye Waters that be above the Firmament, bless ye the Lord:
> O all ye Powers of the Lord, bless ye the Lord: . . .
> O ye Sun and Moon, bless ye the Lord: . . .
> O ye Stars of Heaven, bless ye the Lord:
> O ye Showers and Dew, bless ye the Lord:
> O ye Winds of God, bless ye the Lord:
> O ye Fire and Heat, bless ye the Lord:
> O ye Winter and Summer, bless ye the Lord: . . .
> O ye Dews and Frosts, bless ye the Lord:
> O ye Frost and Cold, bless ye the Lord:
> O ye Ice and Snow, bless ye the Lord:
> O ye Nights and Days, bless ye the Lord: . . .
> O ye Light and Darkness, bless ye the Lord: . . .
> O ye Lightnings and Clouds, bless ye the Lord: . . .
> O let the Earth bless the Lord: yea, let it praise Him and magnify
> Him for ever.

[7] Hymn III. Cf. W. S. Crawford, *Synesius the Hellene* (London, 1901),
pp. 196, 496–497.

O ye Mountains and Hills, bless ye the Lord: . . .
O all ye Green Things upon the Earth, bless ye the Lord: . . .
O ye Wells, bless ye the Lord: . . .
O ye Seas and Floods, bless ye the Lord: . . .
O ye Whales, and all that move in the Waters: . . .
O all ye Fowls of the Air, bless ye the Lord: . . .
O all ye Beasts and Cattle, bless ye the Lord: . . .
O ye Children of Men, bless ye the Lord: . . .
O let Israel bless the Lord: . . .
O ye Priests of the Lord, bless ye the Lord: . . .
O ye Servants of the Lord, bless ye the Lord: . . .
O ye Spirits and Souls of the Righteous, bless ye the Lord: . . .
O ye holy and humble Men of Heart, bless ye the Lord: . . .
O Ananaias, Azarias and Misael, bless ye the Lord: praise
       Him and glorify Him for ever.

This song of praise, inspired by the story of Creation (Gen. i)
may be regarded as elaborating the themes of Psalms xcvi and cxlviii.
It also reflects the adoring wonder expressed in Job xxxviii and xxxix
and has affinities with Psalm civ which, in turn, has some similarities
to the Hymn of Akhenaten, the reforming Egyptian pharaoh. The
Benedicite thus voices man's immemorial exultation as he appre-
hends and responds to Creation's splendour and thrills with joy
beholding the beauty and variety of nature. As Francis, with his
companions read or sang it daily from their Breviaries year after
year, we may be sure this hymn influenced the composition of the
Canticle of Brother Sun. He may have been aware that others before him had been inspired to compose poetry and hymns based
on it.
    Among elaborated paraphrases or developments of the theme
glorifying the Creator and Creation there is a splendid canticle
which came into liturgical use in Swabia during the early tenth century. It begins by invoking clouds, lightning, and thunder to join in
the *Alleluia* and continues:

    Rolling seas and waves,
    rain and surging storms,
    tempest and calm days,

forest and glades, sing
Alleluia.

From hence, all ye birds
the Lord who made you
praise in concert of
Alleluia.

From thence, make reply
the full-throated voice
of beasts of the field,
Alleluia.[8]

Thus birds and beasts are represented as singing antiphonally, hymning the Lord. We are reminded of Saint Francis's delight in alternating his songs with the strophes of a nightingale.

From a quite different quarter of Europe a poem with similar sentiments has come down to us. Written in Welsh it dates from the twelfth century and is included in the *Black Book of Carmarthen.* Birds, bees, and fish join in Creation's offering of adoration:

Hail, all glorious Lord! with holy mirth
May Church and chancel bless Thy good counsel!
Each chancel and church,
All plains and mountains,
And ye three fountains—
Two above wind,
    And one above earth!
May light and darkness bless Thee
Fine silk, and green forest confess Thee!
Thus did Abraham father
Of faith with joy possess Thee,
Bird and bee-song bless Thee.
    Among the lilies and roses!

There follow lines calling on young and old, the days and the stars, the air, the denizens of the waters, brooks, and green things to bless and confess the Lord.[9] But we find similar sentiments expressed in

[8] Cited in L. E. S. Duckett, *Death and Life in the Tenth Century* (Ann Arbor, 1967), pp. 225–243.

[9] A. P. Graves, A *Celtic Psaltery* (London, 1917), p. 75.

the yet earlier Irish *loricae* or invocatory prayers in which "the forces of nature, which played so great a part in Celtic mythology are called upon to praise God, who is blessed for creating them." [10] The description would apply equally well to the Canticle of the Sun.

It would not be difficult to compile an anthology on this theme extending from the beginnings of Christianity to the present day, but one further quotation must suffice. Henry Vaughan wrote in "The Morning-watch":

> . . . the quick world
> Awakes, and sings;
> The rising winds,
> And falling springs,
> Birds, beasts, all things
> Adore Him in their kinds.[11]

Many a hymn sung regularly in church and chapel continues and extends this tradition.[12]

At this distance in time we cannot expect to disentangle neatly the strands of tradition and ancient motifs which, as constituents of the ethos of his age, had an influence on Francis, from the ideas and inspirations contributed by his own experience and insight. The Song of the Creatures of God has the stamp of his genius upon it, but it is the culmination of centuries of devotion expressed in poetry. Probably, it was written, not in Latin, but in Tuscan dialect. Before the century was out, Dante had begun the *Divina Commedia* in the vernacular.

[10] J. Leclercq, F. Vandenbroucke, and L. Bouger, *The Spirituality of the Middle Ages*, trans. Benedictines of Holme Eden Abbey (London, 1968), p. 95.

[11] *The Complete Poems of Henry Vaughan*, ed. F. Fogle (New York: New York University Press, 1965), p. 176.

[12] Notably in the Anglican *Hymns Ancient and Modern*, nos. 371, 372, 374, 379, and 380. The revised edition includes hymns of this character ranging in date from No. 158, earlier than the tenth century, with the lines,

> All Thy creation serveth its Creator,
> Thee every creature praiseth without ceasing,

to W. H. Draper's modern paraphrase of the Canticle of the Sun "All creatures of our God and King" (no. 172).

Passing on from some of the variations on the theme of the Hymn of Creation which preceded the *Laudes Creaturarum*, we turn to Francis's own hymn which Renan, making bold comparisons, called the finest religious poetry since the Gospels: [13]

> Most High, Omnipotent Lord,
> Praise, glory and honour be given to Thee with one accord!
>
> To Thee alone, Most High, does praise belong,
> Yet none is worthy to make of Thee his song.
>
> Be praised, my Lord, with all Thy works whate'er they be,
> Our noble Brother Sun especially,
> Whose brightness makes the light by which we see,
> And he is fair and radiant, splendid and free,
> A likeness and a. type, Most High of Thee.
>
> Be praised, my Lord, for Sister Moon and every Star
> That Thou hast formed to shine so clear from heaven afar.
>
> Be praised, my Lord, for Brother Wind and Air,
> Breezes and clouds and weather foul or fair—
> To every one that breathes Thou givest a share.
>
> Be praised, my Lord, for Sister Water, sure
> None is so useful, lowly, chaste and pure.
>
> Be praised, my Lord, for Brother Fire, whose light
> Thou madest to illuminate the night,
> And he is fair and jolly and strong and bright.
>
> Be praised, my Lord, for Sister Earth, our Mother,
> Who nourishes and gives us food and fodder,
> And the green grass and flowers of every colour.[14]

Francis reflected how splendid it would be if Brother Pacifico who had been a famous troubadour could sing this song throughout the world.

[13] *Nouvelles études d'histoire religieuse* (Paris, 1884), p. 331. It has also been claimed to be the oldest extant poem in any modern language but this is incorrect.

[14] Trans. by F. C. Burkitt, *The Song of Brother Sun in English Rime* (London, 1926). A more familiar translation is by Matthew Arnold.

Unfortunately there is ambiguity in the wording of the Canticle so that it is not entirely clear whether its theme is thanksgiving for all the wonderful works of Creation or these works are called upon to praise the Creator. Celano (2 *Cel.* 217), as mentioned above, states that Francis invited all creatures to praise God, and this is in accordance with what he tells us of the saint's attitude to Nature in his *Vita Prima* and elsewhere in the *Vita Secunda*. The ambiguity resides in the use of *per* which can mean "for" or "by" as it can have the significance of "pour" or "par" in French.[15]

Thus

Laudato si, mi signore per sora luna e le stelle . . .

could be interpreted,

Praised be Thou, my Lord for (or by) sister moon and stars . . .

but in the preceding verse we read,

Laudato sie, mio signore, cum tucte le tue creature . . .
Praised be Thou, my Lord, with all thy creatures . . .

which suggests thanksgiving for all Creation.

The *Mirror of Perfection* (118) tells us that Francis "composed certain Praises of the Lord for His creatures, to incite the hearts of those who should hear them to the praise of God, and that the Lord Himself should be praised by men in His creatures" and that he wished "to make to His praise and to our consolation and to the edification of our neighbour a new Praise of the creatures of the Lord." He was wont to say "we ought specially to praise the Creator Himself for these (sunlight and fire) and the other creatures which we daily use." The *Mirror* also quotes him as remarking: "Every creature cries aloud, 'God made me for thee, O man.'" Thus the emphasis is somewhat utilitarian. Thankfulness for benefits conferred is given more prominence than in Celano's account of

[15] L. Bracaloni, *Il Cantico di Frate Sole* (Todi, 1925). L Salvatorelli considers it absurd to regard *per* as equivalent to *da*. Cf. "Movimenti Francescano e Gioachismo," in *Relazione del X Congressa Int. di Scienze Storiche* III, p. 430. The quotations in Italian are as cited by Sabatier (*op. cit.*, p. 304) after the Assisan MS 338, fol. 33*a*.

Francis's rapturous enjoyment of Creation. His picture of the Poverello is, as we have seen, of one so entranced by God's manifestation of Himself in His creatures that, losing himself in worship, he
finds himself singing to His glory together with all Creation. This
picture seems more authentic than any in which the magnifying of
God is represented as less evident in the saint's thought than man's
convenience.

However, as it is difficult even in our own thought to separate
these two attitudes, it is academic to regard them as set against one
another in the minds of men of the thirteenth century and we are
justified in regarding the poem as voicing an intense personal experience of God's goodness in providing for man and placing him
in so magnificent and friendly a setting. Adoration and thanksgiving
mingle in the manner of themes in a musical harmony. In these
closing years, months, or days of the saint's life, he approaches ever
closer to a unitive experience of Christ and Creation. He is overwhelmed by the realization of God's bounty and the beauty and
beneficence of which He is the Author. The morning stars sing together, and the sons of God shout for joy.

In the Canticle the Creatures of God are differentiated according to the accepted qualities of male and female. Ancient traditions
transmitted from classical mythology and absorbed unconsciously
underlie the distinctions, but, no doubt, the human mind has an
innate tendency to find such analogies and contrasts. The sun and
moon readily suggest contrasting qualities, and in most cultures that
have given the heavenly bodies prominence in their religious or
magical beliefs, they have been regarded as respectively male and
female.[16]

[16] Among the Eskimo the sun and moon are sister and brother running a
race. Cf. Burland, North American Indian Mythology (London, 1965), p. 18.
Observation suggests that the moon outruns the sun. Living in high latitudes the
moon attracts special attention during the prolonged winter darkness. Many
primitive hunting peoples feel an affinity with animals and may consider themselves related to them and even call beasts "brother" or "sister," but pastoral and
agricultural folk do not think in these terms. It is extremely unlikely that any
reminiscence of this primitive usuage influenced Francis. "Brother" and "sister"
as applied to the "creatures" expressed sympathy and some sense of affinity, with
a nuance of endearment.

Of the Creatures in the Canticle, sun, fire, wind, and weather are masculine because the qualities associated with them are power and robustness; the moon, water, and earth are praised for their gentleness and generosity, the moon for her clarity, water for her cleanliness, earth for her fecundity. Underlying the contrasts is the conception of male and female being complementary to one another, involving recognition of the feminine as no less significant in God's scheme than the masculine—a sisterhood and brotherhood cooperating with one another. This would be to labour the obvious were it not that, as has already been pointed out, Celano's views were very different. He implies hardly less than that God made a mistake in creating the female sex. Women are scarcely better than bait by which the devil lures man to destruction. He was not alone in exaggerating the Jewish tradition: "Woman is the origin of sin, and it is through her that we all die" (Ecclus. xxv. 24).[17] Celano, and

[17] Although the relationship between Francis and women can be discussed only briefly, the subject cannot be avoided by those seeking to "see him plain" or assess the veracity of his early biographers. It is difficult to believe that the man who regarded beasts and birds as his brothers and sisters could have treated women in the harsh and boorish way they describe. The reader will have realized that although, strangely, some recent biographers have hesitated to say so, the accounts given by Celano and Bonaventura are, in many respects, unreliable. That they could misrepresent him in this matter must weaken our faith in their accuracy on some other topics.

After reporting the saint's alleged remark that Saint Clare and Lady Jacopa de' Settesoli were the only women he could recognize, Celano (2 *Cel.* 112) takes it upon himself to interpolate his impertinent approval: "Well said, father, for the sight of them makes no man holy." He states that Francis "enjoined the absolute avoidance of that honeyed poison, familiarity with women." After a pious woman and her daughter brought him refreshments when he was in a feeble condition, he is said to have commented that all talk with women was worthless except hearing confession and giving brief admonition (2 *Cel.* 114). For good measure Celano adds that "to such a degree was a woman unwelcome to him that you would suppose her to be not so much a warning or example as an object of dread and horror." Bonaventura (v. 5) simply paraphrases this remark. Celano depicts, not the saint's, but his own warped attitude. He tells a story of a noblewoman on bad terms with her husband who sought his advice (2 *Cel.* 38). When he had reconciled them, they "led a celibate life" and eventually died on the same day. This is a variant of a story that was popular in that age and is introduced to teach that sexual intercourse within marriage is a concession to evil. In a less tendentious and more poetic version, Saint Lucchesio, the first Brother of

not the man who spoke tenderly of Sister Water and Sister Earth, was the misogynist. Perhaps recognition of the deep emotive forces lurking in man's mind which gave rise to a host of myths such as those of the Sirens and the Medusa may enable us to understand

Penitence, is said to have given his goods to the poor. His wife aided him in succouring the wretched but became mortally ill. When she had received the last sacraments, he, too, received them and, as was his wish, they passed away together, holding hands. Cf. Sabatier, *op. cit.*, pp. 269–270. Celano's unthrifty attitude to truth is apparent in his description (2 *Cel.* 86; cf. *Spec. Perf.* 29), so contrary to all he says about the saint's modesty, of Francis and a companion stripping before a woman who importuned him to supply her with material for a gown.

This biographer's peculiar mentality is revealed in his relish for anecdotes about giving clothes away and references to nakedness. Francis strips himself completely naked before the Bishop of Assisi (1 *Cel.* 15). He points to a naked man as an example to the friars (2 *Cel.* 83), tells one of them to take off his habit and prostrate himself before a poor man (cf. *Bon* viii. 5), and himself gives his cloak (88, 89). He donates his breeches (underpants) (90) and a cloak bought for him (92)—a tortuous story which reads like a rehash of a previous anecdote (1 *Cel.* 79). Rufino is ordered to preach in Assisi naked but for his drawers (1 *Cel.* 73). To show his contrition, Brother Juniper strips, except for his breeches and carrying his clothes on his head walks into the market-place at Viterbo (*Fioretti. Friar Juniper*, 8).

Celano (2 *Cel.* 5) compares Saint Martin unfavourably with Saint Francis because Saint Martin gave up all his possessions and last of all his clothes, whereas Francis first relinquished his clothes and then his possessions. Rather strange reasoning, but to be understood, like a number of other anecdotes in the Franciscan Legend, as prompted by the wish to show that Francis's saintliness was even greater than that of Saint Martin and other holy men mentioned in the *Dialogues* of Sulpicius Severus and his *Life of Saint Martin*. Francis subdued wild beasts like Martin (I. xxv), straw on which Martin had lain cured a madman (II. viii) as straw from the Greccio Crib cured the sick, holy men were untouched by fire (I. xviii) as Francis was unscathed on the burning hearth, both saints rescued a hare (II. ix) and tamed a wolf (I. xiv), and in both Legends we hear of saintliness being effective in deflecting storms (III. vii). These ancient legends set the patterns for motifs in the biographies of subsequent saints to such an extent that it is no easy matter to distinguish how directly later stories are derived from them. Celano's tale was evidently influenced by an anecdote cited by Caesarius Heisterbacensis (*Dial. Mir.* VI. v.). Brother Ensfrid, the model for Brother Juniper, gave his breeches to a poor man, and the comment is made that his charity exceeded Saint Martin's. Celano reached fantastic extremes in his story of Francis's stripping naked to make snowmen (p. 128) and the repulsive fable that he compelled a friar to walk naked through miles of deep snow as a penance for visiting a nunnery on an errand of mercy (2 *Cel.* 206), (p. 130).

the attitude of medieval Christendom to womanhood, but we do not
have to scrutinize Celano's manuscripts very closely to perceive the
stains of Eastern dualism on them. So far as the sexes were concerned, the distinction in Francis's mind as indicated by the Canticle

---

In such anecdotes Celano, wishing to show that Francis's devotion to poverty and renunciation surpassed all others, was exaggerating actual penitential
practices. Shortly after his ordination, Saint Bernardino, stripped half naked
and carrying a cross, walked into a village and preached on the Passion.
When the abbot of Bury St. Edmunds threatened the servants of the abbey
and the burghers with excommunication, they prostrated themselves at his
door naked save for their underclothes. Cf. A. Bryant, *The Medieval Foundation* (London, 1966), pp. 91–92.

Three influences contributed to the introduction of these motifs into the Franciscan Legend: tradition, the contemporary ecclesiastical attitude to women and
sex, and the biographers' own prejudices and obsessions.

We hear of hermits, naked among the animals, in the stories of the Desert
Fathers. No doubt these are based on fact, for some of these men isolated
themselves in the wilderness until their scanty clothes dropped to pieces. Cassian mentions that a youth entering a monastery removed all his clothes and
gives an account of a man who, renouncing the world, threw off his garments
and fled to a monastery. Cf. N. Tamassia, *Saint Francis of Assisi and his Legend*
(London, 1940), p. 68; A. N. Tommasini, *Irish Saints in Italy* (London, 1937),
p. 477. This tradition evidently reached Ireland. Saint Cadoc insisted that all
entering his monastery should strip naked. A legend states that Saint Patrick and
his disciple Saint Uindic or Saint Fynnan agreed that they were bound to give
their garments to the needy. As it appears that they were both naked, they had
evidently done so. When a cloak descended miraculously, each insisted the other
should wear it. The dilemma was resolved when the cloak rose heavenward and
was replaced by two cloaks. Cf. E. Neeson, *The Book of Irish Saints* (Cork,
1967), p. 154. Saint Guido gave all his clothes to the poor.

In contemporary ecclesiastical circles it was considered appropriate and even
virtuous to denigrate women. Salimbene, who had what Coulton called "piquant and dangerous Platonic friendships" with women, was religious director
to a number of attractive ladies, yet he loads his pages with a catena of vitu-
perative quotations from the Fathers representing the fair sex in the most
unfavourable terms, such as: "Where women are with men, there shall be no
lack of the devil's birdlime" and, "Would'st thou define or know what woman
is; She is glittering mud, a stinking rose, sweet poison . . ." and so forth.
Only one of these alleged quotations is not spurious. Forbidden fruit had to be
represented as sour. But this jaundiced outlook pervaded monastic thought
and discipline. Bonaventura's secretary, Bernard de Besse, declared that women
were not fit objects to gaze upon, and the manuals of Bonaventura's school
forbade novices to laugh or sing. No friar should look at a woman if he could
avoid it. Cf. C. G. Coulton, *From St. Francis to Dante* (London, 1906), pp.
59–60, 91–93. We have moved far from the friend of Saint Clare and Lady

was not between good and evil impulses but between the gentler and more forceful virtues, with no assumption that one group was superior to the other. This is sound biologically as well as ethically. The Canticle of the Creatures of God epitomizes what Francis

Jacopa, the man who exalted *cortesia* and went singing through the woods. (The lady's name, is variously rendered Jacopa, Jacoba, Giacomina, and Jacqueline.)

Celano and Bonaventura were conforming to an antifeminist tradition accentuated by the stringent efforts initiated in the eleventh century to enforce the celibacy of the clergy, but Celano's own obsessions are apparent in his imagery. His tendency to mention nakedness in contexts where women appear suggests an obsessive streak. These biographers found Francis's known associations with women embarrassing, and involved themselves in exaggerations, inconsistencies, and even falsehoods in trying to explain them away. Celano had written in the Vita Prima that until Francis was twenty-five he surpassed "all his coevals in bad progress in vanity" and "strutted along amid the open places of Babylon" (1 *Cel.* 1–2)—a phrase from Saint Augustine's *Confessions* —but he modified this later (2 *Cel.* 7), and Bonaventura (i. 1) took care to emphasize in his official biography that "he went not astray among the wanton youths after the lusts of the flesh." He omitted references to the Poverello's visits to Saint Clare and the attendance of Lady Jacopa at his deathbed. But there is no mention that, when Francis met the Ladies Chastity, Obedience, and Poverty, he avoided looking at them before they disclosed their true nature and disappeared (vii. 6).

In spite of the evident unreliabilty of these sources, one of the most recent of Francis's biographers declares: "What is quite certain is that Francis was always highly suspicious of women and avoided their company as much as possible." He remarks that when obliged to speak to a woman he gazed at the sky or the ground. Cf. Moorman, *op. cit.* (1946), p. 35 (1963), pp. 85–86. However, Moorman himself has argued (*Sources for the Life of S. Francis of Assisi* [Manchester, 1940], p. 47) that the rule against familiarity with women cannot have been included in the *Regula Primitiva* of 1210.

An interesting parallel may be drawn between the manner in which the life of Saint Francis was recorded and the additions and distortions to which later chroniclers subjected the biographical material concerning an earlier animal lover, Saint Cuthbert. Like Francis the Northumbrian saint had women friends, among whom was Ebba, the abbess of the double monastery of Coldingham. Through horror of some Celtic ecclesiastical customs which they misunderstood, biographers invented tales illustrating Cuthbert's detestation of women. For example, in 1333 an apparition of the saint is said to have made known his displeasure at finding Edward III sleeping with his queen in the priory. Although it was an extremely cold night, she was driven out in her underclothes. Cf. D. J. Hall, *English Mediaeval Pilgrimage* (London, 1966), pp. 86–87. The hagiographer could not resist bringing in the motif of low temperature as a remedy or punishment for sexual desire, however legitimate.

Saint Francis's biographers, in spite of themselves, reveal that they are not

THE CANTICLE OF BROTHER SUN 235

had been exemplifying ever since his conversion. Because God has granted us so much, we should gratefully treat all Creation with reverential delight and compassion. In connexion with a reference to his ablutions, we are told: "After fire, he most singularly loved

telling the whole truth about Francis's relationships with women. Celano (1 Cel. 36) refers to women running to see and hear him. The author of the *Mirror of Perfection* (26) remarks: "He saluted men and women on the road, and those who were in the fields saying: 'The Lord give you peace.'" At Poggio Bustone a white stone in a wall records the saint's greeting when he entered the village in 1209, and on 4 October, observed as the anniversary of his death, a man with a tambourine goes from house to house knocking on the doors and calling this greeting: "Buon giorno, buona gente"; "Good morning, good people." Cf. E. Raymond, *In the Steps of St. Francis* (London, 1938), p. 94. Traditions of this kind do not grow up about people known to have treated women as abhorrent.

Sabatier many years ago exposed these fallacies. He argued that the earliest friars sometimes shared meals with the Sisters and that according to the Rule of 1221 (chap. xii) the Order included Sisters as well as Brothers (*op. cit.*, pp. 158–167, 252). He affirmed: "If before long sickly minds fancied that they interpreted his thought in making the union of the sexes an evil, and all that concerns the physical activity of man a fall . . . ; if married persons condemned themselves to the senseless martyrdom of virginity, he should certainly not be made responsible. The basis of an irrational asceticism came from the dualist ideas of the Catharists, not from the inspired poet who sang nature and her fecundity, who made nests for doves, inviting them to multiply under the watch of God" (*op. cit.*, p. 266). Justified as this is so far as Francis is concerned, it does not take sufficient account of the evidence that throughout history sexual asceticism, sometimes reaching strange extremes, has been approved not only in some orthodox and heretical Christian circles but by the devotees of religions other than Christianity. The highest ideal of Buddhism involves celibacy. Gandhi's ascetic ideal included the avoidance of sexual intercourse in marriage, and recently an Indian holy man paid £4000 to return to India by air in conditions such that he would be unable to see a woman. An ambivalent attitude to women is characteristic of the human male.

Sabatier rightly considered that Catharist doctrines and the reaction to them should be taken into account by those dealing with the origins of Franciscanism, but such influences can be misconstrued. Sir Steven Runciman states: "By the middle of the fourteenth century . . . the only trace of Catharist doctrine was now to be found in certain of St. Francis' own teachings. Consciously or unconsciously he had absorbed something of their ideas of the evil of matter and of the identity of the human with the animal soul." Cf. *The Medieval Manichee* (Cambridge, 1947), p. 129. He confounds what the hagiographers said of him with what he was and fails to take account of the confusion that existed in the medieval mind in regard to the natures of man and animal. Francis was very far from believing that matter was evil. At

water" because it symbolized penitence and the soul-cleansing of baptism (*Spec. Perf.* 118).[18] The saint's delight in nature which burst forth in the Canticle is apparent in another reminiscence:

that time and later, extreme Catharist views in regard to both sex and animal life encouraged ecclesiastical reactions that resulted in the denigration of sex and contempt for women and animals. Dante did not accept such ideas, as is apparent to the reader of Canto I of the *Paradiso*, in which he emphasizes that the glory of God is reflected throughout the whole range of Creation. Unfortunately these perverse notions were widely propagated and have persisted into modern times. A Jesuit expounding Thomist moral philosophy states that, because pity for animals increases compassion for people, it is commendable, but that man has no more obligation to them than to stocks and stones because they are soulless. Cf. J. Rickaby, *Moral Philosophy* (London, 1918), pp. 248–249. Needless to say such views are no longer acceptable among enlightened Christians. They are unfair to Aquinas's teaching, for he wrote that since God is the true object of charity it should be extended to all that He has created, including "the creatures without reason . . . the fish and birds, the beasts and plants." Cf. *Summa theologica*, Charity, I. q. xx. 5, 3. Never has the relationship between man's views on sex and animal life been more obviously important than today because the increase in human population is rapidly reducing the numbers of other forms of life, menacing the balance of nature, and restricting opportunities for the spiritual, mental, and physical refreshment among natural things which are essential to man's fulfilment.

[18] This appreciation and the laudation of water in the Canticle indicate that criticisms of Francis as "a dirty monk" made in the past are unjustified. Celano's statement (2 *Cel.* 136) that after the stigmatization Francis rarely washed his hands and feet in order to prevent the stigmata being seen is so typical of his method of supplying circumstantial detail to provide edification and authentication that it need not be taken seriously. Even so it provides evidence, supplementing other such in the Legend, that among the friars, regular washing was normal.

Recently a geneticist, C. D. Darlington, in *The Evolution of Man and Society* (London, 1969), p. 300, quoted Saint Jerome, "The man who has bathed in Christ needed no second bath," adding the bold assertion that Christendom has been "permanently deflected away from southern countries by its neglect of cleanliness, its opposition to nudity and washing." Such simplifications are fallacious. Throughout much of the world until recently washing was often difficult or in some circumstances hazardous, as in high latitudes, arid regions, and where rivers were infested by crocodiles, piranhas or the vectors of bilharzia. Travellers in inland China today encounter conditions in this respect similar to those in medieval Europe: spitting, wiping the nose on one's garments, vermin, and lack of washing facilities. As Arthur Bryant has pointed out (*The Medieval Foundation* [London, 1966], p. 89), the sanitary and hygienic conditions in medieval monasteries were far in advance of those in the houses of the wealthiest laymen. Cf. D. H. S. Cranage, *The Home of the Monk* (London,

He used to say to the friar who did the garden, not to till the whole ground for pot-herbs; but to leave some part of it to produce green herbs, which in their time should produce flowers for the friars. . . . Nay, he used to say to the brother gardener that he ought always to make a fair pleasaunce in some part of the garden; setting and planting there all sweet-smelling herbs and all herbs which bring forth fair flowers, that in their time they might call them that looked upon those herbs and flowers to the praise of God [*Spec. Perf.* 118].

Celano endorses this (2 *Cel.* II. 165):

He exulted in all the works of the Lord's hands, and penetrated through those pleasant sights to their Life-giving Cause and Principle. In beautiful things he recognized Him who is supremely beautiful; all good things cried out to him, "He who made us is the Best." Everywhere he followed the Beloved by the traces He has impressed on all things; he made for himself a ladder whereby he might reach the Throne. He embraced all things with an unheard-of rapture of devotion, speaking to them of the Lord and exhorting them to praise Him.

Many centuries earlier Plato, in the *Symposium*, had emphasized in more philosophic terms the power of beautiful things to exalt man's spirit: "The true order of going to the things of Love," he wrote, "is to use the beauties of earth as steps along which one mounts upward for the sake of that other Beauty—until from fair notions he arrives at the notion of absolute Beauty and at last

---

1934), pp. 28–29. The frontispiece to vol. II of the translation of *The Dialogue on Miracles* illustrates the massive ornamental *lavatorium* at Heisterbach. Nor was opposition to nudity as typical of medieval Christendom as is suggested. It has already been pointed out that in the thirteenth century, when artists began to represent flowers and birds naturalistically, they also commenced to depict nude male and female figures in some cathedral sculptures, as at Bourges. This followed the ruling by Vincent of Beauvais in his *Speculum* that figures in Resurrection and Last Judgement scenes should be shown naked. Even discounting Celano's exaggerations nudity or semi-nudity is mentioned frequently enough in the Franciscan Legend to indicate that in appropriate circumstances it was not regarded as abhorrent. During the later Middle Ages nude women representing goddesses or nymphs were sometimes posed at vantage points on festive occasions such as the visit of some celebrity to a city. Cf. J. Huizinga, *The Waning of the Middle Ages* (Penguin Books, 1955), pp. 313–315.

knows what the essence of Beauty is." But with Francis it was not inference from the particular to the general but spiritual ardour kindled by God within his soul which enabled him to see nature as expressing divine loveliness. Beauty was apprehended mystically as God's inestimable bounty granted to His children inspiring them to know and worship Him, and teaching them gentleness, consideration, and love. It was not by philosophy that this insight came to the Poverello. God had spoken to him and touched his spirit to flame; therefore he was able to perceive that He who is Absolute Love had adorned Creation with beauty and endowed man with the ability and duty to revel in it. He could have said in the words attributed by Dante to Saint John:

> And through the garden of the world I rove,
> Enamoured of its leaves in measure solely
> As God the Gardener nurtures them above.
> [*Paradiso* xxvi. 64–66]

The Earthly Paradise prefigures the Heavenly.

The Canticle as originally composed was concerned with the natural world, using the term in a rather narrow sense, but the saint added to it later a thanksgiving for God's gifts of insight and moral order— for all that makes for peace. When a dispute arose between the Bishop and the Podestá of Assisi, Francis bade two friars go to the piazza in front of the bishop's palace, where nineteen years earlier he had given back his clothes to his father, and there sing the Canticle of the Creatures of God with this additional verse:

> Be praised, my Lord, for those who for Thy love forgive,
> Contented unavenged in quiet to live.
> Blest those who in the way of peace are found—
> By Thee, O Lord most High, they shall be crowned.

The happy outcome was that in front of a great concourse Bishop and Podestá embraced and kissed each other (*Spec. Perf.* 101; *Leg. Ant.* 44). As quoted in the *Mirror of Perfection* the verse praises God not only for those who pardon for love of Him but also for all who endure sickness and tribulation with faith and fortitude. Francis had always seen the hand of God in suffering and regarded it as a challenge, not merely to be endured but to be triumphed over. His sufferings had been his "sisters" (2 *Cel.* 212). Like Kierkegaard, so similar to him in utter dedication but so different in his view of the function of joy in the Christian life, he had sought to live as Christ's contemporary, sharing His humiliation and agony. He was very far from considering death an evil or an anomaly in God's world. When he had been told that he had but a short time to live, he stretched out his hands and cried: "Then be welcome Sister Death!" (2 *Cel.* 217). He sang:

> Be praised, my Lord, for our Sister Bodily Death,
> From whom none can escape that has drawn breath.
> "Woe to those dying in mortal sin!" He saith.
> Blest those who find that in Thy Holy Will
> The second Death to them will bring no ill.
>   [*Spec. Perf.* 120, 123]

It was as the devoted disciple of Christ that succeeding generations rightly honoured Saint Francis. Dante exalted him over the Doctors of the Church and the founders of the monastic Orders as the most perfect imitator of Christ (*Paradiso* xxxii. 34–36). In the *Paradiso* Saint Thomas Aquinas, the Angelic Doctor, speaks in eulogy of him as a sun born into the world at Assisi "where a fertile slope hangs from a hill," a place that, because of the light and warmth he brought to the world, might be called a new East. There he wedded Lady Poverty:

> *La lor concordia e i lor lieti sembianti*
> *amore e maraviglia e dolce sguardo*
> *facieno esser cagion di pensier santi.*
>   [*Paradiso,* xi. 76–8]

Their harmony and joyous bearing made love, wonder, and gentle looks arouse holy thoughts, and so the world gains courage to believe that holiness, wonder, love, and joy may dwell together in harmony.[19] This is the saint, declares Saint Thomas, whose achievement can best be sung in heaven's glory.

---

[19] Cf. 1 *Cel.* 39. Tamassia (*op. cit.*, pp. 87–88) regards Dante's lines as based on this passage.

Dante, with unerring inspiration, singles out wonder as among the saint's most striking and commendable virtues. It underlies his whole attitude to nature. Wonder naturally leads to worship. He looked at the sunrise, the woods, fields, and vineyards, he listened to the birds and streams, he savoured the perfumes of flowers in an ecstasy of wonder, and his heart-strings vibrated to immemorial melodies: "O Lord how great are Thy works! and Thy thoughts are very deep" (Psalm xcii. 5); "Great and marvellous are Thy works, Lord God Almighty" (Psalm cxxxix. 14; Rev. xv. 3); "O Lord how manifold are Thy works! in wisdom hast Thou made them all; the earth is full of Thy riches" (Psalm civ. 24). This song of the soul is indeed old but ever new. Of the Franciscan Roger Bacon it has been said: "He was a man consumed with wonder at the mechanism of the Universe," and in our time the Jesuit Teilhard de Chardin referred to his faith being "inspired and supported by his inability to contain his sense of wonder." [20]

It is not within our present scope to review or evaluate how Saint Francis's influence affected later generations. We cannot expect to be able to distinguish clearly between trends of his time and the effect of his personal influence in directing them into paths which they would not otherwise have followed nor to estimate the influence of his simplicity, integrity, and piety on generations of faithful folk; but certainly his tenderness for nature, manifested in his taking notice of and caring for humble and sometimes despised living things, ultimately affected visual art, literature, and science. Perhaps our familiarity with reproductions of the fresco in the Upper Church at Assisi of Francis preaching to the birds tends to dull our realization of how novel was such a representation showing a saint concerned for the welfare of birds, delineated so carefully that it is possible to identify some of the species. Franciscan birds show unwonted docility but they belong among trees, not libraries. Here, for all who walked or worshipped in Assisi throughout the centuries was inspiration to compassion together with encouragement to observe. Attention was no longer concentrated on mythical creatures or morals

[20] Bryant, op. cit., p. 100; P. Grenet, Teilhard de Chardin: The Man and His Theories, trans. R. A. Rudorff (London, 1965), p. 164.

drawn from their imaginary qualities. A path had been opened out which others followed. "Chose étrange!" said Renan, "ce sordide mendiant fut le père de l'art italien." A primitive form of drama was initiated by some Franciscans from Assisi and Perugia. They impersonated saints and prophets while proclaiming their merits. In Florence these developed into religious plays before the end of the thirteenth century. Each autumn men from the countryside gathered at the Porto Romano for a competition in which they whistled imitations of bird song. Possibly these, like the popular songs and sketches called *stornelli* had arisen as an off-shoot of the medieval *laude*.[21]

The keen observation of animals and natural phenomena in Dante's *Divina Commedia* foreshadowed scientific advance. He mentioned, for example, that the colours of the rainbow were due to light shining through moist air (*Purg.* xxv. 91–93); and Roger Bacon, who set forth the principles of experimental science in his *Opus Tertium*, included a penetrating exposition of this phenomenon. Adventurousness of a different kind was shown by the heroic Franciscans who penetrated to the Mongol court and established the church in Peking.[22] The walls of convention had been breached, and the successors of these pioneers advanced to new enterprises.

[21] J. Macleod, *People of Florence* (London, 1963), p. 148. Cf. P. Bargellino, *Vedere e Capire Firenze* (Florence, 1958).

[22] In 1245, Innocent III commissioned John of Pian de Carpini, one of Francis's disciples as emissary to the Mongol court. He returned in 1247 after enduring many hardships. William of Rubruck who set out in 1253 for the court of the Great Khan near Karakoram returned two years later. Yet another Franciscan, John of Montecorvino, reached Cambaluc (Peking) in 1294 and was able to report eleven years later that he had baptized about six thousand converts. He was created Archbishop. Friar Odoric, sent on a mission to the East, reached India about 1321 and went on to China where he stayed three years. John of Marignolli reached Cambaluc in 1342 and when he returned to Avignon in 1353 reported that he had "made a great harvest of souls" and that the Franciscans had a cathedral and other churches in the city. At Zaitun he found three churches of the Friars Minor, "passing rich and elegant." Cf. C. Dawson, ed., *The Mongol Mission* (London and New York, 1955); M. Komroff, ed., *Contemporaries of Marco Polo* (New York, 1928); K. S. Latourette, *A History of Christian Missions in China* (London, 1929); A. van den Wyngaert, *Jean de Mont Corvin* (Lille, 1924); *Sinica Franciscana* I (Quaracchi, 1922).

Saint Francis has been called "the Orpheus of the Middle Ages," [23] but the comparison, while having the merit of linking him with the ancient myth of harmony between man and beast, is superficial. He, indeed, was a sweet singer, and we envisage him with friendly birds and beasts around him; but his attitude was always that of an unworthy guest and immensely privileged participant amid the miracles of beauty by means of which God is constantly manifesting Himself. He proclaimed that all created things minister to man through God's grace; therefore, for humanity and the rest of Creation, true joy and fulfilment lie in setting forth His glory. He sang, not to charm Creation, but because he was charmed by it. Worship being the highest expression of wonder and reverence, man's lowlier brethren might not be able to offer such explicit, heartfelt, and understanding adoration; but they could join with him according to their several sensibilities and endowments in reverence and praise. The Little Poor Man loosed the tongues of rocks and meadows to raise their voices in brotherly concord singing "Glory to God in the Highest and on earth peace."

Enthralled by the beauty and mystery of Creation, he believed and showed that love of God, love of man, and love of nature were not only compatible with one another but the natural, divinely purposed state of humanity. The love and joy resulting from devotion to God and the creatures of God should augment love and enjoyment each of the others because all is of God. He did not separate the interests of God, man, and nature, as we do, to our detriment spiritually and the earth's impoverishment. It is a measure of how materialistically minded we have become that conservationists' arguments for the preservation of the earth's flora and fauna are so often based on self-interest, the need to preserve plants and animals for man's use and enjoyment. The argument is valid and cogent so far as it goes, but implies an impoverished concept of man, for he alone is able to look beyond personal and social advantage and cherish heavenly ideals.

Nature is to be preserved and revered because of its variety and

[23] F. Ozanam, *The Franciscan Poets in Italy of the Thirteenth Century*, trans. A. E. Nellen and N. C. Craig (London, 1914), p. 78.

beauty—for its own sake as the handiwork of God—only secondarily for our benefit, though the two ideals cannot be separated. The lady Matilda, whom Dante hears singing as she gathers flowers in the rich meadows of the Earthly Paradise, may be taken to represent ideally man's attitude to nature, for she picks the flowers in appreciation of their beauty as God's gifts (*Purg.* xxviii. 34–69). Thus the poet symbolizes not only nature in perfection but the ideal Christian attitude to nature.

We should recognize that, so long as men fail to be seized of the wonder and glory of the universe, they will regard proximate ends as more important than long-term considerations, and the beauty and interest of the world will be eroded, not merely on account of human selfishness nor because men do not know nor care about them, but simply by default. In the labour and stress, tedium and trivialities, distresses and diversions of life, people will neglect them unless they have been startled awake to a heavenly vision. Such a vision in transforming splendour as was granted to Saint Francis is vouchsafed to few but is available in some measure to all; for who is without the gifts exalted by Dante in his panegyric on Saint Francis: wonder, love, joy, and an appreciation of harmony? And none of us is unable to augment them. It is possible for us to enter into the experience of being new-created in a new-created world. To those to whom that experience is granted in however lowly a degree, the beauty of the world remains an ever-present consolation and illumination.

Notes to Illustrations

1. One of five designs illustrating the life of St. Francis. Another window shows St. Francis cutting off St. Clare's hair. The windows date from the first half of the fourteenth century but were extensively renovated at the end of the last century. The cock represents the birds of the day, the owl those of the night. There is a barn owl in a Stigmatization by Bartholommeo della Gatta and also in the Gilbert White memorial window of Saint Francis at Selborne which depicts all the birds mentioned by him.

2a. This drawing was made a few years after the sketch in the Eton College MS. Here in his *Chronica Majora* (C.C.C. MS XVI. f.66r) Matthew Paris portrayed the birds as large and powerful, including among them an eagle and a stork.

2b. This is believed to be the earliest English representation of St. Francis preaching to the birds and is in a MS (Eton 96. f. 22) containing the summary of world history up to 1243 by Peter of Poitiers, Chancellor of Paris (ca. 1200). It dates from about 1244. A sketch of the saint's head appears beside this drawing.

2c. This elegant illustration in the Luttrell Psalter (B.M. Add. 42130. f. 60v) dates from about 1340. The leaves of one of the highly conventionalized trees resemble oak leaves. The artist has drawn the birds in a rather rule of thumb style, not representing them clasping the branches. In medieval art the lion often symbolizes Resurrection.

A. G. Little, in *Franciscan History and Legend in English Medieval Art* (Manchester University Press, 1937) cites a number of other illustrations of the Sermon. Francis Klingender, in *Animals in Art and Thought* (London, 1971) attributes the popularity of this theme in England to the Englishman's love of birds during the thirteenth and fourteenth century. In support the wall paintings in Longthorpe Tower, Peterborough, might be cited, indicating as they do that a man of this period liked to have pictures indoors of birds such as the curlew and heron which he could see from his windows. But the popularity of the Sermon to the Birds in Italy continued into the beginning of the fifteenth century, as the painting by Taddeo di

Bartoli, now in Hanover, indicates. In this the birds are sufficiently realistic for a hoopoe, magpie, pheasant, flying partridge, and quacking duck to be identified. Klingender includes in his list of birds which figure in fourteenth century illuminated MSS, wrens, robins, finches, and larks, commenting that "they represent such harmless species as those mentioned in Celano's and Bonaventura's accounts of the bird sermon by St. Francis"; but Bonaventura does not refer to particular species and Celano mentions only doves, rooks and jackdaws. It would seem that the artists who depicted large birds were acquainted with his account, though Klingender is probably correct in supposing that there was some interchange between artistic conceptions of the Bird of the Apocalypse and those represented as constituting Francis's congregation.

Judging by the bird dishes served at medieval feasts in England and elsewhere, the appointment of "bird-catchers" to the staffs of big houses, and illustrations of fowling in MSS, birds were treated with scant compassion. But certainly from the eighteenth century to the present time there has been more interest in birds and greater compassion for them in England than in Italy.

Perhaps the emphasis on two details of the Franciscan Legend in England, the Sermon and the Stigmatization, may be attributed in large part to the loss of some motifs which any legend is liable to undergo as it travels further from its centre of origin. The Sermon called attention to the importance of gratitude toward God and compassion among men and for all Creation, the Stigmatization emphasized God's love as shown in Christ's Cross and the significance of sacrifice in the Christian life.

3. This scene is one of three on the predella of an altar-piece representing the Stigmatization, brought by Napoleon from Pisa as booty to Paris. The panel bears Giotto's name, but expert opinion inclines to the view that the artist was a member of his *bottega*. It was painted about 1300. The design resembles the fresco in the Upper Basilica of San Francesco at Assisi but includes larger birds, a cock, geese, magpies, and egret-like species. Cf. B. Berenson, *Italian Painters of the Renaissance: Florentine School*, 1 (London, 1963), 82; A. Martindale and E. Baccheschi, *The Complete Paintings of Giotto* (London, 1969), p. 95; A. Smart, *The Assisi Problem and the Art of Giotto* (Oxford, 1971), pp. 106–117, 192–193.

4. Assisi is shown at the top of the fresco, but a portion depicting the gate of the city is missing. The incident illustrates the saint's charity, humility, and love of chivalry. The horse is the knight's. After his conversion Francis usually rode an ass.

5. Vines and roses cover the arched trellis. Fanciful decorative birds perch on it. In the background swans swim on a river. Imaginative incongruities vary from a heron-like bird with plumed tail to a bird with a man's head and an apelike figure reading (Lat. 9473 f. 186v). A monkey is represented on a page of Mary of St. Pol's breviary which depicts St. Clare holding a book (Cambridge University Library, Dd. 5.5). The illuminations in this breviary are by a French artist. Monkeys appear as decorative motifs in a number of fourteenth-century manuscripts.

6. The Psalter of John de Beaufort dates from the early fifteenth century (B.M. Royal 2.A. XVIII. f. 9. v). St. Francis, enraptured, is depicted in a flower-spangled meadow with a grove of trees represented in a stereotyped manner, in the background.

7. The portrait of St. Francis is life size. This altar painting illustrates the new vigour which the Byzantine style acquired on reaching Italy. In the detail showing St. Francis preaching to the birds, the trees and birds are conventionalized, according to this style. The painting is signed by the artist and dated 1235.

8. This painting dates from the second half of the thirteenth century and resembles more than any other the portrait of St. Francis at Subiaco made during the saint's lifetime. Experts esteem highly the simple beauties of the whole work. The scenes represented are: (1) The Sermon to the Birds; (2) The Dream of Honorius; (3) The Crucifix of St. Damian; (4) St. Francis renounces his Father; (5) The Vision of the Chariot of Fire; (6) The Stigmatization; (7) The Crib at Greccio; and (8) The Death of the Saint.

9. The Wolf places its paw in the saint's hand in token of his pact of peace while alarmed citizens look out from the walls of Gubbio. Scattered bones and a dismembered body in the background indicate the extent of the Wolf's depredations. In the sky are migrating cranes —birds also shown in the artist's Journey of the Magi. The painting was executed between 1437 and 1444. There is a bas-relief in wood of St. Francis and the Wolf in the Lower Church of Assisi.

10a & b. These illustrations (B.M. Royal 2 B. VII ["Queen Mary's

Psalter"] *ff*. 176v, 177) may represent idealistically the joyous spirit of the first Franciscans rather than real life. They might serve to illustrate the burden of a fourteenth-century carol:

Hand in hand we shall us take
And joy and bliss we shall us make
For the Devil of Hell hath man forsaked
And God His Son our mate is maked.

The Franciscans enacted scenes illustrating the Life of St. Francis to educate illiterate folk; there is a record of a masque or revel at Oseney Abbey in 1504. For their notable contributions to music and poetry, cf. H. Goad, *Greyfriars* (London, 1947).

11. On his way from Mount La Verna after the Stigmatization and not long before he composed the Canticle of the Sun, St. Francis stayed at Città di Castello. If he prayed in the church, and composed the Canticle of the Sun later, as is probable, the heavenly bodies depicted on the altar may have provided inspiration.

12. In the background, outside the walled town with a river flowing by, a shepherd tends his flock—a scene recalling St. Francis' care for sheep as symbolizing the Lamb of God. The stigmata on the saint's hands are faintly visible. The ass represents his humility. The heron is perched in an unusual situation, on a cliff top, but it may here symbolize penitence, as in other pictures, and is appropriately shown in austere surroundings. Long-necked birds were traditional in pictures of the Sermon to the Birds, partly because of their decorative appearance (pls. 2a, 3, 14). Behind Francis is a spike of mullein (Verbascum) indicating his delight in flowers (1 *Cel.* 80, 81). The rabbit that, according to Bonaventura (viii. 8), was brought to him when on an island in the lake at Perugia, peeps from the masonry below the sleeve of the saint's light brown habit. A small bird in the left foreground is probably not a little bittern, as suggested by Meiss.

The cliff face rising from a meadow is true to the scene at La Verna. The hermitage—a grotto with vine-entwined lattice—is designed to accord with statements that the friars dwelt in caves as well as huts made of boughs. Warm light bathes the scene, suggesting the radiance of the seraphic vision.

This is one of the earliest pictures of St. Francis in which a skull is depicted. It was painted about 1480. Later representations, such as those by Velazquez in the Louvre and Zurbaran in Madrid, show him rapt in contemplation before a skull without any indication of his joy in nature.

Giovanni Bellini was the first Venetian painter to appreciate landscape. Cf. M. Meiss, *Giovanni Bellini's St. Francis in the Frick Collection* (New York, 1964).

13. According to the account given by Corrado, Bishop of Assisi in 1335, Satan came one January night urging Francis to reduce the amount of time he spent on nocturnal prayer. The saint, perceiving that the temptation was of the devil, went out naked and crawled through a thorny hedge, whereupon a wonderful light shone, angels appeared and the wood was filled with white and crimson roses. He found himself clothed in dazzling raiment and entered the Portiuncula chapel with a bouquet of the flowers and laid them on the altar. While doing so he had a vision of Christ and His Mother above it together with the angelic host.

14. Jan Breughel II (1601–1678) was one of three artists of this name, father, son, and grandson. His father (ca. 1568–1625), one of the two sons of Pieter, lived in Cologne and travelled in Italy, where his pictures were much admired. He painted flowers and landscapes with small human and animal figures in the background. The style of Jan Breughel II followed closely that of his father. His interest in flowers, foliage, and animal life is apparent in this picture which would seem to have been influenced by the painting at Cologne by the Master of St. Severin (pl. 19). The two herons, one standing and the other in flight, in the left-hand bottom corner are probably without symbolical significance. Similar birds are shown in other paintings by this artist, but in this picture and Bellini's painting (pl. 12) the heron, as a bird often feeding alone by the waterside in desolate country, may have been introduced not only for its decorative effect but as appropriate to a scene representing the isolation of a saint undergoing a transcendent experience. As the Stigmatization took place on La Verna, painters such as Giotto (1276–1337), Lorenzo di Credi (1459–1537), and other artists depicted craggy scenery and trees in the background. Comparison of a series of such pictures illustrates the development of sensitivity to scenic beauty.

15. One of the series of frescoes illustrating the Legend of St. Francis with which Gozzoli decorated the apse of the church at Montefalco. He worked as an assistant to Fra Angelico, whose influence is apparent in this and other pictures of the series. As in the illustration

of the scene in San Francesco, Assisi (pl. 18) the Crib is represented in church. Celano evidently envisaged the Praesepe in a grotto or the open air as he mentions that the woodland and rocks echoed the jubilation of the congregation. According to his account an altar was raised and a church dedicated at the place where the manger was hallowed. Gozzoli painted Francis's birth in a stable.

16. The tonsured saint holds a crossed staff in one hand and extends the other as if to emphasize his remarks, as in the Eton MS (pl. 2a). The birds, of different species, are perched on a tree, the branches of which are delineated by typical thirteenth-century scroll-work. A small unidentifiable animal stands on its hind legs at the foot of the tree, apparently trying to climb it. The artist, whose technical skill suggests that he was permanently employed in creating such works, may have added a predatory beast to emphasize the worldly perils to which the members of any congregation are exposed. Probably the painting, which is high on the north wall and for which various tints of ochre were used, was executed between 1260 and 1280 by a craftsman whose skill was such that he is thought to have been permanently employed on such works. Cf. E. W. Tristram in Little, 1937.

17. St. Francis wears a brown habit with a thrice-knotted girdle and, as in other pictures, his hand is raised in a gesture toward his bird congregation. Among the birds, which are carefully delineated, are a robin and an owl. The owl is one of the species with tufts on its head. In size it approximates to the little owl rather than the long-eared or short-eared, but the little owl was not in England at this period. Evidently the painter was influenced by current convention-alized pictures of owls (pl. 1). The work is in ochre and black, and dates from about 1300. Portions of it cannot be deciphered. A figure holding a book on the west side of the same window splay, may, possibly, be St. Clare. Other associated wall paintings depict St. George, St. Christopher, a History of St. Margaret and a Doom. One of the birds with St. Francis is singing.

18. It is believed that this fresco was designed by Giotto but executed by his assistants, but cf. works cited in note 2. The scene is set in the church of the village of Greccio. A remarkable feature is the panelled reverse of the crucifix. Exigencies of composition have resulted in the ox and ass being represented as diminutive in the foreground.

19. St. Francis is shown enraptured while receiving the stigmata.

Brother Leo's posture suggests that he is overcome or obeying the saint's instructions not to watch him. In other pictures he watches from a distance or appears bewildered (pl. 14). The seraph appears "with six resplendent and flaming wings having the form of a man crucified" as described in the *Fioretti*. St. Francis and Leo wear the habit which gave rise to the name "Grey Friars." The distant scene represents a northern landscape rather than Assisi. On the left, Francis is taming the Wolf of Gubbio which is placing a paw in his hand as in Sassetta's picture (pl. 9) while on the right the Sermon to the Birds is depicted. Perhaps the figure at the upper right hand corner represents the saint bestowing his blessing. A butterfly, of the family Nymphalidae, has alighted on a rock in the foreground. It may have been added as a decorative detail rather than as a symbol of the Resurrection.

The Master of St. Severin was one of the two main representatives of the School of Cologne at the end of the fifteenth and beginning of the sixteenth century. His style is reminiscent of the Dutch primitives, suggesting that he was brought up in the Low countries.

Bibliographical Note

Quotations from the Lives of Saint Francis are, with a few exceptions, from translations readily available in English:

Fioretti: The Little Flowers of St. Francis, translated by T. Okey (London, 1944). (*Fioretti*)

Speculum Perfectionis: The Mirror of Perfection, translated by R. Steele (London, 1944). (*Spec. Perf.*)

Legenda Maior: The Life of St. Francis by St. Bonaventura, translated by E. G. Salter (London, 1944). (*Bon.*)

These translations are published conveniently in one volume in Everyman's Library by J. M. Dent and Sons, Ltd., 10–13 Bedford St., London, W.C. 2, and E. P. Dutton and Co., Inc., 286–302 Fourth Avenue, New York. There is a more recent edition.

The *Fioretti* is based on the *Actus B. Francisci et Sociorum eius*, edited by P. Sabatier in *Collection d'Études et des Documents* IV (Paris, 1902). The most recent translations of the *Fioretti* and the *Speculum* are by L. Sherley-Price (Penguin Books, 1959) and in *S. Francis of Assisi, his Life and Writings* (London, 1959). The Italian text used is that published by Hoepli (1920).

Vita Prima and Vita Secunda: The Lives of S. Francis of Assisi by Thomas of Celano, translated by A. G. Ferrers Howell (London, 1908). (1 *Cel.* and 2 *Cel.*)

Legenda Trium Sociorum: The Legend of S. Francis by the Three Companions, translated by E. G. Salter (London, 1902). (3 *Soc.*)

Legenda Antiqua S. Francisci, edited by F. Delorme in *Archivum Franciscanum Historicum* XV (Quaracchi, 1922). (*Leg. Ant.*)

Celano's *Vita Prima* was written between 1228 and 1230. His *Vita Secunda* was approved by the Chapter General in 1247. In view of the divisions that had arisen within the Order, Bonaventura was authorized in 1260 to compile a Life designed to reconcile the opposing parties. He presented the *Legenda Maior* to the Chapter at Pisa in 1263, and at the Assembly General of 1266, Bonaventura himself presiding, orders were given that the writings of other biographers should be destroyed. The

Actus seems to have been compiled between 1322 and 1328. Some years later when the *Fioretti di San Francesco* was published fifty-three chapters were added with the *Considerazioni sulle sacre stimmata* and the Lives of Brothers Juniper and Giles. As the popular concept of Saint Francis and his companions is largely based on this attractive compilation, it is important to bear in mind that it dates from a century after the saint's death and contains much that is unhistorical but of importance as illustrating the outlook of the first Franciscans, faithful to their founder's ideals.

Scripta Leonis, Rufini et Angeli, sociorum S. Francisci. Ed. and trans. R. B. Brooke (Oxford, 1970). This important critical study was not available until after this book was in the publisher's hands. It provides the Latin text as well as the English translation and considers the relationships of the documents to one another.

Index

The names of individual saints are listed under Saint, and animals are indexed under Organisms.

255